Springer Series on Social Work

Albert R. Roberts, D.S.W., Series Editor

School of Social Work, Indiana University, Indianapolis

Advisory Board: Joseph D. Anderson, D.S.W., Barbara Berkman, D.S.W., Paul H. Ephross, Ph.D., Sheldon R. Gelman, Ph.D., Nancy A. Humphreys, D.S.W., Sheldon Siegel, Ph.D., and Julia Watkins, Ph.D.

Joseph Anderson, D.S.W., A.C.S.W., is Professor of Social Work at Shippensburg University and a Senior Teaching Fellow at the National University of Singapore. He received his doctoral degree from the University of Maryland, where he has also taught. Dr. Anderson has been president of the Central Pennsylvania Chapter of the National Association of Social Workers, chair of the Educational Planning Commission of the Council on Social Work Education (CSWE), and a member of CSWE's Commission on Accreditation. Currently, he is a member of the Academy of Certified Social Workers, a consulting editor of the *Journal of Education for Social Workers*, and on the editorial boards of *Social Work with Groups* and Springer Publishing Company's Social Work Series. Dr. Anderson is the author of *Social Work Methods and Processes* and *Counseling Through Group Process* (Springer Publishing Company, 1984), as well as numerous articles on group counseling and social work practice and education.

Foundations
of
Social Work Practice

Joseph Anderson, D.S.W., A.C.S.W.

Springer Publishing Company
New York

Springer Publishing Company, Inc.
536 Broadway
New York, NY 10012

88 89 90 91 92/5 4 3 2 1

LIBRARY OF CONGRESS
Library of Congress Cataloging-in-Publication Data

Anderson, Joseph, 1941-
    Foundations of social work practice / Joseph Anderson.
        p.   cm.—(Springer series on social work : v. 12)
    Bibliography: p.
    Includes index.
    ISBN 0-8261-5500-6
    1. Social service.   I. Title.   II. Series.
HV40.A77 1988
361—dc19   87-33404
                                                               CIP

Printed in the United States of America

To the memory and works of William Schwartz, who has been an inspiration for my work; and to Wanda, in whose love my soul soars.

Contents

PART II   Generic Social Work Process Competencies

Foreword

The renowned philosopher Mortimer Adler, the Editor of a widely acclaimed edition of the Encyclopedia Britannica, enjoys talking about giving away knowledge. He views the transmission of knowledge as potentially most effective when it is put in a form that others can absorb. Dr. Joseph D. Anderson has a similar overriding objective—to capture the foundation competencies needed by the skilled social worker and to provide a method for communicating them to B.S.W. and M.S.W. students in basic practice courses. In an articulate and exceptionally well-written manner, Dr. Anderson has identified and illustrated the foundation competencies basic to effective social work intervention at the beginning and the advanced levels. The basic skills he identifies are applicable to all client systems—individual, family, group, organization, or community. The skills are thoroughly grounded in disciplined theory and research. Joseph Anderson provides the reader with a generic model that can contribute significantly to the professional development of entry-level social workers by identifying specific competencies and performance objectives and ways in which beginning social workers can assess and evaluate their actual practice, catch their mistakes early, and correct them.

In recent years the social work literature has produced several notable texts on generalist social work practice and the ecological model. Included among these notable texts is Dr. Anderson's 1981 book, *Social Work Methods and Processes*. The generalist and ecological perspectives have had an enormous impact on all the areas of social work practice. The reason for this substantial impact has primarily been that these practice models have proven to have great practical application in a number of practice settings ranging from child welfare to mental health. This social work text will further extend the value of these models by developing and conceptualizing Anderson's Foundation

Practice Model. His model integrates the ecological and phenomenological perspectives for practice with an interactional model. Taken together, the principles, concepts, and skills provide a unifying framework for defining both the generic components of clinical practice and for identifying the generic skills for this practice.

Part I of this book is comprised of the author's presentation of social work's interactional perspective combined with both the ecological and self-awareness perspectives as prerequisites to the development of foundation competencies. In Part II he expands upon his examination of the theoretical perspectives undergirding social work practice. Each of the seven chapters in this part of the book focuses on a specific foundation competence.

I highly recommend this book to professors who teach social work practice to B.S.W. seniors and M.S.W. students. Dr. Anderson's book stands out as a uniquely systematic, comprehensive, lucid, well-organized, and practical text. Because of the author's knowledge and skill at synthesizing phenomenological theory, ecological and generalist perspectives, symbolic interactionism, and Eastern philosophy, this book will become a classic contribution to social work education.

The other eleven books in the Springer Series on Social Work have focused on a specific area of practice such as social work practice in the emergency room or elder abuse and neglect or social work in the workplace. These original reference volumes have filled a gap in the social work literature on specialization areas. I welcome Dr. Anderson's new book to the Series on Social Work and note that it is the first book in the series that was written as both a reference volume and a basic social work text. I anticipate that this book will come to be viewed as an illuminating and practical text and an exemplar of a step-by-step module learning approach for future social workers.

ALBERT R. ROBERTS, D.S.W.

Editor, Springer Series on Social Work
Associate Professor and Chairperson
Planning and Management Curriculum
School of Social Work
Indiana University at Indianapolis
November, 1987

Preface

This book is about foundation competencies for social work practice. The dictionary suggests that the shared element in the meaning of such synonyms as *able, capable, qualified,* and *competent* is a quality of fitness. Competence implies a good fit among tasks, expectations for the performance of tasks, and actual performance. As such, competence is an interactional concept. It is also an integrative concept. Competence refers to a set of abilities that integrate thinking, feeling, and doing through reliable and creative skill. Social work *competence,* then, is defined as *the integrated mastery of analytical and interactional skills through which the purpose and principles of social work that guide practice are applied in the effective performance of tasks.*

This definition incorporates aspects of the many meanings of the term *competence* as found in the social work literature (Anderson, 1985). Competence translates knowledge and values into a set of analytical and interactional skills that are artfully applied in the situational contexts of practice. The use of these skills in practice contributes simultaneously to the achievement of professional purpose, effective performance of job tasks, and positive client outcomes.

Foundation competencies are the skills that are basic to both beginning and advanced practice. The 1983 curriculum policy statement of the Council on Social Work Education (CSWE) for BSW and MSW program accreditation establishes the principle that social work education and practice build on a *common professional foundation.* This foundation is the major objective of BSW programs and the base for concentration learning in MSW programs. Foundation competencies translate social work knowledge and values into generic principles and skills for work with individuals, families, small groups, organizations, and communities. This practice, carried out through a variety of intervention systems, is called "generalist" practice.

Thus this book focuses on the skills that provide a generic foundation for generalist practice. These skills include two major types: analytical and interactional. Analytical skills require ways of looking at and thinking about service situations and one's use of oneself in practice. Interactional skills combine this "thinking" and "feeling" in the "doing" of face-to-face work. The foundation analytical skills include the use of the ecological perspective, self-awareness, "tuning-in," differential assessment, and service planning, the use of practice models for intervention, and evaluation. The interactional skills entail establishing helping relationships, contracting, elaborating and clarifying, empathizing, sustaining work, sharing one's own feelings, providing information, linking, advocacy, and ending. This book presents and integrates these skills as competencies for foundation practice through a conception of social work process as the generic phases of work. These four phases are: preliminary (tuning-up), beginning, work, and ending.

Social work practice is principle-based and not rule- or technique-governed. Therefore, social work practice is, and always will be, both a science and an art. All skills, at their best, are both disciplined and creative. The discipline comes from the theory and research base that translates knowledge and values into informed skills. The creative elements of competence come from adapting principles and skills to one's own personal style and to the assessed understanding of particular client systems (individual, family, group, organization, or community). The intent of this book is to present skills that can lead to both disciplined and creative entry-level practice. Therefore, the skills are grounded in disciplined theory and research, as well as in procedures that can be integrated creatively with professional purpose, personal styles, and client system needs.

The theory and research base for these foundation competencies combines the ecological and phenomenological perspectives for practice with an interactional model. Together, these provide the conceptual framework for defining the generic elements of practice and for identifying the generic skills for this practice.

I have tried to present these competencies in a way that introduces them to beginning students in social work (as "foundation"), yet also contributes to continuing professional development in review and independent learning (as "core"). As students initially master the breadth of these skills for their use in practice, they can have a base for developing a depth of competence through their disciplined and creative use. The integrative thread that weaves these skills to create a competent practitioner is the focus on social work process as this informs the generic foundation of practice.

No book can teach practice. Practice is learned by attempting to apply these principles, concepts, and skills in the real world of providing services. Therefore, the book includes suggestions for the practice of these competencies. This book, as a theoretical base for practice, can contribute most to professional development if it provides a useful model for assessing and evaluating what students do in actual practice. The professional social worker is not a person free of mistakes. Rather, the professional is a person who shortens the time between making a mistake and catching and learning from it. This book will be useful if it provides a model that helps students catch their mistakes in practice quickly and gives them some direction on how to correct these.

After establishing the theoretical perspectives in Part I, each chapter in Part II focuses on a specific foundation competence. The chapters develop the conceptual base for each particular competence and state the skills in terms of performance objectives. This organization promotes the use of this book in module teaching and learning in social work education (Brennen, 1978; Dea, 1971; Price, 1976). Module learning has the potential for balancing self-directed adult learning styles and required content (Price, 1976); for integrating content areas (Brennen, 1978); and for applying integrated content to practice in field experiences (Dea, 1971). A module is a self-contained learning unit that integrates conceptual themes around specific performance (observable and measurable) objectives, specific content and skills necessary for achieving the objectives, and specific ways of evaluating the mastery of the objectives.

The chapters in Part I develop the underlying perspectives for social work foundation competencies. These include the interactional-generalist perspective (Chapter 1), the theoretical perspectives and foundation competencies (Chapter 2), the ecological perspective (Chapter 3), and the self-awareness perspective (Chapter 4). Part II covers the competencies of generic social work process, as consistent with these perspectives, in the four phases of direct service practice: preliminary (Chapter 5), beginning (Chapters 6 and 7), work (Chapters 8 and 9), and ending (Chapter 10). A final chapter (Chapter 11) covers how we learn competence for practice.

Perspectives

1 Social Work's Interactional Perspective and Foundation Practice

Kim Koh had practiced with his sword ever since he could remember. Now, as a young man, he had become a fairly skillful swordsman. But he was not a samurai.

Thus Kim went to Master Ito to learn to be a samurai swordsman. Ito put Kim through a complex set of highly detailed training exercises. Each aspect of the process of masterful swordsmanship was presented in theory, broken down into specific components, and studied carefully, one at a time.

During this process of technical mastery, Kim found handling the sword very awkward. He felt he was losing his naturally developed skills. In fact, his performance seemed to drop increasingly during his practice of each of the single skills. In his impatience and frustration, Kim went to Ito to complain: "Master, I am a worse swordsman now than when I first came to you. Where once I could handle my sword like a swan, graceful and natural, I now feel like a wounded grasshopper, uncoordinated and jumpy."

Ito responded, "You are so impatient, Kim, and you want to be a samurai? Once you become totally aware of each part of the skill for mastering swordsmanship and practice these to perfection, you have taken the first step. You may be ready to move from grasshopper to swan to true samurai. Go now and practice and say no more."

Kim complied. He worked hard at each individual skill, developing his awareness of the skill and practicing it to perfection. He then returned to Ito and demonstrated his newly acquired skills.

3

"You have taken the first major step to become samurai, Kim. Now you must take another very important step. Go to the top of that mountain and meditate. When you have found a perspective that makes everything you've learned seem unimportant, return to me."

Kim meditated for three days and nights, until he seemed to have forgotten everything he had learned from Ito. Then a clear picture formed in his mind's eye, and his whole being knew he had found the perspective of a samurai. He was not a grasshopper, nor a swan. He and the sword were one.

When Kim returned with this perspective, now so much of his style of being, and with his perfectly developed skills integrated into this perspective, Ito knew instantly. "You are samurai," he confirmed. "Go now and see things clearly."

Learning the skills and competencies in this book may be very similar to Kim's experience in learning samurai swordsmanship. This learning requires understanding the parts of social work practice and integrating these parts into a meaningful and useful whole. The theory for both these parts and the whole informs individual skills, overall competencies, and the core social work process. Most chapters of this book detail the individual skills and competencies for study and practice. This practice at times will seem unnatural and awkward. Together, though, these skills form the base for foundation-level social work practice. Central to this foundation, however, is the perspective from which these skills evolve and to which they contribute. This chapter presents this perspective.

Professions differ in their domain, their focus, and their perspective for this focus. The physician focuses on the physical person and the biological environmental influences that contribute to physical illness. The lawyer focuses on the rights of individuals and groups and their legal institutions. The social worker focuses on the intricate interactional processes between people and their social environment in their social living. And this social focus is more difficult to define than the physical or legal one. The social focus is more precisely a biopsychosocial one; that is, one in which the individual as an organism and personality interacts with the multilayers of social systems in which people are born, live, struggle, grow, and die. This focus requires a special and unique perspective, or frame of reference.

A frame of reference frames our view of the world. In social work practice, it focuses our attention on the elements of the world we intend to influence by what we do. *Webster* defines perspective as the "capacity to view things in their true relations or relative importance."

A social work perspective must direct our attention and intention to the realities in any practice situation upon which we wish to place primary importance. These are the interactions we want to understand in assessment and to influence in intervention. All foundation competencies flow from this central frame of reference. What is the social work perspective, which assures our capacity to best view things in their relative importance? This book bases all foundation competencies on *social work's interactional perspective*.

SOCIAL WORK'S INTERACTIONAL PERSPECTIVE

Social work's perspective is the simultaneous dual focus on people and their environment. Social work concerns not merely the biology and psychology of the individual nor the sociology of the environment. Instead, the relational processes between the individual and society receive primary attention. This view considers how people affect environments and how environments affect people in their mutual need for each other. Thus social work focuses on *interactions*.

Historically, this perspective concerned the "person-in-situation." The person-in-situation notion has a long and consistent history as the most fundamental component of a framework for social work practice. For example, the *Report of the Milford Conference* (Social Casework, 1928) tentatively agreed that social work "concerned the individual's capacity for self-maintenance which . . . is always relative to a given setting" (p. 8). Almost all more recent attempts to define social work take as their starting place the interaction between people and their environment and then translate this into ideas about our unique professional purpose and function (Anderson, 1981; Bartlett, 1970; Billups, 1984; Germain, 1979; Gordon, 1983; NASW, 1977; Rosenfeld, 1983; Siporin, 1980). For instance, this focus finds recent affirmation in the latest curriculum policy statement of the Council on Social Work Education (1982): "Professional practice thus focuses on the transactions between people and their environments that affect their ability to accomplish life tasks, alleviate distress, and realize individual and collective aspirations" (p. 6). This focus greatly determines our knowledge and values and constitutes a frame of reference that is both unique and unifying for social work as a profession.

There is an interesting historical aside to this central frame of reference and social work's development as a profession. Abraham Flexner (1905), less than a decade after he revolutionized the medical profession by recommending a common educational foundation, took the podium at the National Conference of Charities and Corrections to address the question, "Is Social Work a Profession?" He applied his six criteria of professional activity to social work and found it wanting. To Flexner, professional activity was basically *intellectual*, carrying with it great personal responsibility; it was *learned*, being based on great knowledge and not merely routine; it was *practical* rather than purely theoretical or academic; its *technique* could be taught as the major basis for professional education; it was strongly *organized* internally; and it was motivated by *altruism*, with professionals viewing themselves as working for some aspect of the good of society.

Most social workers remember Flexner's verdict that social work was *not* a profession. Few, however, seem to recall how he found social work wanting and how he concluded his presentation. Flexner's opinion was that social work had no teachable technique of its own, but only mediated between people with needs and resources to meet these needs. And he concluded this classic presentation with these words: "The unselfish devotion of those who have chosen to give themselves to making the world a fitter place to live in can fill social work with the professional spirit and thus to some extent lift it above all the distinctions which I have been at such pains to make" (Flexner, 1905, p. 590).

Following Flexner, social work did not soon develop a unifying frame of reference for the knowledge and values to match its purpose and mediating skills. Instead, the profession unfortunately sought individual treatment techniques, largely outside of social work, and at times waivered in its professional spirit to make the world a fitter place to live (Borenzweig, 1971; Rothman, 1985). Some of the past and much of the present work on clarifying this perspective asserts not that social work *only* mediates, but that social work *distinctively* mediates the interactions between people and environments to match needs and resources in order to make the world "fitter." This evolving view can now provide a generic core that marks all professional practice.

GENERIC FRAMEWORK

The point at which the individual and environment make direct and active contact is the domain of social work. All social work practice concerns the interactions at the interface of individuals and their immediate, impinging environment. Here, the interactional exchange becomes apparent and sometimes problematic. Social work's central *purpose* is to reduce current mismatches between needs and resources in this interaction and to prevent potential mismatches. Our professional *function*, then, is mediating the interactions in the specific context of those services that are designed to bring together individual needs and social resources. This purpose and function direct the social work *focus* in any practice situation upon the interactions between people and the various systems through which they relate with society—the family, peer group, social agency, neighborhood, school, job, and others.

For instance, social work practice with an adolescent substance abuser concerns not just how the adolescent meets particular needs through his or her self-destructive and socially irresponsible behavior. It considers how these needs reflect particular problems in the interface between this adolescent and pertinent environmental systems. These likely include the family, the peer group, the school, and the community, among others. The adolescent's interaction with these systems creates the needs behind substance abuse, and it can also provide the resources to promote and/or alleviate the problematic behavior. Such a professional focus affects both how we view this adolescent's problems and what we do to enable a better match between interactional needs and resources. If our definition of the problem is not based solely on the person's behavior, our intervention is likely to include work with the family and the peer group as well as with the individual adolescent.

In this view, interactions refer to reciprocal processes: One party influences another and, in turn, is also influenced by the other. Many refer to this reciprocity when they write about "transactional exchanges" (Germain, 1981; Siporin, 1980; Vigilante et al., 1981). Interactions reflect some mutual exchange of energy and information with one or more other parties.

The relationship between the individual and the environment is always a reciprocal process, even though it is often not experienced as such by many clients. Our clients may experience themselves as at odds with their environment, overwhelmed by its demands and pollutants, and victims of its inhumanity and injustice. Most often, these situations reflect an exchange that devitalizes both people and their environments. They evolve from destructive reciprocal processes. On the other hand, a better match in the interaction between the person and environment is vitalizing and constructive for both. This is called *synergistic* interaction. Enabling more synergistic interactions, therefore, is the primary *objective* of all social work practice.

A social worker with an interactional perspective may direct activities primarily to either the person or the environment. Over time in any direct practice situation, this same practitioner will most likely direct these activities at both—usually in a "more-or-less" rather than "either-or" manner—to enable a more synergistic match. This can involve the promotion, restoration, maintenance, or enhancement of these interactions through the competent provision of direct service. It can also involve the indirect advocating, planning, developing, and implementing of social policies, services, and programs that provide resources to meet basic needs and support the development of people's capacities and abilities. A synergistic match promotes the simultaneous development of both people and their interactive social systems.

These objectives place primary *value* on the following qualities of reciprocal interactions. We value interactions that balance individual autonomy and interdependence with others. These interactions respect individual dignity and worth, self-determination, the potential for self-actualization, *and* social responsibility (maximizing the realization of the potential of other individuals). In other words, we value and therefore promote synergistic social systems in all of our activities. Synergistic social systems are families, small groups, organizations, and communities that function simultaneously for the good of both the individual and the system.

These values require that all social workers possess fundamental *knowledge* of the potential for and obstacles to synergistic social interactions as well as the processes, methods, and skills to enable such interactions. This foundation knowledge, then, includes the theory, principles, and skills for assessing mismatches, mediating to enable matches, and evaluating the degree of synergy that results from our practice.

Thus the generic framework of social work practice (as illustrated in Figure 1-1) evolves from a configuration of our domain, purpose, function, focus, and objectives, as well as some aspects of our knowledge and skills. Harriet Bartlett (1971) has likewise defined what is generic in social work practice in such a configuration:

> Social work practice . . . is recognized by a constellation of value, purpose, knowledge, and interventive techniques. Some social work practice shows more extensive use of one or the other of the components, but it is social work practice only when all are present to some degree. (p. 1479)

This constellation is the common core of all social work practice in its very diverse forms and makes this practice unique to the social work profession. That is, these components *together* make all social workers more similar to each other and more different from other helping professionals.

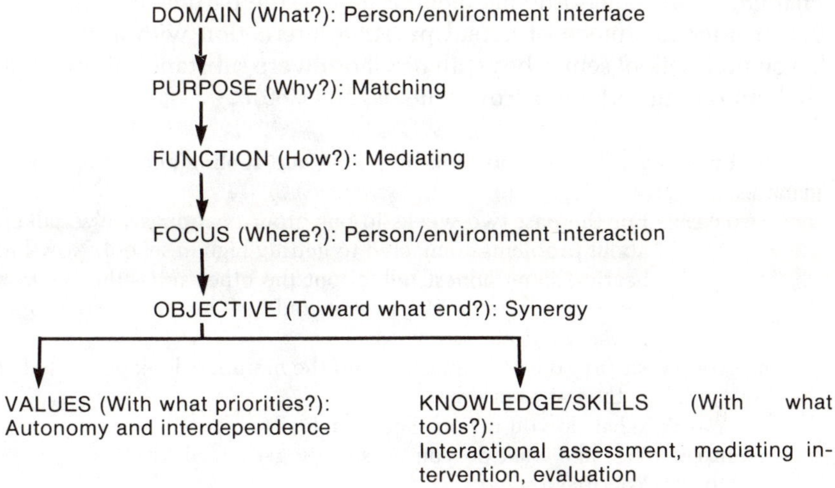

DOMAIN (What?): Person/environment interface

↓

PURPOSE (Why?): Matching

↓

FUNCTION (How?): Mediating

↓

FOCUS (Where?): Person/environment interaction

↓

OBJECTIVE (Toward what end?): Synergy

VALUES (With what priorities?): Autonomy and interdependence

KNOWLEDGE/SKILLS (With what tools?): Interactional assessment, mediating intervention, evaluation

FIGURE 1-1 Generic framework for social work practice.

As these generic components of social work practice come together in our work with the adolescent substance abuser mentioned earlier, we would be bringing a unique combination of "cause" and "function" to what is both an individual and social problem. An outsider observing the work with this youth, the family, and peers might be hard-pressed to distinguish the uniqueness of what we as social workers are doing in our practice. It is not really *what* we do—our specific intervention activities—that differentiates social work practice from other helping professions. It is why we do what we do—our domain, purpose, focus, and objectives—and how we do what we do—our translation of a particular set of values, knowledge, and skills into professional intents and actions.

Thus if we observe a social worker loading up a station wagon with this adolescent and his peers for a picnic trip to the country on a sunny Saturday afternoon, we may wonder how this differs from the actions of a scout leader, a Sunday school teacher, a parent, or a child-care worker. We might ask: "What is really professional about this? Why does one have to be trained for this? Can't any good-hearted person enjoy an afternoon with a group of adolescents and therefore 'help' them?" What may not be seen is how this outing was planned to promote more mutual aid among the group. Or how the social worker responded with a particular mixture of empathic support and honest challenge, or confrontation, to the banter among the youths during the ride. Or how the picnic was purposefully planned and engaged in as an activity for enabling more synergistic interactions among the participants.

Consider this piece of actual practice interaction with a group of seven high school senior boys, all of whom were substance abusers, on such an outing (adapted from Shields, 1985/86):

(The boys began the conversation by joking and fooling about their marijuana use.)

SOCIAL WORKER: For the past two weeks in our group meetings we've talked about problems connected to getting high in school. Now I'm hearing some honest talk about the other side—the fun you see in getting high. Maybe you could tell me more about some of the good parts.

(The group is surprised by the question and the members look perplexed at the social worker, then at each other.)

ANDY: What do you mean? The benefits?

SOCIAL WORKER: Yes, like what do you personally get out of it?

DAN: You mean why?

RON: Well, music sounds better—I have more fun.

TIM: Yeah, you have a better time.

(All agree.)

LARRY: (hesitantly) I haven't smoked in two weeks.

RICHIE: Me either.

(Members start joking and teasing each other about trying to "go straight.")

SOCIAL WORKER: (asks Richie and Larry) How come you haven't smoked?

LARRY: I had no money.

RICHIE: I got drunk instead.

SOCIAL WORKER: Oh, that doesn't count?

RICHIE: No, it's different.

(The group laughs.)

DAN: Oh, come off it Rich, it's no different.

RICHIE: I think it is.

SOCIAL WORKER: How is it different for you?

RICHIE: Well, I don't worry about it. (pause) Like sometimes I'm afraid if I smoke too much I'll become a burnout.

CARL: Sometimes, I don't even want to do it. But I do.

LARRY: It's something to look forward to.

TIM: Like on a nice day like today—you get stoned outside—it's real nice.

CARL: I wouldn't.

TIM: Why not?

CARL: It's too nice out. I can get high on this—on our being out and being together.

DAN: I would, just to relax. I'm so tense after school.

SOCIAL WORKER: What do you mean, tense?

(Dan begins to talk about the pressure he feels in school. He shares with the group his worry that he won't graduate and how ashamed his parents will be. The others listen intently to these words and feelings, obviously so strong for Dan.)

SOCIAL WORKER: Does anyone else feel discouraged and worried about gradua-
                tion?

(Others share their particular concerns, and a discussion ensues about the particular pressures of senior year and the weight of future decisions they have to face.)

As we delve more into this piece of practice, we can identify how this social worker applied her generic professional foundation to bring a unique difference to this work. She uses her overriding purpose to enable this peer group system to match better with each member's developmental needs, her function to mediate the interactions among these youths and their impinging social worlds (peers, family, school, future, and so on), her values of acceptance and mutual aid, and the knowledge that translates these into action. Thus she starts where the group is—their somewhat bravado attitude and coping pattern—and challenges them to use each other and their process together toward more serious work on the drug theme. Again, nothing unique to social work marks what this social worker says or does. Rather, why she says or does this, how she maintains a focus on the work consistent with this purpose, and the integration of the knowledge, values, and skills with what she says and does—all these reflect what is uniquely and signifi- cantly *social work* in her practice. This configuration of the generics of social work in her foundation for practice is what she shares in com- mon with the best of practice in all of social work.

GENERALIST FRAMEWORK

Not only is all social work practice generic, but, to some degree, it is generalist. To achieve our social work purpose through a focus on the interactions between individuals and their impinging environments, we need a variety of methods to promote good matches and prevent mismatches. Thus, our very perspective for practice is a generalist one. This *generalist perspective*, then, is another generic element of all practice (Schatz & Jenkins, 1987). Even specialists within social work use a generalist base. Their practice demands versatility of methods as well as specific knowledge relevant to particular populations-at-risk, contexts, and fields. Those specializing in delivering direct services, such as BSW graduates and clinical or direct practice social workers, must be especially well-prepared for generalist practice. This is true regardless of any additional specialization in population-at-risk, context, or fields. (See Anderson, 1985; Carroll, 1977; Constable, 1978; Costin, 1981; Hartman, 1983; Gordon & Schutz, 1977; Martinez-Brawley, 1986; Meares, 1981; Meyer, Garber, & Williams, 1979; Vice-Irey, 1980.)

In direct-service generalist practice, the practitioner uses all prevailing social work methods either singly or in combination to strengthen the inherent capacities for reciprocal interactions in both individuals and their social systems. Intervention activities target problems in these interactions at all levels—intrapersonal, familial, interpersonal, organizational, communal, institutional, and societal. Most often, practitioners attend to more than one aspect of a given problem simultaneously, as they are discovered in the problem-solving process. The service evolves from an assessment of needs, goals, and intervention systems, as determined through a relationship process with the practitioner, to the planning of methods and approaches most appropriate to influence selected targets. The intervention draws from any one or any combination of methods, each with a set of specific models or approaches. The practitioner attempts to match specific methods and approaches to each problem situation. In this way, already established knowledge is used eclectically, and additional modes can be developed to meet new challenges to the profession.

Any model of direct-service generalist social work practice, therefore, must account for these three primary dimensions of all social work practice: the generic, the specific, and the generalist. It needs to incorporate these dimensions in their separate "parts" and their interrelationship in the "whole." Finally, it needs to be heuristic in its applicability for the study of practice and its potential to serve as a guide for learning to practice effectively. Figure 1-2 diagrams one such conceptual framework.

This direct-service generalist framework begins with the recognition that we use methods that depend upon the nature of client systems and intervention systems. In direct-service practice, "client systems" are "people who sanction or ask for the . . . services, who are expected beneficiaries of service, and who have a working agreement or contract" (Pincus & Minahan, 1976, p. 63). "Intervention systems" are people and interactions that need to be influenced to accomplish the goals in the contract with client systems. These intervention systems at times include and at times are different from the direct client system (individuals, families, or small groups). For example, in protective services for the elderly, we may gear many of our initial activities to individuals who are

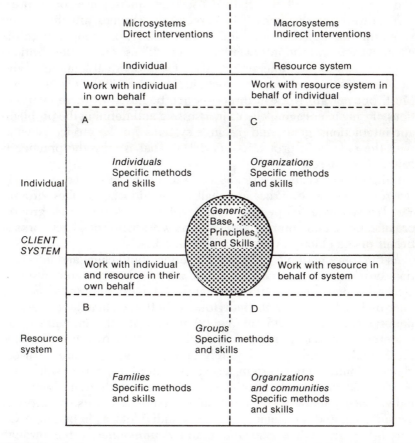

FIGURE 1-2 Generalist framework for direct-service social work practice.

"at-risk" (the client system) to increase their self-concern and willingness to consider behaviors and resources that better assure their safety and security (also, then, the intervention system). As we work with neighbors and extended family to establish a social network for this protection and security, our intervention system (these networks) is different from our direct client system (individual elderly who are at-risk).

The second dimension in this framework for direct-service practice is the generalist one (depicted in the dotted line running vertically through the middle of Figure 1-2). As this diagram depicts, the generalist concept is based on two major, interrelated assumptions: (1) at times the direct client system and the intervention system are the same and at times they differ; (2) direct-service practice uses both direct and indirect interventions. The direct interventions are those used when the microsystem of an individual, family, or group is both the client system and the intervention system. Thus, direct interventions refer to face-to-face interactions with the individuals, families, and small groups themselves for changes in the system in their own behalf. Most, but not all, work in direct service begins with these interventions, if only in engaging clients in assessing and defining the problematic interactions, goals, and resource systems for the service (such as with the elderly in protective services). That is why the practice is called *direct service*.

Indirect interventions are those designed to influence people in macrosystems as resources in behalf of individuals, families, groups, and larger classes of people. This involves work with task groups, organizations, and communities (such as work with social networks in behalf of the elderly in protective services).

As the four quadrants in Figure 1-2 reflect, both client and intervention systems can involve the individual or other resource systems. Generalist practice, therefore, demands: (1) work with *individuals* in their own behalf (when the individual is both the client and intervention system, as in quadrant A); (2) work with the individual and resource systems as in *families* and *groups* in their own behalf (when the individual and system—family and small groups—are both the client and intervention system, as in quadrant B); (3) work with others in informal or formal organizational resource systems in behalf of individual clients (when the intervention system is a formal or informal *organization* and the client system is an individual, as in quadrant C); and (4) work with *organizations* and *communities*, often through groups, in behalf of the resource system members (when the intervention system and the client system are the organization or community, as in quadrant D). Thus, all direct-service generalist social work practice requires a repertoire of methods to inform direct and indirect interventions with individuals, families, groups, organizations, and communities (as depicted in the four quadrants in Figure 1-2).

The methods themselves provide the specific dimension for this framework. There are models for the use of each method that inform specific principles and skills for effective generalist practice. Work with individuals requires specific as well as generic skills for establishing helping relationships, interviewing, and problem solving. Work with families requires specific knowledge and skills for assessment, enabling family process and family system competence in behalf of all

members and enhancing the family system's interaction with its ecological environment. Work with groups, when the group itself is a
major resource for meeting members' needs, requires specific knowledge and skills for assessment and for enabling group process toward
mutual aid in behalf of its members. When the group is a resource for
organizational and community change, the specific knowledge and
skills for practice involve assessments and leadership designed to
enable the group to develop its competence to influence targeted
aspects of organizations and communities. Work with organizations in
behalf of individuals requires specific knowledge and skills for networking in informal resource systems and for case consultation, linking, referral, and case advocacy in formal organizational resource
systems. Work with organizations and communities in behalf of their
members requires specific knowledge and skills for assessing organizations and communities, for developing strategies for the development of programs, policies, and services, for cause (or class) advocacy, and for enabling organizational and community development.

There are also specific models for adapting methods to the needs of
special populations. The beginning direct-service generalist needs
models that are theoretically compatible and readily integrated with
the concepts of the generic base of social work practice. The advanced
practitioner can draw on an eclectic variety of approaches within
methods and across methods with more knowledge and experience of
the use of theory and research in practice.

CONCLUSION

The generalist framework has as its core the ability to apply the
generic base of social work principles and skills, or foundation competencies. These generic principles and skills include those that combine the basic knowledge and values that are significant elements of all
social work methods into guidelines for action. Models of generic
interactional skills, ecological analytical skills, and generic social work
process further define this core and are presented in this text.

There are particular methods and practice models that are the
essential minimum needed for specific work in each of the four quadrants of generalist practice shown in Figure 1-2. Mastery of these
assures sufficient depth as well as breadth of skill for work with
individuals, families, groups, organizations, and communities. The
more advanced the level of preparation for generalist practice, the
greater the variety of approaches we might learn for this practice. At a

minimal level of competence for direct-service generalist practice, we need models that can fit into a less complex and potentially less contradictory overriding theoretical perspective. The process-oriented, interactional, problem-solving model of this book provides one such integrative theory base.

2 Theoretical Perspectives and Competencies

One day Winnie-the-Pooh dropped in at Rabbit's hole unannounced, in hope of finding a Little Something. Rabbit was, of course, too polite to turn Pooh down. He was too polite even to stop Pooh when Pooh was eating every bit of honey, condensed milk, and bread in Rabbit's hole. At last, when there was nothing more to eat, Pooh attempted to leave. He only "attempted" because by now Pooh was so stuffed that he could only get halfway through the entrance to Rabbit's hole.

And there, halfway through, stuck Pooh until Christopher Robin, his Wise Friend, came along. It was clear that Pooh would remain stuck for quite a while—a whole week suggested Christopher Robin—before he would be thin enough to get free again.

"A week!" said Pooh gloomily. "What about meals?"

"I'm afraid no meals," said Christopher Robin, "because of getting thin quicker. But we will read to you."

Bear began to sigh, and then found he couldn't because he was so tightly stuck; and a tear rolled down his eye, as he said: "Then would you read a Sustaining Book, such as would help and comfort a Wedged Bear in Great Tightness?"

In this tale, adapted from A. A. Milne's *Winnie-the-Pooh* (1954), we find some instructive metaphors for the use of theory in social work practice. Like Pooh, our need for theory can lead us to fill our heads with so many conflicting ideas that we get stuck about what to do when we confront the real challenge of practice. Or we can weld ourselves to a particular theoretical approach that does not really fit the demands of practice, thus sticking our clients in the Rabbit hole, trying to force their lives to fit our theory.

17

We, however, do need theory, defined as generalized propositions and concepts that explain and predict the interactional events in practice, and we will use some form of it. A useful practice theory can be most sustaining, like the book that Christopher Robin read to Pooh. Such a theory translates our basic social work knowledge and values into principles and skills; it provides us with guidelines that really help those we serve. This chapter presents the theory used to determine the foundation competencies described in this text. This theory seems especially fruitful for informing foundation-level practice; it combines the ecological and phenomenological perspectives with the interactional model.

PRACTICE THEORY

Practicing social work requires two types of practice theories: a theory *for* practice and a theory *of* practice (Vigilante et al., 1981). A theory *for* practice is a metatheory. Metatheory establishes the overriding framework in which to view the many possible kinds of realities that occur in practice. In social work, this metatheory must provide a perspective on the nature of person–environment interactions that is consistent with the profession's philosophical (what we believe) and epistemological (what and how we know) foundations. It is the basis for combining values and knowledge with the analytical tasks of practice: problem identification, assessment, planning, and evaluation. Metatheory, then, illuminates what we look for, how we look at it, and therefore how we understand the people and events we face in practice. It also explains why we focus in these particular ways on the people and events.

A theory *of* practice is more accurately a "practice model." A practice model translates the *whys* and *whats* and *hows* of what we believe and know into direction of what to *do* in specific practice situations. A social work practice model applies the metatheory of what occurs in person–environment interactions and scales these ideas to the transactions that occur in actual practice. These include interactions between the practitioner and clients and between clients and their social worlds. Thus practice models translate values and knowledge into informed analytical and interactional skills to direct our practice in specific ways. In this book, theory *for* practice comes from the ecological and phenomenological perspectives. The theory *of* practice comes from an interactional practice model. The remainder of this chapter introduces these perspectives, this model, and the foundation competencies and skills that evolve from them.

THE ECOLOGICAL PERSPECTIVE

Using the ecological perspective, social work practice consistently views the client in relation to the physical and social environments that contain the resources for or obstacles to meeting needs. The key interactional concepts in the ecological perspective, which spotlight the nature of clients' relationships with the environment, are adaptation, stress, and coping.

Adaptation is the interactional process in which people both shape their physical and social environment and are shaped by them. Both self and environment at every level (biological, psychological, social, and cultural) are constantly changing. Adaptation is the continuous effort to fit the ever-changing conditions of existence to ever-changing human needs and aspirations. As an interactional concept, adaptation directs our concerns simultaneously to the qualities of the person and the qualities of the environment that promote or inhibit matching and mutual growth.

This concern brings us to the second interactional concept of the ecological perspective: stress. The concept of stress increases our understanding of transactions that tend to upset the interactional processes between people and their environments in a way that is potentially damaging to either or both. Stress comes from people's perception of an imbalance between the demands upon them and their capabilities in meeting those demands.

The first aspect of stress is the demand. Demand on the individual, family, group, organization, or community can initiate from environmental events and processes or internal (biological and/or psychological) needs and processes, and often from both. Demands call forth capabilities. Capability refers to the abilities, capacities, and resources available for meeting the demand. Research suggests the important distinction that what is more critical than actual demand and actual capability are *perceived* demand and the *perceived* capability (Coelho et al., 1974; Cox, 1978; Monat & Lazarus, 1977). A perception of an imbalance between demand and capability leads to the emotional experience of stress and to change in one's physiological state. These experiences and changes, in turn, lead to psychological and physiological coping responses.

Therefore, coping is also an interactional concept. Coping responses can reduce, eliminate, or accelerate stress. Successful coping draws upon particular personality attributes and situational elements. Social work intervention that is stress- and coping-oriented enables both autonomy and interdependence. It must "help people to discover their inner resources, reconnect to past or present environments, and enhance adaptive relatedness and a sense of identity and self-esteem, competence, and autonomy. Such qualities are, after all, outcomes of adaptive transactions between people and environments" (Germain, 1981, p. 330).

This ecological perspective is a central metatheory for the selection of the major analytical skills of the foundation competencies in this book. As the next chapter will elaborate, this metatheory informs significant prerequisite competencies in the foundation for social work practice.

PHENOMENOLOGICAL PERSPECTIVE

As a complement to the ecological perspective, the phenomenological one asserts that the reality of person–environment interactions lies in its meaning to the persons experiencing them. In other words, we comprehend the nature of interactions by understanding the meaning to the persons involved, including ourselves as practitioners. This understanding comes from subjective and self-reflexive participation and not from objective study alone. The key concepts, here, are experience, meaning, perception, and process.

The phenomenological perspective is a holistic view of human-beings-in-the-world, in which person and world together are constantly experiencing change in their being and becoming. Human behavior and development is neither "inside" a person's head nor "outside" in the environment. The human being is not a container that spills contents into the environment, nor is he or she a blank slate on which the environment inscribes the story of his or her life. Rather, individual and milieu comprise inseparable psychosocial events, or experiences. Events are not "inner" or "outer," but meaningful exchanges between people and their social worlds. We both find meaning in and bring meaning to our psychosocial experiences.

The phenomenological perspective conceives of the individual as a conscious, thinking, feeling, and willing being, actively involved in interchanges with others. These interactions are the basis for altering the phenomenal world. People live in an ongoing process of experience in which they perceive and develop meanings for themselves and for their worlds. As practitioners, our observations and participation are part of the person's experience of the psychosocial field. We alter the nature of that field by our very perceptions and the meaning we bring to it.

This perspective suggests that our practice models must connect subjective human experience, including our own as practitioners, to our understanding and influencing of person–environment interactions. So, too, the models need to be process-based. That is, they need to inform how we can enable process to promote change and growth.

Social work consistently attends to several dialectical and reciprocal processes. The individual and society comprise a dialectic that any metatheory must both explain and transcend. At the most basic level is the dialectic of process itself. All processes entail both continuity and change. In the relational processes between person and environment both continuity and change can be for better or worse. This includes our own relational processes with clients and their environments—the helping process itself. We need to comprehend this process and enable it to promote the kind of continuity and change that maintain and increase self-fulfillment and worth.

In other words, both psychosocial reality and the social worker's attempts to influence it are process phenomena. We must enhance the process through which the individual and society interact with each other for mutual fulfillment and growth. And most often we face this task at the crisis points when this dialectic can be most pronounced in its interactional process. Thus our practice models must inform our skills for mediation in these interactional processes in a way that promotes more mutual aid, more matching, more synergy. The interactional model is one such approach—most consistent with ecological and phenomenological metatheories—for this practice.

INTERACTIONAL MODEL

The interactional model (Anderson, 1984b; Shulman, 1984; Schwartz, 1971) focuses on the connections among three sets of relational processes in any practice situation. These are the client, the environmental resource systems that impinge on the client, and the social worker. These relational processes can be diagramed as shown in Figure 2-1.

At the left of Figure 2-1 is the client: a person in an ambivalent process of being and becoming whose autonomy can evolve only through interdependent engagement with the resource systems. On the right are these systems (family, work, school, agency, etc.), which are themselves involved in an ambivalent process of continuity and change. Their maintenance and growth are interdependent with those of the client. The interactional model views this ambivalent striving toward health in both individuals and resource systems as the underly-

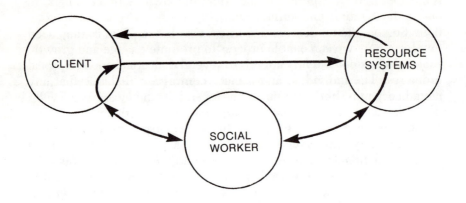

FIGURE 2-1 Interactional model.

ing interdependence with which the social worker, at the middle of the
diagram, mediates to overcome obstacles and promote more mutual
matching in the interaction.

The underlying assumption is that all interaction involves the person
and system "each needing the other for its own life and growth, and
each reaching out to the other with all the strength it can muster at a
given moment" (Schwartz, 1961, p. 15). Practice entails entering these
interdependent relational processes and seeking the common ground,
however diminished, between clients and their resource systems. The
social worker does not motivate or remotivate people and systems.
Rather, the practitioner reaches for the sometimes faint thrusts for life
and growth in the client and in the resource systems at those points
where they currently need each other most. Through mediating functions and skills, the practitioner challenges the obstacles to this mutual
need-meeting process and strengthens the interdependent connections
that enable the life and growth of both. Hence the target is always the
interaction between clients and their ecological systems, regardless of
how much the obstacles have obscured their mutual dependence.

Take, for example, a typical situation in protective services for
children. Three major systems affect this practice: the client/family,
the practitioner/agency, and the court/community. In any practice
situation, these three systems hold both shared and different perceptions of social reality. The Pugnats, the client/family system, may not
perceive child abuse at all. Or they may see their way of parenting

their children as nobody's business but their own. In addition, they see only that you, the practitioner/agency system, are aligned with the court/community system to threaten them and to take away their children. This view of reality at first glance suggests that the Pugnats are in no way motivated to engage in the work needed to assure their children's protection.

You, as the practitioner, may see child abuse. You may also see what you believe are serious problems in the overall family functioning to meet each other's needs. You may see many of these problems reflected in the parents' alcoholism and frequent violence toward each other and their children. Certainly, too, you perceive the family as currently unmotivated to face the abuse and work to lessen and prevent it. Therefore you recommend to the court that the children be removed temporarily from the home.

The court/community system perceives a reality similar to yours. The information you present leads the judge to take legal responsibility temporarily from the Pugnats. The judge determines the abuse "founded," a responsibility to protect the children through the court's authority and the rights of the parents to know what needs to be done to get the children back. The judge therefore orders that the children be placed in a temporary foster home under the supervision and legal custody of your agency, that the parents are required to complete an alcohol rehabilitation program successfully, and that they receive family counseling. The judge also indicates that your agency is to work with the Pugnats on this plan as well as on other needs that arise and to monitor and report progress before the court considers any return of the children to the home.

In this example, we have three interacting systems, each needing the others for meeting the needs of the Pugnat children. The connections of the Pugnats to you and the court are currently strong in resistance and weak in motivation for their engagement in the work that needs to be done. Figure 2-2 illustrates these connections.

Any mediation in this situation must build on the common ground, however faint, among these systems. As you stand between the Pugnats and the court/community, you are in a special position to reach for these diminished connections and to begin the work there. For instance, the Pugnats do not want to lose their children. Whenever possible, the court/community system does not want children permanently lost to their family of origin. Both the Pugnats and the community want the children to be protected and nurtured as much as possible in their own home. The reality of this shared objective and the current gap in its achievement serve as the major points for beginning

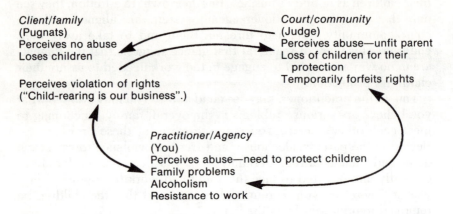

Client/family
(Pugnats)
Perceives no abuse
Loses children

Perceives violation of rights
("Child-rearing is our business".)

Court/community
(Judge)
Perceives abuse—unfit parent
Loss of children for their
    protection
Temporarily forfeits rights

Practitioner/Agency
(You)
Perceives abuse—need to protect children
Family problems
Alcoholism
Resistance to work

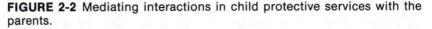

FIGURE 2-2 Mediating interactions in child protective services with the parents.

mediation in this situation. As the Pugnats and the court/community interact with each other and with you and your agency's services—motivated through the common ground and goal of caring for their children in their own home—these different realities may come to contribute less to resistance and troubled connections. All three systems can benefit from understanding these different social realities and seeking and building on the current interdependent connections. In other words, you represent both the Pugnats and the community when everything you do indicates that you want the same thing that the Pugnats and the courts want—the children protected and cared for as much as possible by the Pugnats—and that you are there to help them work toward achieving this reciprocal objective. Even in such a strongly adversarial situation, the practice promotes as much interdependence, or mutual aid, as possible.

The interactional model, as suggested in this example, is therefore consistent with the ecological perspective's focus on interactional stress, coping, and optimal adaptation. It also incorporates the phenomenological perspective in its attention to meaning, experience, perception, and process.

A basic premise of the model is that we can only understand this interaction through its meaning and purpose for those involved. Social reality evolves from individually perceived and consensually agreed upon meanings of events and through empathic participation with those experiencing the events. In other words, the reciprocal processes by which the individual and society reach out for each other in mutual need for survival and growth cannot be known objectively. They can only be known through human encounters.

This view is quite different from the assumption that people can be known through a detached expertise that studies existing problems as known objects, establishes "fix-it" goals, and takes action to set it right. This stance of objectivity has created a science of helping that Rollo May (1958) has described as "so limiting, self-contradictory, and indeed often so destructive . . . , that *the less we are involved in a given situation, the more clearly we can observe the truth*" (italics in original) (p. 27). The interactional model perceives the client as a self-determining, self-actualizing, and energy-producing individual with certain needs to achieve for his or her self-actualization. This person meets with a professional who has a specific function to carry out in their engagement as interdependent partners within a system of relationships. This focus is upon the ways in which each person in the system "reverberates" with others as all of them act upon their respective purposes for and intentions in being together. The tasks are related to these purposes and change as they do—moment to moment. As William Schwartz (1971) proposed, this practice demands that we "emphasize experience and affect, step-by-step processes, and situational rather than structural descriptions of people in difficulty" (p. 1259).

Thus this model is designed to enhance life-promoting, mutual-aid interactions between people and their immediate social systems—at work, at play, in the family, in the neighborhood, within the agency, and so on. The understanding of the match and mismatch in these interactions determines the practitioner's specific interventions at each phase of the work (Anderson, 1984b). This work requires practice skills that "are designed to create not harmony but interaction, based on a sense of strength, feeling, and purpose, drawing on the all-but-forgotten stake of people in their own institutions, and of the institutions in the people they are meant to serve" (Schwartz, 1971, p. 1261).

Practice, therefore, entails competencies for mediating between the needs and resources of individuals and those of others in their interactional systems. This generic function of social work practice was originally stated by Schwartz (1961):

The social work function is to mediate the individual–social transaction as it is worked out in the specific context of those agencies which are designed to bring together individual needs and social resources—the person's urge to belong to society as a full and productive member and the society's ability to provide certain specific means for integrating its people and enriching their social contributions. (p. 15)

This function is translated into method through interactional tasks and skills within four phases of work: preliminary, beginning, work, and ending (Shulman, 1984).

Both tasks and skills are generic, or common. They apply to practice with individuals, families, groups, organizations, and communities. The unique and generic tasks of our mediating function operationalize the purpose of social work practice. They are:

- Searching out the common ground between clients' perceptions of their own needs and the social demands they face.
- Detecting and challenging the obstacles that obscure the common ground and frustrate the efforts of people to identify their own autonomy in relation to their interdependence.
- Actualizing the potential for synergy in the interaction between clients and others.
- Defining the requirements and limits of the situation and encounter in which the client–practitioner relationship is set. These boundaries establish the purpose for the work and a contract that binds the client and agency (or social purpose) to each other and creates the condition under which the client and practitioner assume their respective functions.

These tasks are carried out through phasic, process-oriented generic skills. The *preliminary*, or *tuning-in*, phase requires what Schwartz (1971) called "preliminary empathy"—making oneself sensitive to the phenomenological world of clients, their veiled communications, and social work's knowledge of special needs and issues. The skills are tuning-in to self, tuning-in to client, and tuning-in to client's situation. Knowledge is related to action in preparation for action. The essential question is: "Where might I and this client be?"

The *beginning* phase clearly establishes the conditions of a working contract. The skills require establishing helping relationships, contracting, making an initial assessment, and service planning. The practitioner provides a clear statement of purpose in relation to client need and agency (or social purpose) function, establishes a working consensus about this purpose and about roles and responsibilities in providing the service, solicits feedback and checks mutuality of purposes, engages the client in a partnership for the work in his or her behalf, and determines more specifically the relevant needs and resources. The essential questions are: "What are we going to work on? How are we going to work on this?"

The *work* phase utilizes fully the practitioner's skills in carrying out his or her part of the contract. The questions continually asked are: "Are we working? What are we working on?" The skills require perceiving when work is going on and when it is being avoided and sustaining the work as much as possible. These include sessional tuning-in and contracting, elaborating and clarifying, empathizing, sharing one's own feelings, demanding work, providing information, using practice theory, and helping clients negotiate systems through linking and advocacy.

The *ending* (or *transition*) phase faces the question: "What have we accomplished?" The skills require effectively terminating the relationship process, or a segment of it, and systematically evaluating the service.

Figure 2-3 summarizes the perspectives, models, and concepts presented in this chapter. The ecological perspective provides a way of viewing person–environment interactions in relation to reciprocal adaptation, coping, and stress. These concepts illuminate our central social work focus in these interactions. The phenomenological perspective complements the ecological one in practice. The concepts of subjective experience, perception, and meaning place primary emphases on our use of relationships, understanding, and the enabling process in practice. The interactional model provides guidelines for this practice that are consistent with the metatheories of the ecological and phenomenological perspectives. It defines our function as mediating, our social work helping relationships as encounters, and the social work process as phases of work. A basic set of generic skills derives from this model. This function and its phases and skills generate the competence model of this text.

OVERVIEW OF COMPETENCIES AND SKILLS

In this book, these perspectives and the interactional model integrate into a model of foundation competencies. This model includes two prerequisite and six major social work process competencies. These

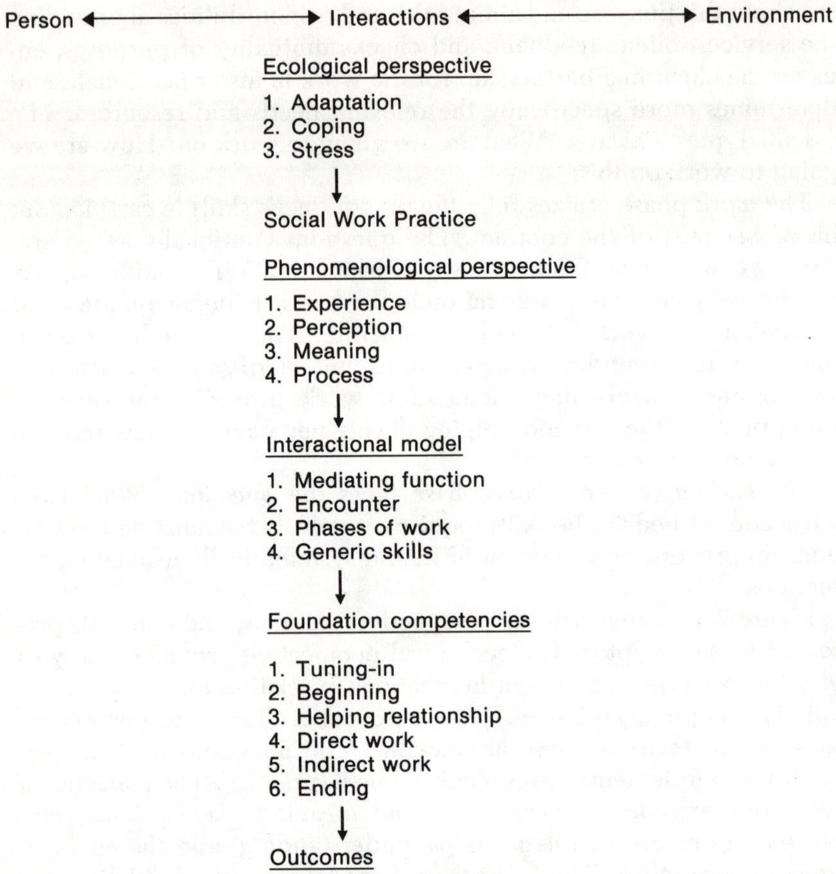

Person ◄————————► Interactions ◄————————► Environment

<u>Ecological perspective</u>

1. Adaptation
2. Coping
3. Stress

↓

Social Work Practice

<u>Phenomenological perspective</u>

1. Experience
2. Perception
3. Meaning
4. Process

↓

<u>Interactional model</u>

1. Mediating function
2. Encounter
3. Phases of work
4. Generic skills

↓

<u>Foundation competencies</u>

1. Tuning-in
2. Beginning
3. Helping relationship
4. Direct work
5. Indirect work
6. Ending

↓

<u>Outcomes</u>

FIGURE 2-3 Foundation practice model.

process competencies entail 20 separate skills. Together, these constitute the foundation for social work practice. In addition there is a seventh competency, which includes how we develop or learn continuous competence in practice. The book is organized around these competencies and skills. The chapters in Part II serve as modules; each one focuses on a particular competency and its skills. Below is an overview of these competencies and skills.

Prerequisite Competence 1: Ability to apply the ecological perspective of person–environment interaction to all direct-service practice situations.

Prerequisite Competence 2: Ability to use self-awareness toward the use of self professionally in all interpersonal practice situations.

Competence #1:   **Ability to tune-in to self, client, client's life situation, and the helping situation consistent with social work perspective in the preliminary phase.**

Skill 1:   Tuning-in to self: recognition of one's own values, feelings, and assumptions in relation to specific clients.

Skill 2:   Tuning-in to client: anticipatory sensitivity to client's concerns and feelings regarding his or her situation and the use of help.

Skill 3:   Tuning-in to client's situation: anticipatory assessment based on holistic and ecological perspectives that focuses on the interactions between people and their environments.

Competence #2:   **Ability to establish helping relationships that enable clients' active engagement in using services in their own behalf.**

Skill 4:   Use of purpose and function: promoting clients' adaptive growth through a consistent focus on the client and his or her situation and functioning to mediate interactions between the client and particular resource systems.

Skill 5:   Integrated use of support and challenge: balancing the acceptance of clients where they are and the challenge for their becoming.

Skill 6:   Responding to and with feelings: reaching for and demonstrating understanding of clients' feelings and sharing own in primary-level empathy.

Competence #3:   **Ability to begin social work process by engaging clients in service use through initial contracting, accurate and comprehensive assessment, and effective service planning.**

Skill 7:   Contracting: clarifying purpose, goals, functions, and mutual roles and responsibilities; reaching for feedback; and seeking agreement on prioritized concerns, goals, targets, and tasks.

Skill 8:   Initial assessment: appraising and understanding the relationship among internal and external needs and resources in clients' interactions with ecological environmental systems.

Skill 9:   Service planning: determining goals, targets, strategies, and methods for generalist intervention consistent with initial assessment.

Competence #4:   **Ability to sustain the social work process through direct client contact in the work phase.**

Skill 10:   Sessional tuning-in and contracting: starting where clients are and establishing agreement about what they are working on during subsequent contacts.

Skill 11:   Elaborating and clarifying: understanding and illuminating the experienced realities of clients' situations for ongoing assessment and service planning.

Skill 12:   Empathy: discriminating among clients' feelings and actively responding to the meaning of these feelings for clients at the advanced level.

Skill 13:   Sharing own feelings: genuinely expressing one's own feelings as related to the purpose and function of the work together.

Skill 14:   Demanding work: assuring that the purpose of the relationship process is work from clients and in their behalf.

Skill 15:   Providing information: clearly giving data pertinent to clients' work.

Skill 16:   Use of practice theory: planning and assessing use of self on the basis of explicated knowledge of what one is doing to help and why.

Competence #5:   **Ability to sustain work through mediation between clients and resource systems during the work phase.**

Skill 17: Linking: linking clients and formal and informal resource people in behalf of both clients and systems.

Skill 18: Advocacy: actively defending or maintaining clients' needs and rights to potential resource systems.

Competence #6: **Ability to enable effective service termination during the ending phase.**

Skill 19: Ending: promoting the process of service termination with attention to the clients' feelings, perceptions, and plans.

Skill 20: Evaluation: determining the effectiveness of the work and appraising what worked and did not work and why to achieve the service goals.

Competence #7: **Ability to use professional development opportunities.**

Skill 21: Deductive learning: ability to apply theory to practice.

Skill 22: Inductive learning: ability to draw theory from practice.

Skill 23: Willingness to risk: openness to self-disclosure and experimentation with change.

Skill 24: Assessment of learning needs: ability to appraise strengths and limitations in relation to competencies and skills demanded for high-level professional practice.

Skill 25: Commitment to competence: continual and considerable effort to increase and expand skill development.

Skill 26: Scholarship: ability to read, study, conceptualize, critically analyze, and use available knowledge.

Skill 27: Collegial learning: ability to learn from and teach others in group learning situations.

CONCLUSION

Upon first reading, these competencies probably seem overwhelming. This book, however, is designed to present each of these more fully and in a manner permitting mastery of them one at a time. As you understand the nature of the skills that constitute these competencies, develop operational principles for using these skills, and practice using them in suggested exercises and field experience, the expectation is that you will accumulate mastery of all six competencies. Each remaining chapter in Parts I and II focuses on one competency and provides conceptual and experiential material for enabling your mastery of it. By the time you finish using this book—and it requires use as well as reading and studying—you should be well on your way to developing a set of competencies for practice. The hope is that this learning will serve as a useful foundation for future learning and professional development as a social worker.

3 Prerequisite Competence 1: The Ecological Perspective

Scientists in the land of Mu were very much perplexed. They had carefully studied the rabbit population in Mu for 25 years and what they found approached the mystery of their most difficult koan. Over this time, they found regular undulations in the frequency curves of the rabbit populations they so carefully observed and recorded. Now there was a bounty crop, now a scarcity. These undulations were regular and predictable; but no matter how hard they looked and how much they studied, contemplated, discussed, and debated, they could not find the causes. These were the best of scientists and not ready to give up easily, especially when such a mystery was involved.

So they scheduled major conferences to discuss and study everything they could about rabbits. They attended such workshops as "The Mating Habits of Rabbits," "Natural Birth Control of Rabbits," "The Demography of Rabbit Birth Patterns," "Anorexia Nervosa Among Rabbits," "The Suicide Rate of Rabbits," and "The Correlation Between Size of Family and Educational Attainment in Rabbit Families"—all to no avail. Now even the most determined and wisest of the scientists in Mu were growing discouraged.

Then one of the greatest scientists of Mu, Professor Newt, grew so tired one evening of thinking about the problem that he decided to forget about rabbits altogether and take a long walk in his garden with his son, Heis. It was a particularly clear night in the land of Mu, and Professor Newt could not resist educating Heis on the constellations. Heis, however, did not enjoy having his head in the stars, preferring to watch what was happening under his own two feet. Just as his father was saying, "Now there is the Little Dipper, known as the . . . ," a rabbit ran right over Heis's feet. Then there followed a fox quickly gaining on the rabbit. "Dad," said Heis, "why do foxes chase rabbits?" At that moment Professor Newt had one big "Aha!" and the mystery, through serendipity, began to be solved.

Professor Newt continued his study of rabbits by charting the fox population in Mu. And he found a most interesting rhythm, similar to that of rabbits, in the foxes—except that the rhythm was exactly opposite. When the foxes were plentiful, the rabbits were scarce, and vice versa. Finally, he realized what had been happening, and soon all of the scientists in Mu understood the causes of such regular fluctuations in the rabbit population. As the plentiful rabbits are harvested by the foxes, the food supply of the foxes declines and they, in turn, eventually decline. The decline in foxes permits the rabbit population to expand again, but, of course, the foxes again grow more abundant with their new food supply of rabbits. And so the cycle is repeated, again and again.

ECOLOGICAL SYSTEMS

An interesting transition in perspective and thought takes place in this story, one that also is taking place in our study and understanding of human behavior. In both instances, investigators have moved from studying an individual or an individual species to studying a set of relationships that seem to be influencing the subject. We shift from thinking about one species, the rabbit, to examining a configuration of relationships within an ecological system.

Of course, the fox–rabbit cycle is only one part of a much larger system in Mu that includes the human population, the soil, the weather, the insects, the animals, and the plants of Mu. So, too, are the patterns of interaction of the individual, like the fluctuations in the rabbit population, much better understood when examined in relationship with other environmental forces such as the family, the group, the organization, the community, the economy, and the culture. Human behavior is admittedly more complicated, but the idea of the ecological system is the common referent. And it is a very useful concept.

All living systems are organized to maintain some kind of boundary, balance, and equilibrium and have some capacity to adapt to their ecological context. The person has more of this adaptive capacity and flexibility in boundary definition and balance. Look, for instance, at a very simple organism—the amoeba, made infamous in so many horror movies under such fear-inspiring names as the "Thing" or the "Giant Blob." The amoeba is a system, but a system with clear boundaries.

Within these boundaries there is an organization of sorts. This organization is active; it "works" to maintain its structure. If the amoeba encounters a hostile chemical or organism, it may dodge or otherwise attempt to elude the intruder to protect the integrity of its own life. The amoeba has a simple version of the complicated mechanism found in all people, and all living systems, to adapt to its environment. It makes changes in its own behavior based on information about its environment through the mechanism called feedback. Feedback permits the system to alter its activity, its structure, its direction, or, in the case of more complicated organisms such as people, its environment (or all of these) in order to further its own needs and goals. For people, this feedback includes not only awareness of resources in the environment but also consciousness of a variety of our simultaneous needs and wants.

In the ecological perspective for human behavior, therefore, we refer to the *interactions* between person and environment. The balance of environmental forces is not the sole determinant of human behavior. The character of the individual also figures significantly. Individuals and environments are mutually shaping, interdependent systems. Each changes over time; each adapts in response to changes in the other. Therefore, while environmental press is the environment's contribution to individual–environment transactions, the individual brings to the situation a unique arrangement of adaptive needs and resources. Different people thus react differently to the same environment, just as different environments react differently to the same person.

Ecological Perspective in Human Interactions

The interactions between individual and environment form the basis of an ecological approach to human behavior and development. Throughout development, the individual and the environment engage in reciprocal interaction, in transaction; each influences the other in an ever-changing interplay of biology and society—with perception, thought, and feeling as the mediators. For example, the relationship between parent and child changes and becomes more complex over time as each continually learns from and responds to the other. Parents do not change children; nor do children change parents. The relationship itself changes and causes change in both, always within the wider relationship of the immediate and more distant cultural environment. When our basic and unique needs match the environmental resources available in the culture and in interpersonal relationships, we have found our "ecological niches." These niches, or fits, are the result of many ecological factors.

By the word *ecological* here, I mean the way the individual and the immediate environment (the "ecological niche") respond to each other. We cannot understand the relationships between children and parents, promote development, and decrease risks without understanding the conditions surrounding the family. These affect interactions between child and parent and define each family's particular experience. Therefore, the ecological perspective reveals connections that might otherwise be missed and turns our attention beyond the immediate and the obvious to where the most significant influences may lie. As in a "shell game," the pea may not be where it most appears. Let us look at a specific example in the Psyche family.

Mrs. Psyche sits down to a family dinner. She is hungry. Her physical needs compel her to eat and are part of explaining her behavior. These, however, are only a part of the explanation. Many of the forces impinging on her are social forces, environmental pressures from her social environment. Her table manners are learned, as was the way she set the table, and the very fact that in line with her role definition, *she* set the table. Additionally, she, rather than Mr. Psyche, prepared the meal. Other interactions are influencing her. She is angry at Mr. Psyche for having been late for dinner, even though she is aware that he was kept late at the office for legitimate reasons. She is even more angry at Storm, her 5-year-old son, whose constant squirming at the table irritates her.

At this meal, both Mr. and Mrs. Psyche are silently anxious about the family's finances. The inflationary economy often leads them to brood about the rising cost of groceries and other essentials to support their family of four.

The tension at the table rises when a telephone call from Mr. Psyche's mother interrupts the meal, increasing Mrs. Psyche's anger. At the end of the meal, Lily, the teenaged daughter, gets a telephone call from her boyfriend, and she asks to be excused from her chores to go to a movie that Mrs. Psyche is sure is X-rated. Mrs. Psyche, the wife and mother, who has not been out in the evening for a month and who by now thoroughly resents what she internally calls the "harried housewife role," finally loses her temper. She snaps out at Lily.

The environmental pressures on Mrs. Psyche (indeed on the whole family) appear to swirl around them in a very chaotic manner. Mrs. Psyche often feels that she is being repeatedly stung by a horde of invisible mosquitoes, so randomly intrusive do these tensions seem.

However, all of these tensions are related to the ecological system with which she transacts.

There is the world economy and society; there is the work system, the teenaged peer group, and the extended family; and, of course, there are the dynamics of the nuclear family, including such subsystems as Mrs. Psyche and Lily's relationship and Mr. and Mrs. Psyche's relationship. Conflicts in all these systems influence the Psyches. Conflicts in the Middle East have fixed oil prices, which have added to world inflation and the Psyche's financial pressures. Ideological conflict within society affecting the woman's role, the man's role, the degree of independence of adolescents, and questions of censorship—all these unresolved social issues bear upon the Psyche's conflicts. Mrs. Psyche is in conflict, but not just with Lily, Storm, or Mr. Psyche. If she would parcel out these tensions as ecological system problems operating on different levels, she might find a way of simplifying some of the complexities she faces and of setting priorities for solving some of the problems. She can alter some of this environment. For instance, Mrs. Psyche may cope more effectively with one of her family's mealtime problems by taking the phone off the hook during dinner.

Work with the Psyches, therefore, requires a perspective and a general theory base that provides a framework for assessing and intervening in pertinent aspects of the environment. We also need interactional concepts for understanding people's problems in living and for generating principles to influence person–environment transactions. The ecological perspective and developing theory promise such a framework.

ECOLOGICAL PERSPECTIVE AND SOCIAL WORK

In the ecological perspective the focus is on both how people are affected by their social and physical environment and how they actively use and change their environments (Germain, 1979). This perspective delineates and distinguishes first between the physical and social environments and their reciprocal influence on each other within the context of a particular culture. The physical environment consists of two layers: the natural world and the built world. The *natural* world comprises plants, animals, landscapes, and climate. The *built* world refers to all the structures and objects created by human beings—from cities, neighborhoods, and houses to complex transportation and communication systems.

The social environment is marked by several levels of social organization. The most immediate layer includes social networks of family, friends, neighbors, and workmates—all of whom have different functions in relation to personal needs and goals. This layer also includes such resources as natural helpers, mutual-aid systems, and self-help groups, as well as such potentially natural helpers as landlords, merchants, and policemen (who may, upon entering a client system's lifespace, represent negatively experienced authority and power to the client, whether it be an individual, a family, or a group).

Beyond the social network lies the layer of organization and institutions designed to provide services and resources. These include the private and public social systems of work, education, welfare, housing, recreation, and health care. In social work practice, this layer includes our own agency. Our agency not only shapes our practice to a great extent; it is also a salient presence in the quality of clients' lives and their problems in living. Finally, the social environment entails the societal layer. This layer includes the cultural value systems, political and economic structures, and laws, statutes, and policies.

The first principle of the ecological perspective is to locate people within the context of the physical and social environment impinging upon them. In social work practice, we consistently view client systems in relation to the salient points in the layers of the physical and social environment. The key interactional concepts that highlight the nature of clients' relationships with the environment are adaptation, stress, and coping.

The ecological perspective concerns the interactions between people and environments that both promote and inhibit growth, development, the release of human potential, and the capacity of the environment to support the diversity of human potential. Social work has its distinct location as a profession, in Carel Germain's (1981) words, in this "transaction area where the actual interchanges between people and environments occur, where qualities of the person intersect with qualities of the environment, with positive or negative consequences for both" (p. 325). From this perspective, the objective of social work practice can be stated as promoting adaptive interactions and preventing or correcting maladaptive ones (Bartlett, 1970; Gordon, 1969; Social Work, 1977).

A second principle of the ecological perspective uses the interactional concepts of adaptation, stress, and coping. According to this principle, once the client system is located within context, we must assess the nature of the interactions between client systems and environmental systems. In particular, we need to note the points of adaptive and maladaptive interactions. This assessment requires identification of the points of stress created by an imbalance between perceived demands and capabilities, the specific outcomes of the current coping responses in use, and the potential resources in the environment and in the client system for more effective coping. Foundation competencies in this model require analytical skills for applying the ecological framework in assessments and in the overall practice paradigm.

The Ecomap

An excellent tool for applying the ecological perspective is the ecomap. An ecomap (Hartman, 1979; Hartman & Laird, 1983) is a drawing that dynamically depicts the person's ecological context and the boundaries in his or her lifespace. These include the major environmental systems that interact with the person in the current situation. It establishes the person's ecological niche at a significant point in time by identifying and characterizing the major resources and obstacles to adaptive growth in the person's interactions with the world. It specifies the flow and nature of the person's connection with aspects of impinging environmental systems. We can use the ecomap in a shared process with the client or simply in our own analysis. This use can assure consideration of not only the more tangible and concrete life connections but also those human, personal, social, psychological, and spiritual influences that shape our lives in holistic ways.

Through ecomapping, we and the client can gain understanding of the deprivations, stress, and at-risk areas of interactions with the environment that sap the client's strengths and coping capacities and restrict growth. This analysis can guide interactions that mediate stress and conflicts, build more adaptive ones, and develop and mobilize resources on behalf of the client. All we need is a piece of paper, a pencil, and an ecological frame of reference that helps client systems (individuals, families, or small groups) think through and describe their particular environments.

The ecomap, as illustrated in Figure 3-1, consists of circles that are convenient fictions, falsely dividing aspects of what cannot be verbalized as inner or outer. Therefore the ecomap serves most efficiently as a broad picture. For instance, it is not so practical for mapping the intricacies of actual inner family relationships and dynamics. Nevertheless, this general charting of the family system often is a picture saving many words.

The ecomap begins with a large circle at its center, representing an individual client. A larger circle, representing the nuclear family system or household, surrounds the original circle. In mapping families,

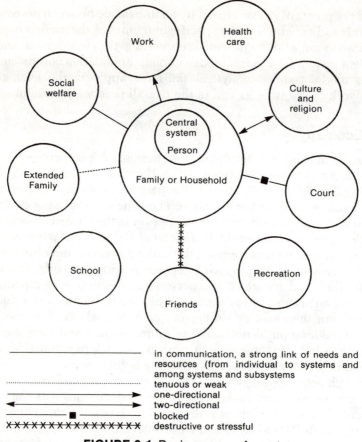

FIGURE 3-1 Basic ecomap format.

you may want to use squares to indicate males and circles to depict females within this larger circle. Then, map the nuclear family as in the traditional family tree or genetic chart. At the minimum, put the person's name and age in the center of the circle or square that represents her or him. You may also want to include other brief information.

When the client and members of the household are drawn within the large middle circle, you are ready to identify those environmental systems that significantly interact with and affect the client's and family's life. These systems (social welfare, work, health care, extended family, recreation, culture and religion, friends, school, agency, worker, and so on) are then depicted in separate, labeled circles revolving around the center circle. As soon as you determine the nature of a client–system or family–system interaction, draw a line to express both the fact and the quality of the connection.

A solid or thick line represents an important, strong, or positive connection. Here the client or resource system is in reciprocal communication. The broken line represents a tenuous or weak connection. Placing xxxx across the line indicates a stressful or conflicted relationship. A block on the line depicts a strong relationship that is currently blocked as a resource. An arrow at one end of the line, or one at both ends, indicates the direction of the flow of communication, resources, energy, and/or interest. A total picture emerges from drawing these lines among individuals, systems, and subsystems.

This code is an efficient shorthand for using the ecomap as an analytical tool in assessment and service planning. For some, this code may be too narrow or constraining and other creative codes could be developed. For example, some may wish to qualify the nature of connections by writing a brief description along the connecting line. Others may develop other types of lines, or use two different lines to describe a particularly ambivalent or complicated connection. The basic ecomap, however it is coded, serves well to promote an ecological perspective of the service situation and enable a beginning ecological assessment of the client's adaptive relationship with his or her world.

The Dual Perspective

We often need an important addition to the ecomap when assessing and working with the adaptive interactions of special populations, such as minority-group members. This framework is the "dual perspective" (Chestang, 1980; Norton, 1978), which asserts that all of us to some degree, and most especially blacks, women, and other oppressed groups in the United States, live simultaneously in two worlds. Members of these groups live a dual experience and possess a dual culture, emanating from such social conditions as institutionalized racism and sexism. They consistently confront blocks that are systematically and structurally designed to restrict opportunities for goal achievement in the larger social system. These conditions consist of the denial of legal rights, the inconsistency of societal demands and expectations, and the possible resulting sense of personal impotence from the lack of power to achieve their goals or to influence their environment. Blacks, women, and other oppressed groups, therefore, must develop adaptive and coping strategies consistent with their own cultural world. This coping behavior may often be at variance with that considered "normal" by the white, male-dominated culture. The dual perspective fosters understanding of a minority-group member's dual cultural experience.

Norton (1978) defines the conceptual tool of the dual perspective as our capacity to take into account the attitude of another in assessment and practice:

> The dual perspective is the conscious and systematic process of perceiving, understanding, and comparing simultaneously the values, attitudes, and behavior of the larger societal system with those of the client's immediate family and community system. It is the conscious awareness of the cognitive and attitudinal levels of the similarities and differences in the two systems. (p. 3)

Incorporating this dual perspective into initial and ongoing ecomapping requires specific identifications of: (1) the similarities and differences between nurturing environmental systems and sustaining environmental systems; (2) the nature of interactions between and among these systems and the individual client; and (3) the client's *perceived* areas of stress in attempts to adapt to and cope with dual cultural experiences. The notions of nurturing and sustaining environmental systems aid understanding of this dual cultural experience. We all live in at least these two environments or systems. The most immediate is the nurturing system, which houses family, friends, and the supportive institutions of our immediate community. From these "immediate generalized others" we acquire and express values, norms, and traditions that foster our sense of self-worth and self-actualization. Therefore we invest positive feelings and profound caring in this system.

The nurturing system, and our significant investment in it, holds the greatest resources to meet our emotional needs and achieve our humanizing goals. They are the most powerful influence on our identity and sense of dignity. Our relationships in this world contribute enormously to our basic sense of security and personal worth. We share, too, the pride in the collective history and identity and in the achievements of our own cultural group. We also share, particularly if we are members of oppressed groups, the sorrows and degradations group members have borne, and must bear, in their interactions with the other world of the wider society.

This other world is the sustaining environmental system. It is here that resources are found for instrumental and pragmatic needs, for physical survival, and for increases in the quality of life—goods and services, political power, shelter, employment and other economic resources, education, health, and such. This wider society is peopled by the powerful and influential. For ethnic minorities, these "major generalized others," these people of power, most often differ from those in one's nurturing environment in skin color, in speech patterns, in habits, in attitudes toward the minority-group person, and perhaps even in language.

We must all learn to leave the security of family, friends, and neighborhood and go into the dominant society to secure our survival needs. The benefit of using the dual perspective to work with minority persons is the understanding it gives of the quantum leap they must make from a nurturing world "into a world where the attitudes of its inhabitants and the structure of its institutions are *systematically designed* to inhibit, prohibit, and otherwise block their goal achievement" (Chestang, 1980, p. 4). Depending upon the individual's experience and perception of living in these two spheres and the gaps and fences between them, the minority person develops particular coping attitudes and behaviors that are part of his or her strengths and that can only be understood from this dual perspective. We must take the role of the other as he or she lives in these two worlds, "moving back and forth between them through an invisible shield which bounds them, so that their separatism is clearly understood by those who must travel between them, although it is vaguely perceived, if at all, by those whose lives are lived primarily in one sphere" (Chestang, 1982, p. 3) Figure 3-2 depicts the dual perspective as a useful conceptual tool for aspects of ecomapping with minority clients and women.

To use the dual perspective we need (1) knowledge of specific minority cultures; (2) knowledge of the dominant culture; (3) knowledge of the client's unique and individualized perception and experiences of both the nurturing and sustaining environmental systems; (4) knowledge of our own values, attitudes, and stereotypes; and (5) a "reversible mind set" (Piaget, 1957, cited in Norton, 1978), or "the ability and conscious motivation to think about the situation being observed and to look for points of difference, conflict, or congruence with the larger society" (Norton, 1978, p. 6). For instance, work with a minority person who is an adolescent requires knowledge of adolescent development in our society as well as specific knowledge of his or her ethnic or cultural group, the opportunities available to them, and the norms prescribing behavior within this nurturing system. This knowledge needs to be synthesized and evaluated against our own values and attitudes to determine our own possible bias and our ability to entertain difference. It also needs to be weighed against the individualized perceptions of this particular adolescent. The whole process consciously uses the reversible mind set to specify and understand

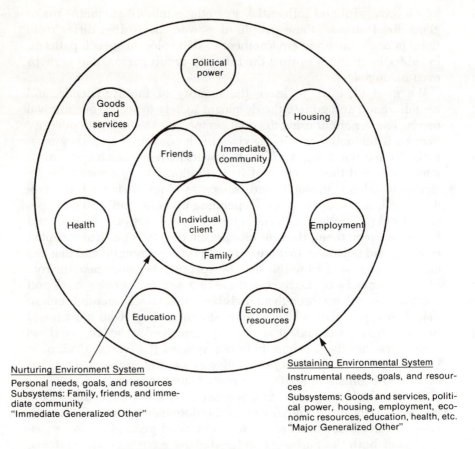

FIGURE 3-2 Dual perspective ecomap.

transactions between the immediate generalized other and the major generalized other within the person as well as between his or her environmental systems. Together, this knowledge has a validity that prevents stereotyping. Acceptance of any behavioral characteristics because of generalized stereotypes about specific minority groups is antithetical to use of the dual perspective. Among its major uses in ecomapping are identifying, challenging, and preventing these stereotypes and understanding the strengths inherent in coping in situations that challenge one's sense of dignity and worth.

The case study in the next section demonstrates the use of the ecological perspective through both the ecomap and the dual perspective. This study comes from the description of "A Systems Dilemma" by Lynn Hoffman and Lorence Long (1969). It involves an urban black family whose father and the family system as a whole are caught in an "ecological niche" that restricts adaptive coping by an elaborate interplay of ecological systems.

Case Study: A System Dilemma

The central character of our story, Charles Johnson, is a 52-year-old black man who worked for 11 years as a chef in a proprietary nursing home. His wife, Bernice, works in a home for brain-damaged children. Before he quit his job, they made enough to keep their 15-year-old daughter, Lorna, in private school, and their 19-year-old daughter, Gail, in college. Mr. Johnson was brought to the attention of the social services department of a neighborhood health center because of the following dilemma.

Mr. and Mrs. Johnson's combined income was above the limit for the low-income housing apartment that they had occupied for 17 years, and the Housing Authority was trying to evict them. The neighborhood was in the throes of a severe housing shortage. Thus there was little prospect of finding decent housing at a rent they could afford. Mr. Johnson for some years had experienced dizzy spells, and he drank a sizable amount of liquor each day. Twice he had fallen while at work. The second time, three years earlier, he had been taken to a psychiatric hospital. There, they told his wife he was an epileptic. In the past months, these dizzy spells had occurred more frequently. This prompted the Housing Authority agent, who wished to help the Johnsons, to suggest that he get a statement from a doctor saying that the spells were serious enough to put his working future in doubt. This statement would allow him to quit work and collect disability payment. At the same time, the family's income would be sufficiently reduced to enable them to stay on in their apartment.

Mr. Johnson agreed with the Housing agent that this might be the best thing to do. So did his wife. Unfortunately, the drop in income would mean that the family could no longer continue to keep the two girls in school without extra financing. Also, quitting work would seriously undermine Mr. Johnson's status both outside of and within his family, particularly in regard to his wife.

The Housing agent contacted the social services department of the community health service for advice in locating a doctor who would certify Mr. Johnson as too ill to work. A social worker was assigned to the case and talked to the Housing agent about it. The worker then called the Johnsons' home. Only Mrs. Johnson was in, but she was glad to speak to the worker. The worker's case report stated:

"Mrs. J. spoke anxiously of her husband's condition. She equated him with the brain-damaged children with whom she works. His drinking complicated the seizure problem, and it seemed to be getting worse. He had been missing work more lately. Worker arranged for Mr. and Mrs. J. to meet with him."

When meeting with the couple together for the first time, the worker's impression was one of a "dominating" wife and "passive" husband. During the interview, the wife took over as spokesperson for the husband. The matter of what to do in relation to the eviction threat was discussed, with Mr. Johnson saying that he had thought of quitting his job to maintain housing. Mrs. Johnson then suggested that she quit instead. The worker asked them how they would decide who should quit work, remarking later in his notes: "There seemed to be no answer." Mr. Johnson next turned to the subject of his dizzy spells and how they affected his working. The worker asked him to tell the full story of his illness to the doctor the Housing agent had arranged for him to see at the health service, because the medical opinion could help to stave off the impending eviction. He stressed that Mr. Johnson should tell his own story, not let his wife tell it for him.

At this point, Mr. Johnson took his leave, explaining that he had to babysit for their youngest, preschool daughter, Maureen. After her husband had gone, Mrs. Johnson again expressed anxiety about his "seizures" and his increased drinking and said that he slept most of the time when he was at home. She went on to explain that she preferred his sleeping, because when he was awake he would often explode over nothing, and his "grouchiness," as she termed his behavior, was hard to take. Sometimes he would even try to hit her, but she claimed she was the stronger and got the better of him in any physical fight. Thus the message from Mrs. Johnson seemed to be: Stay at home and sleep and we'll have less trouble. On the other hand, it was Mrs. Johnson who was most committed to seeing that her daughters got good educations, and if this commitment were to be fulfilled, she could not afford to let her husband stay at home and sleep.

Up to now, Mr. Johnson had not talked very much for himself. However, during an interview with Mr. Johnson alone, just before the appointment with the doctor, the worker was able to uncover points of pride in Mr. Johnson's opinion of himself. He was proud of his skills as a cook and proud of his position of responsibility as supervisor of a large and busy kitchen where complicated diets for sick people had to be adhered to. He had held the same position for many years. He was naturally disheartened by the increased frequency of the dizzy spells and unnerved by the fear that one more "seizure" at work might cause him to be fired. Caught in the grip of a self-fulfilling prophecy, in that his fear of having the seizures was part of what provoked them, Mr. Johnson would clearly be vulnerable to messages from others confirming these fears. As an example of Mr. Johnson's easily crumbled sense of personal rights and gloomy expectations, here is an excerpt from the worker's account of the interview:

WORKER: Your wife said the other day that you had had two seizures on the job, and that one more would mean the end of the job. Is that so?

MR. J.:   Yes.

WORKER: Who made that ruling? The insurance company? (Wife had previously mentioned the insurance company in that connection.)

MR. J.:   No, well, you see when I had the last seizure at work—when I had my head injury—as the Hospitals Department inspector was coming in the door, I was going out on a stretcher. My boss told me that the inspector said that one more seizure and he'd have to let me go.

WORKER: Is that just the inspector's idea, or is that a ruling by the Department of Hospitals?

MR. J.:   I don't know.

WORKER: Exactly how did your boss tell it to you?

MR. J.:   He said the inspector said, if a man falls out like that, you can't keep him, can you?

WORKER: Would you like me to try to find out if there really is such a regulation, or if this was just an offhand remark by the inspector?

MR. J.:   I'd be delighted.

The next chapter of the story concerns Mr. Johnson's visit to the doctor. A new set of opinions now came out, containing a new proliferation of contradictory meanings. Mr. Johnson had been coming to the health service for 3 years for physical complaints, and in the course of his first workup, the doctor learned and noted down that he customarily drank up to a quart of liquor a day. A look at the medical chart revealed that the statement "chronic alcoholic" was written at the bottom of every subsequent entry in the chart, no matter which department in the clinic Mr. Johnson came to, or for what reason. In discussing his "drinking problem" with the social worker, Mr. Johnson said that he usually kept whiskey by him on the job, "because if I feel shaky, I take a drink, and then I'm usually all right." However, Mr. Johnson's doctor had told him that "anyone who takes a drink before six o'clock in the evening is an alcoholic."

This confusion reappeared, with a new twist, in the encounter with the different doctor who examined Mr. Johnson at the time of the referral to the social service department. The worker had sent this doctor a long memo explaining the importance the medical recommendations would have in regard to the family's housing. Initially, the worker had accepted the request from the Housing agent: "Certify this man as unable to work." But the conversation with Mr. Johnson raised doubts in the worker's mind about the advisability of removing the support that work represented to him, and the memo reflected the worker's ambivalence. The following statement was issued by the doctor:

> Apparently patient is a lazy, indifferent, passive, immature, dependent, inadequate personality who cannot maintain a responsible position for any appreciable length of time. He prefers alcohol to anticonvulsive medications and, indeed, at times his convulsions may be merely "rum fits" or delirium tremens. Apparently the best that can be expected from this individual is that he can be productive on occasions as long as he is "mothered" by his wife and society. I would suggest that he not be moved from his present apartment, since his present income is likely to vanish at any moment of stress.

Perhaps the worker's memo had sounded too protective to the doctor. It may have called forth this "antimothering" response. The worker then phoned Mr. Johnson, expecting him to be upset. On the contrary, Mr. Johnson said that his interview with the doctor had gone very well. The doctor had behaved in a kind and benevolent manner to him and had told him that he would not have to worry about being moved after the Housing Authority read what he was going to write in his statement.

The worker then called the doctor, who said that he was only willing to sign a statement that Mr. Johnson was a chronic alcoholic. The worker called a lawyer at an antipoverty agency, who told him that to show this diagnosis to the Housing Authority would not stop the family's eviction; on the contrary, it would ensure it. The worker then appealed to a doctor further up in the clinic hierarchy, who issued a diagnosis of "chronic seizure disorders and labile hypertension" and stated that Mr. Johnson should be permitted to remain in his present apartment, since the stress of moving at this time might prove harmful. The wording here was important, since it did not tie the Johnsons' continuing occupancy of their apartment to Mr. Johnson's decision about work.

The worker was just about to mail this statement to the Housing Authority when he learned that Mr. Johnson had just had a bad dizzy spell at work and had decided to quit for good. In view of the situation, this event was not surprising. There were many conflicting pressures for and against his continuing to work, both within the circle of Mr. Johnson's immediate and daily relationships and within the circle of helpers around the family. The explanation that a human being cannot continue to function under the strain of this kind of "mosquito storm" may be as reasonable a way to see his collapse as to trace it to a single aspect, whether this be a "dependent personality," a "dominating wife," the "overmothering of society," or some mysterious physical condition such as "chronic seizure disorder."

Whatever its cause, Mr. Johnson's decision to quit his job, which occurred a little more than 2 weeks after the Housing agent first called the health service, created a new configuration. Now, not loss of housing but a far more difficult loss to repair came into question: Mr. Johnson's loss of social place. In particular, a shift in the relationship between husband and wife had taken place, leaving the wife on top and the husband on the bottom. This shift had been hanging in the air for a long time, but it was only now, when the outer social systems finally got into the act, that it became sanctioned and fixed. Three doctors, a Housing agent, Mrs. Johnson, Mr. Johnson, possibly his boss, and to some extent the social worker all became implicated in the process that caused Mr. Johnson to accept, or to provoke, a label of helplessness.

Now a twofold job presented itself: first, to get Mr. Johnson out of the sick person's seat and back on his feet; second, while this was being attempted, to work out the changed economics of family life now that Mr. Johnson no longer contributed an income. This second task alone meant endless time that had to be devoted to dealing with a multitude of institutions and agencies. A list of these institutions will give an idea of the forest of helpers that had sprung up around the Johnson family: the health service, with its various departments; OEO legal services; the Housing Authority; Mr. Johnson's union; the Veterans Administration; Workmen's Compensation; a private loan company; All Saints Parish; Franklin Settlement; and Southern College.

Rather than describe in detail how the worker helped the Johnsons to deal with all these agencies, one single example will be presented: the raising of funds so that the oldest girl could finish the year at Southern College, where she was now a junior. Neither Gail nor Lorna was doing too well at school, and Mrs. Johnson said she had never tried to look for scholarship aid for Gail, "because my daughter is not the brightest person in the world." It seemed that Gail had been in a subdued struggle with her mother for some time. The main issue had become the low-status black college in the South that Gail had chosen to go to, which affronted the mother's scholarly and social expectations for her. Two years before, the girl had begun to get migraine headaches, and the psychiatrist she saw commented to Mrs. Johnson that they might stem from the mother's feelings about Gail's college. The mother denied this, but the headaches stopped after this suggestion was made, and Gail was allowed to attend the college. The worker, sensing the importance of keeping Gail in school, offered to help Mrs. Johnson find a source of scholarship funds. The tactic was to build on the upwardly-mobile motivation of Mrs. Johnson, which required her to keep her daughter in college at any price. The alternate current in Mrs. Johnson—let daughter fail and come back home to reconstitute an unhealthy family triangle—was strong, all the more so because it was not recognized. Insight therapy was not particularly suited to this family, and it seemed more logical to strengthen the conscious drive toward achievement by offspring.

In order to give an idea of the number of fundraising operations that took place over a two-and-a-half-month period, a chronological list of transactions over one instance follows. Multiply this sequence many times, and we begin to see how much time and energy of persons and agencies have to be poured into the vacuum left when even an unassuming cook like Mr. Johnson relinquishes his share of the social burden.

Number of Operations Needed to Secure College Assistance Funds for Miss J., November 28 to February 12:

1. 11/28—Mrs. J. speaks to worker about problem of college assistance for daughter. Illness of Mr. J. has made it impossible for family to provide this money.
2. 12/7—Worker calls Urban League for information. He is referred to College Assistance Program.
3. Same date—Worker gives information to Mrs. J., who makes appointment with College Assistance Program for December 19. Persons in that office give her conflicting information about who to go to, but someone finally comes in and makes an appointment with the right person.
4. 12/11—Mrs. J. calls Sam Arcaro, who used to work for Franklin Settlement House and who is in touch with a donor interested in Miss J.
5. 12/12—Mr. J. and worker go to see Father Arcy at All Saints Parish. The family are members of that parish and Mr. J. is a well-known figure there.
6. Same date—Father Arcy writes to president of Southern College, where Miss J. is a student. Father Arcy tells Mr. J. to get in touch with Mrs. Xavier, who is head of the parish Scholarship

Fund. Since Mr. J. and Mrs. Xavier have a feud going, the worker and the family decide that Mrs. J. might be the best one to approach her.

7. Same week—The president of Southern College refers the matter to college loan officer and writes Father Arcy to that effect.

8. 12/18—Miss J. comes home from college. Worker talks with her; she is not particularly happy at school, but she wants to continue.

9. 12/19—Miss J. and her mother go to College Assistance Program, where she is given an application for a National Defense Loan.

10. Same week—Miss J. goes to see Mr. Watson at Franklin Settlement.

11. Same week—Miss J. goes to see Sam Arcaro.

12. Same week—Miss J. goes to see Father Arcy, too. She is sick with the flu during the last part of her vacation, and does not follow up on any of these appointments.

13. Same week—Miss J. returns to college in South Carolina.

14. 1/4—Mrs. J. calls Mr. Watson, finds that he is waiting for Miss J. to return.

15. 1/5—Mrs. J. goes to see Mr. Watson, who says that Franklin Settlement will help with some money but cannot give the whole amount.

16. Same date—Mrs. J. contacts Sam Arcaro, who says that Miss J. gave him the impression that she wanted to transfer when she talked to him. He will not act until this is clarified.

17. Same date—Mrs. J. writes to Miss J. at college, asking her to contact Mr. Arcaro.

18. 1/14—Mrs. J. has been trying to reach Mrs. Xavier for weeks. Finally she succeeds, only to learn that Mrs. Xavier only raises money; she does not dispense it. Mrs. J. is referred to the Diocesan Scholarship Fund, represented by Father Chipworth and Mrs. York.

19. Week of 1/14—Worker calls Mrs. York and finds that Miss J. must apply herself. They only have limited funds and cannot give the whole amount.

20. 1/22—Worker calls Miss J. in South Carolina, asking her to respond to Mr. Arcaro and the Diocesan Scholarship Committee. Miss J. is not in; worker does not reach her.

21. Same date—A letter arrives from Miss J. She very much wants to live off campus, and has made arrangements to do so; her mother approves. Miss J. thinks this will solve the problem of her unhappiness at school.

22. 1/23—Worker calls Father Chipworth, a friend, who also knows the family. He agrees to give $300.
23. 1/23 to 1/26—Mrs. J. makes a number of attempts to reach the college business manager to get postponement of the date when fees are due. He is never in when she calls.
24. 1/24—Miss J. calls worker 2 days after his call. Worker tells her that the logjam has been broken.
25. 1/28—Diocesan Scholarship Committee votes the $300 that Father Chipworth had promised.
26. 1/30—Father Borden, pastor of All Saints Parish, writes the $300 check and sends it to Miss J. at college. He sends it to the dormitory, which instead of forwarding it to her new address, returns it to her home address.
27. Same date—Mrs. J. contacts Franklin Settlement, which immediately comes through with the remaining funds.
28. Same date—Worker writes to college business manager to arrange for delay in fee-due date.
29. 2/2—Returned scholarship check sent by Mrs. J. to Miss J. Fees are not paid.
30. 2/12—Worker receives letter from college business manager, dated February 9, granting delay in due date for fees. (See step 29.)

During this period the worker had 12 family interviews with the parents, parts of which were spent working out the next step in the above process. However, the worker's main business during this time was related to the health of Mr. J. and other issues arising from that. Our society expects low-income, sometimes disorganized families, under stress from illness and other factors, to negotiate a complex assortment of systems in order to survive. It is a remarkable achievement that the members of the Johnson family were able to play such a significant part in this particular issue of raising scholarship funds.

Figure 3-3 is an ecomap depicting these transactions at this point in the work. This ecological assessment suggests the number of targets that need to be addressed in order to reverse the machinery that has assailed the dignity of Mr. Johnson and made an invalid of him. These targets include the health care system, in order to confront a racist attitude and get an accurate diagnosis and treatment for Mr. Johnson's seizures; the family system, in order to increase communication between Mr. and Mrs. Johnson as concerned partners; the employment system, in order to get Mr. Johnson back to work; the housing system, in order to permit the Johnsons to maintain their current level of

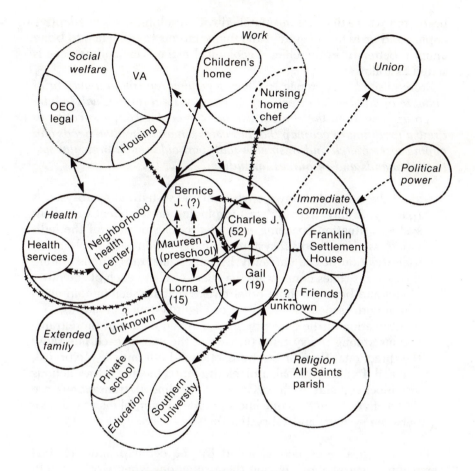

FIGURE 3-3 Johnson family ecomap.

housing; and Mr. Johnson himself, in order to reaffirm his dignity, worth, and competence.

CONCLUSION

This first prerequisite competence concerns the ability to apply the ecological perspective in all direct-service generalist situations. Specifically, this competence requires skills for ecomapping. Ecomapping depicts the transactions among people and their impinging environmental systems. It emphasizes areas where coping resources match needs and where they are mismatched with resulting stress in adaptive coping and growth. It signifies the major targets to influence to bring about a better fit in the client's ecological niche. This competence is stated as follows:

Prerequisite Competence 1: *Given a general referral or a very brief vignette of a potential direct-service client system (individual, family, or group) situation, the student can use the ecological perspective to draw a preliminary ecomap that indicates where individual needs and coping tasks match and mismatch with particular environmental systems demands and resources, including*:

- all of the currently known environmental systems and subsystems (partner, family, agency, etc.) impinging on the client's or client system's situation (systems as labeled circles outside of the individual as circle, and subsystems as parts within each circle);
- identification of the currently hypothesized transactions among the systems (lines connecting the client circle to each of the other circles and between those other circles that are seen in communication with respect to the client or client system's situation);
- identification of the currently hypothesized nature of these transactions among the systems (arrows at the end of each line show the directional flow of the transactions—both ends if reciprocal, one end if unidirectional, a block drawn on the line if transactions are blocked, and with xxxxx over the line if transactions are destructive; more than one line and type of symbol may be drawn between systems and subsystems).

The ecological perspective, aided by the ecomap and the dual perspective, is a way of viewing these situations when working with minority groups, as in the case of the Johnson family. This application implies a number of significant resource systems to target intervention in direct-service generalist work with Mr. Johnson and his family.

SUGGESTED LEARNING EXERCISE 3-1: JOHNSON ECOMAP

Let us continue with our story of the work with Charles Johnson and his family—at the end of which you will be required to draw your own ecomap. The last part of the story (Hoffman & Long, 1968, pp. 318–329) describes what the worker did at the point of the earlier assessment. The objective of this work is to reverse the machinery that had created an invalid of Mr. Johnson. The story continues as follows.

The worker had been consulting with a psychiatrist at the health service about the Johnsons and has now asked the psychiatrist to meet with Mr. and Mrs. Johnson. This psychiatrist looked at the situation through two sets of glasses: the medical one, which would support the assumption that Mr. Johnson suffered from some physical condition—epilepsy or alcoholism or some combination of both; and the "ecological" one, which would widen the focus of the investigation to include nonbiological factors. What he found tended to support the hypothesis that social and environmental factors rather than purely physical ones were at work.

First of all, he discovered that ever since the "seizure" three years before, Mr. Johnson had been taking large dosages of Dilantin and Librium (tranquilizers) and phenobarbital. It was only after this time that the dizzy spells began to manifest themselves. When Mr. Johnson sought further medical advice, his dosages were increased. He was now constantly feeling dizzy and constantly terrified that another seizure was coming on. He found that a drink of whiskey would dispel the dizziness for a while and gradually increased his liquor consumption to about a quart a day. The dizzy spells continued, now augmented by the large amounts of medication and the large amounts of alcohol. Further visits to doctors brought increased dosages of drugs, which brought on more dizziness, which prompted him to drink more. There was also some doubt as to the nature of Mr. Johnson's seizures. The psychiatrist summed up his opinion on the medical aspects of Mr. Johnson's condition thus:

> In a review of the chart, and on careful questioning, I can find no evidence that Mr. Johnson has ever had a seizure since the first one that brought him to Bellevue. There is a notation that he had a couple of blackout spells which turn out, on questioning both Mr. Johnson and his wife, to be fainting spells, not seizures. These can be reasonably explained as resulting at least in part from the combination of sedative and anesthetic (alcoholic) drugs he was taking, as can his dizzy spells. His EEG is normal (slow, but this is compatible with sedation).

The psychiatrist pointed out to Mr. Johnson the possibility that, far from helping him, the drugs were in part responsible for the dizzy spells. A few days later, an incident occurred that helped Mr. Johnson see that he could do without medication. Mrs. Johnson interpreted a vague remark on the part of the husband, mistakenly as it turned out, as a suicide threat. She took away the store of medication he had amassed, fearing that he would overdose. Mr. Johnson reported to the worker that while he was deprived of his usual medication he had no serious dizzy spells.

At the same time, the psychiatrist looked at the family factors that might be contributing to Mr. Johnson's difficulties. He learned that the onset of Mr. Johnson's heavy drinking had coincided with the birth of his youngest daughter, 6 years before, at which time his wife stopped having sexual relations with him. His drinking was opposed by Mrs. Johnson until he had his second "seizure." After that, he was able to defend his drinking on the ground that it kept him from having his spells. At the same time, Mr. Johnson was more and more accepting the position of a sick and disabled person. This at least brought him concern from his wife. She also seemed to be more comfortable in a situation in which she held the reins.

The psychiatrist presented his overall impression of the case as follows:

In my opinion, Mr. Johnson is a passive dependent man who has gradually accepted the role of an epileptic individual provided for him by those about him. There is no evidence that he is epileptic. He is an alcoholic. But even his alcoholism seems to be secondary to his sense of exclusion from his family resulting from his wife's sexual withdrawal and what seems to be a coalition of females (wife and three daughters) who find it easier for him to be powerless than to deal with him as the head of the household. Secondary gain is provided for him as the result of the actions of the Department of Public Housing and his wife's provision of mothering for her "sick" husband (child).

The psychiatrist recommended to Mr. Johnson's doctor that he withdraw all sedative drugs and suggested that the worker confront the family with the dynamics that were placing Mr. Johnson in the invalid role and work to reestablish Mr. Johnson's status as man of the house. He stressed particularly the need to get Mr. and Mrs. Johnson back together as a married pair.

At this point, a disagreement arose between the psychiatrist and the social worker. Acting on a cue from Mr. Johnson, who had said he wanted to get "dried out," the worker suggested that he be hospitalized for this purpose. This would also allow Mr. Johnson's physical condition to be assessed in a setting where his intake of both drugs and alcohol would be controlled. The psychiatrist argued that hospitalization might reinforce the label of invalid that was already hanging over

Mr. Johnson's head. He also feared that a new set of medical authorities might pick up and reaffirm the old label of epileptic from Mr. Johnson's previous hospital record. For these reasons, he felt it would be best to hold off on hospitalization. Until, as will be seen, Mr. Johnson himself broke the stalemate, the worker continued to see the family every week, and the question of hospitalization remained open.

For the next two and a half months, an uneasy stasis prevailed in the family, perhaps related to the uneasy stasis between the psychiatrist and the worker, who still differed on the subject of hospitalization. Mr. Johnson lay around the house and continued to drink, and Mrs. Johnson complained to the worker about his drinking but continued to supply him with his daily allotment. Even though she also complained about the fact that Mr. Johnson's drinking cost her $40 a week, it was clear that she had a stake in keeping alive the idea that her husband needed to drink. Once, for instance, in the period just after Mr. Johnson had quit work, the worker called and was told by Mrs. Johnson that they had had a terrible weekend. Mr. Johnson had accidentally spilled the bottle of liquor she had bought him to last the weekend, and she had had no money to replace it. She said he was in great pain, which was hard on her, too, as she could not bear to see him suffer. Also, he was difficult to handle when he could not get his liquor. During his next meeting with the couple, the worker asked Mr. Johnson about what had happened. Mr. Johnson said that he had knocked the bottle onto the kitchen floor. "I washed the kitchen floor with gin," he said. "I felt real bad about that." The worker asked, "How did you feel without the liquor?" Mr. Johnson said, "Lonely." Otherwise he had apparently got through the weekend quite well.

Mrs. Johnson also preferred to have her husband stay at home, drinking or doped up, because she had less trouble keeping the upper hand. In a later interview with the worker, she said (the interview record is being quoted):

"One thing that has been better since he's been home is that we've had fewer arguments. We used to argue all the time. My whole married life has been nothing but arguments. . . ."

Worker: "These arguments, who wins them—half and half, or do you win most, or does he?" Mr. J. said quickly, "She wins them all."

Mrs. J. said, "Well, there's never any agreement, so nobody wins."

Worker said, "But usually you do what you feel must be done, whatever happens about the argument." Mrs. J. said, "Yes."

During this time, the worker kept pushing on a number of fronts, all designed to move the seesaw that had locked with Mrs. Johnson above and Mr. Johnson below. During an interview in mid-February, the seesaw started to loosen. Among other things, the worker was trying to get Mr. Johnson to think about going back to work. If he had part-time work, it would not affect his housing eligibility. Mr. Johnson countered by describing all the panicky feelings and dizziness he was getting whenever he ventured out. Mrs. Johnson moved in, too, saying that work was out of the question until Mr. Johnson stopped drinking. Her fear was that Mr. Johnson would get a job, they would lose their housing, he would collapse, and they would then be left without sufficient income to pay for more expensive quarters. She brought up hospitalization again and said with some feeling that she would like to see progress. The worker said that it appeared that progress for Mr. Johnson was tied to two things: working and having sexual relations with his wife. The couple started talking about the difficulties they had in being intimate together, a subject they were not accustomed to discussing and that made Mrs. Johnson anxious.

The worker further put her on the spot by bringing up her failure to register their youngest child for a Head Start program, an intention she had expressed in the first interview, months before. Of course, her not having done this meant that her husband, who was now at home all the time, was perpetually babysitting. Mrs. Johnson promised to try to register the child but ended the meeting by complaining about her husband's growing resentment of having to babysit.

The meeting seemed to have broken some kind of dam. The next day, Mr. Johnson had another "seizure" as he went out to buy some liquor. He was taken to the health service, where a doctor gave him a prescription for sedative drugs and sent him home. The worker came to see him as soon as possible, feeling now that not talk but action was required, and pushed for hospitalization. Mr. Johnson seemed genuinely eager to go ahead. He said that he seemed to be going down the drain and he wanted to prevent that. Mrs. Johnson for the first time began to show signs of doubt about hospitalizing her husband, but the worker agreed to go ahead and make plans, because Mr. Johnson had said he was ready. The wife called the worker several days later and said that if Mr. Johnson did not stop drinking, she herself was going to have to quit work; she had come home that evening and found him asleep when he should have been taking care of the little girl. It was an interesting message: "I want my husband to stop drinking so that he can babysit for me better." But it seemed her way of supporting the decision to go ahead with hospitalization.

The worker now turned his efforts to finding a hospital that would allow the clinic some measure of control over Mr. Johnson's case. The hospital he found was satisfactory in this respect to the psychiatrist, who now supported the plan. However, the psychiatrist still wished to guard against the danger that the wife might interpret the move as further proof that her husband was sick and thus offset any good it might do. Before Mr. Johnson went into the hospital, the psychiatrist had one more meeting with the couple. In it he pointed out that Mrs. Johnson, by supplying her husband with liquor, had helped to incapacitate him, as both a breadwinner and a bed-partner. He was particularly concerned to expose the wife's share in the husband's problems, which both preferred to define as belonging to the husband alone. He did this, not by telling the wife all the ways in which she was dominating or babying her husband, but by putting her on the other end of a fulcrum. If Mr. Johnson was willing to give up drinking as well as the benefits of the invalid position, Mrs. Johnson must make some concessions that would prevent him from lapsing back and would help to restore his sense of worth as a husband and head of the house. This particularly meant sex, as the psychiatrist emphasized strongly.

In a subsequent interview with the worker, Mrs. Johnson said that she could understand why the psychiatrist had criticized her, but that she did not give Mr. Johnson liquor to hurt him, only because it was easier for her when she did so. She thought he ought to be strong enough to resist it. She also brought up the question of sex, which the psychiatrist had pushed her on; she said she did not want to seem uncooperative, but she could not promise to begin sleeping with Mr. Johnson because she did not want to promise anything that was not going to happen. The worker said that it was not so much a matter of her sleeping or not sleeping with her husband; but if she was going to work at keeping him a nonparticipant in family life, then this whole effort would be for nothing. If, on the other hand, Mr. Johnson was going to be helped to regain his place in the family, then they could work with his being hard to get along with. Mrs. Johnson seemingly got the point and agreed, but the worker did not feel her heart was in it.

The evening of Mr. Johnson's departure for the hospital did not go smoothly. Mrs. Johnson kept postponing their leaving, even though Mr. Johnson and the worker, who was accompanying them, were anxious to get going. After an elaborate dinner, which the worker shared, Mr. Johnson got up just as coffee was being served and said that he was nervous and wanted to go. The worker got up with him and they began to put on their coats. Mrs. Johnson stopped them, saying to Mr. Johnson that it was not polite to drag people off before

they had had a chance to finish their coffee. Everybody sat down
again until coffee was finished. Several other distractions were engi-
neered by Mrs. Johnson, including the temporary loss of her house
keys. The worker said later that he had expected some resistance on
the wife's part, but that he had not been prepared for such a dazzling
display.

In the first days after Mr. Johnson came home from getting "dried
out," he felt poorly, and his wife seemed especially remote and down-
cast. Efforts to plug him into Alcoholics Anonymous were not successful, and within a month he was drinking again with his old cronies,
who during his period of abstinence had begun to call him "the
preacher." However, he was much happier, was eating well for the
first time in years, and had actively begun to look for work. The
worker had to terminate the case at this point, after arranging for it to
be taken over by another caseworker. Subsequent developments were
both hopeful and unhopeful.

On the unhopeful side, as Mr. Johnson began to act more self-
assured, his wife became more and more unhappy. At one point, she
threatened to desert the family if Mr. Johnson did not stop drinking
totally. There was a possibility that she might replace Mr. Johnson as
the invalid; 5 years before she had been seeing a psychiatrist inten-
sively and had nearly been hospitalized at that time. However, she
began to see the new social worker regularly, and this seemed to help
her keep going.

Another unfortunate event was that the Housing Authority agent
had expressed opposition to Mr. Johnson's working full-time again,
telling him that if he did, the family would have to leave their apartment. The original worker phoned the agent to check on this, and the
agent, after trying to get him to agree that Mrs. Johnson was a terrible
housekeeper (also grounds for ineligibility), said that it might be
"more humane" to tell Mr. Johnson that it was the end of the line as far
as his ever working again was concerned rather than let him get his
hopes up. This was particularly discouraging from the worker's point
of view. Even if some changes could be brought about in the family
system, it was difficult to believe that much permanent good could be
done when the systems outside the family remained so fixed.

However, Mr. Johnson turned the tables on those who had con-
signed him to the dustbin. He found a summer job cooking for a camp.
When he returned from camp, the owner of the camp offered him
another job in the city at a very good wage. His old employer was also
asking him to come back, arranging for him to work in such a way that
his income level would no longer be a problem. Mr. Johnson decided

to accept the second alternative but was faced with the task of turning down the first. The worker was prepared to do the task for Mr. Johnson, on the premise that it was so difficult that it might immobilize him and the downward spiral would begin all over again. But the next time Mr. Johnson came in, he told the worker that he had settled the matter himself and was already back at work.

The major—and unexpected—development was that Gail, who had been doing marginally at college, was getting A's and B's at midterm. It would be encouraging to believe, and consistent with family theory, that the airing of difficulties between husband and wife had set Gail free from the family triangle she seemed to have been caught in, thus allowing her to succeed on her own. It would also be encouraging to believe that the 30 operations described earlier were not in vain.

Now, draw an ecomap depicting the current ecological situation for Charles Johnson and his family. Compare your ecomap to Figure 3-3. Where are the current matches and mismatches, the current areas of adaptive coping and stress in this situation? What goals and targets for maintaining this coping and addressing stress areas do you see? Determine what you, as the worker, would want to do in relation to terminating work with the Johnsons at this point. Use your ecomap to defend your position regarding these termination plans.

SUGGESTED LEARNING EXERCISE 3-2:
FIELD ECOMAP

Select a case situation assigned in your field practicum or experience and draw an ecomap that describes this situation from the ecological perspective. Use the ecomap to determine the major goals and targets you plan to address in improving the match between the client's coping needs and resources and the coping resources in the impinging environment. (You might want to draw another ecomap of this situation after you have implemented this interventive plan. This before-and-after ecomapping is a useful tool to assess your practice by attention to the various transactions involved. In this way, the ecomap, consistent with the ecological perspective, serves as both an assessment and evaluation tool.)

4 Prerequisite Competence 2: The Self-Awareness Perspective

One bright winter morning Piglet came upon Pooh Bear in the snowy woods. Piglet's curiosity peaked as he watched Pooh Bear walking around a spinnet bush with his head down, staring intently at the snow. "What are you doing, Pooh Bear?" Piglet asked. "Tracking," replied Pooh Bear. "Tracking what?" retorted Piglet. "I don't really know," said Pooh Bear, "You can't always tell with paw marks."

So Piglet joined him since he didn't have anything else to do until Friday anyway. The paw marks they were following continued to lead around the spinnet bush. "I wonder if this creature we're tracking might be a Woozle or a Wizzle," asked Piglet with a tremor of fear in his voice. "I don't know," whispered Pooh Bear. "But, look!" Suddenly it appeared that whatever it was had been joined by another Woozle or Wizzle. And to their mounting astonishment they found as they continued that they were evidently pursuing more and more Woozles and Wizzles!

In fact, Piglet became so befuddled that, judging the time to be twelve o'clock, he was suddenly moved to recall he had something to do between the hours twelve and five past twelve. So he left Pooh Bear to his tracking, sizing up the situation as: "He who tracks and runs away will live to track another day."

And so it was Pooh who had the great discovery. After a while he stopped going around the spinnet bush and looked closely at all the tracks made by the Woozles and Wizzles. Now he looked at them for a very long while, as he was a bear of very small brain. Then, he carefully placed his own paw snugly down into one of the Woozle tracks! And when Pooh Bear did that he did a very remarkable thing from which he learned a very important lesson. Pooh Bear got wise to himself (Milne, 1954).

SELF-AWARENESS

Getting wise to ourselves, or self-awareness, is among the most important prerequisite foundation competencies for social work practice. The major instrument we use in practice is our selves. Just as the violinist needs to know his or her particular violin and keep it as finely tuned as possible to produce music, so must the social worker know the self and tune that self to resonate effectively with others in practice situations.

What is self-awareness and how do we learn it? These questions are difficult to answer. Almost all models of social work practice promote self-awareness as a basic skill, but only a few (Brill, 1973; Keith-Lucas, 1972) have attempted to define the components of this skill. This chapter defines self-awareness as the ability to identify one's patterns in interpersonal relationships in such areas as one's purposes, values, styles, strengths, limitations, assumptions, thoughts, feelings, perceptions, and communications. In the colloquial, self-awareness is "knowing where you are coming from." Much of social work learning at its best is designed to develop congruence between your personal self and your professional self through self-awareness.

The professional self is marked by discipline (Brill, 1973) and reliability (Avila & Combs, 1985), born from knowledge and self-awareness and the authenticity (Tropp, 1970) and creativity (Keith-Lucas, 1972) generated from trust in one's discipline, knowledge, and self. For instance, Brill (1973) views education for the helping professions as education for the use of self, or "progression from freedom through discipline, to greater freedom" (p. 2). In her questions for the helping person, Brill asks us to be aware of our needs and value systems, their sources, and the strengths and limitations in our own personality patterns. Understanding them requires an ability to recognize and accept our own imperfections as human beings and our capability of change. This acceptance frees us to perceive with clarity and relate with honesty—both to ourselves and to others.

To Keith-Lucas (1972) this self-acceptance is primarily "a quality of not being afraid of oneself" (p. 91). In fact, accepting and facing fear of oneself is the first major step toward self-awareness. When we can see who we are in any given moment, we can admit both our strengths and our imperfections and work on our inevitable limitations more resourcefully—if we choose. We will likely grant more courage, humility, and concern to ourselves as well as to others. We will see more clearly what is in ourselves and others—realizing when "the emperor has no clothes"—and relate more fully and authentically. As we relate this self-awareness to what constitutes the professional self, we can develop the creativity that springs from self-discipline. These professional elements of self-awareness, then, are presented in this chapter: professional purpose and values, preferred styles of interacting, levels of commitment and responsibility, and "theories-in-use"—or the perceptions, thoughts, feelings, and communications that evolve in practice situations.

PURPOSE AND VALUES

A continuous set of research studies (Avila & Combs, 1985; Combs et al., 1969) reveals some significant findings on the relation of underlying purpose and values to effective helping. In these studies, the most effective helpers in a variety of professions differed from less effective ones in their beliefs or values about their purpose, themselves, the people they served, and the primary tasks of helping. Their training, knowledge, methods, and/or techniques did not appear to make any difference in helping outcomes; what effective helpers shared were four basic beliefs about their purposes and values.

First, effective helpers view the *purpose of help as freeing* (assisting, releasing, facilitating, enabling, empowering) rather than controlling (manipulating, changing, coercing, blocking, or inhibiting). While addressing narrow concerns in particular target problems, the purpose of the help is to enable the other to develop coping capacities in a manner that stimulates his or her individual growth process. The help aims to develop motivation, capacity, and opportunity for future competence and growth. To achieve this purpose, the helping situation requires personal involvement and self-revelation rather than self-concealing aloofness. The focus is on furthering the other's process toward competence and growth rather than rigidly focusing on preconceived goals. The basic orientation is altruistic concern for the other's welfare rather than narcissistic attendance to one's own personal goals.

This finding implies that we must be clear in every practice situation about "where we are coming from" in perceiving our purpose. If we integrate the social work purpose of "matching" into all of our work, we will view every situation as one in which we can free the client and environmental resources to meet current and future needs in our absence. In short, we will try to work ourselves out of a job. The questions we need to explore are: To what degree am I concerned with this person's growth as well as amelioration of the specific problematic situation? Whose needs am I meeting in this interaction and in the planning and implementation of the intervention? What have I shared with the other in clarifying my purpose and my stake in this helping process? Where might my own needs (to be liked, to feel competent, to be wanted, to please my supervisor, etc.) potentially block my ability to focus on the other's needs and goals and to enable the other to develop his or her own coping capacities and adaptive growth?

Second, effective helpers *value people* as having the inner capacity to deal with their own problems. They are motivated to facilitate wholeness, competence, and self-determination. The value of self-determination derives from the belief that people possess dignity and integrity; that they are creative and dynamic rather than passive or inert participants in psychosocial events; that their behavior is trustworthy, dependable, and purposeful, rather than capricious or unpredictable; and that, when aware of their own needs and the needs of others, they make choices for action that are potentially fulfilling and enhancing to themselves and others, rather than impeding, threatening, or self-destructive.

This finding implies that we must monitor our views of those we serve in terms of our general assumptions about people and our particular assumptions about the motivation and capacity of specific individuals. As we identify those values that contradict our trust in the dignity and integrity of others, it is often best to explore their source: Which of these values did I learn in my family? In my culture? In frustrating relationships with people I tend to view (stereotype) as like these? In my beliefs about my own motivation and capacities? This initial awareness, which is often the first step in "value clarification" programs, can often free us to consider the possibility of different values, or other ways of viewing people. This openness to change in our own values can lead to helping behavior that seeks the strengths of motivation, capacities, and opportunities and respects self-determination in situations where we heretofore did not see them.

Third, effective helpers *value themselves*. They identify with, rather than see themselves as apart from, humanity in general. They believe they are basically adequate to the task at hand and see themselves as essentially trustworthy, dependable, reliable, and able to cope with most events in their own lives and in practice. They have a strong sense of themselves as possessing dignity and integrity, not as persons of little consequence who can be overlooked and discounted.

This finding implies that we must also be aware of our beliefs about ourselves as helpers. How do we assess our own place in humanity? How do we experience and "own" our own competence? What are our rights as human beings, and how do we assert these? What is it that we particularly can offer to others, or to this specific other in this specific situation? When we find that our own sense of autonomy, wholeness, self-esteem, and self-respect are thwarted, we must look for the sources of their violence to our dignity and integrity. If we tend to blame ourselves we will likely also tend to blame our clients, rather than target activities to address the systems that produce these assaults on our own and our clients' sense of dignity and worth. This finding does not imply that either we or our clients are perfect. Rather, we work to transcend our imperfections in our thrust to become the best possible, yet imperfect, person we can be.

Fourth, effective helpers *value process*. They view their tasks as directed more to people and their needs than to things (objects, events, rules, and so on). The objectives of the tasks are clearly related to the benefits of those they serve. The means, or tasks, do not become ends in themselves. Therefore, people and tasks are not viewed as objects but as subjective processes that have purpose and meaning in the phenomenological world of those we serve. People are approached from a subjective perspective that emphasizes their perceptions of reality rather than from an emphasis on objective "facts" of reality.

This finding implies that we must examine our practice with attention to how we conceive our tasks and the reality of those we serve. The basic questions are: To what degree do we see tasks as ends in themselves rather than tools to meet others' needs? What does the other define as reality, and how are we defining this reality? What pressures do we experience from our setting, our supervisor, our colleagues, ourselves, and/or our clients to complete tasks as ends in themselves rather than as means to serve our clients? How does my client view his or her situation, the tasks of this helping process, and his or her own motivation, capacity, and opportunities for coping and adaptive growth?

In sum, effective helpers value empowering and humanizing means and ends—for both their clients and themselves. What do you value?

VALUE CONFLICTS AND ETHICAL DILEMMAS

Value conflicts and ethical dilemmas in social work practice demand special self-awareness. Developing personal values into professional values is necessary but not sufficient for the effective use of self in practice. The nature of social work's professional values can lead to painful value conflicts and ethical dilemmas in practice. The Council on Social Work Education's (1982) curriculum policy statement asserts that the primary value of social work is that "people should have equal access to the resources, services, and opportunities for the accomplishment of life tasks, alleviation of distress, and the realization of their aspirations and values in relation to themselves, the rights of others, the general welfare, and social justice" (p. 3).

Five secondary, or "instrumental" (Pincus & Minahan, 1973), values evolve from this primary one (CSWE, 1982, p. 3):

1. Professional relationships are built upon the social worker's regard for individual growth and dignity. These relationships are characterized by mutual participation, acceptance, confidentiality, honesty, and open handling of conflict.
2. Social workers respect people's rights to choose, to contract for services, and to participate in the helping process.
3. Social workers contribute to making social institutions more humane and responsive to human needs.
4. Social workers demonstrate respect for and acceptance of the unique characteristics of diverse populations.
5. Social workers are responsible for their own ethical conduct and competence.

These instrumental values suggest that in all practice situations, social workers strive toward: (1) honesty; (2) recognizing and appreciating—rather than judging—differences; (3) confidentiality of communications; (4) maintaining an open, accepting attitude; and (5) maximizing the involvement and self-determination of those with whom they work. These values are considered "instrumental" because they provide ethical principles that can serve as practice guidelines to actualize our primary values. Building relationships based on these "core conditions" (Rogers, 1957) is necessary but not necessarily sufficient for positive change in clients, not only from a value base but also from the perspective of empirical research (for reviews of this extensive research on empathy, genuineness, or honesty, and unconditional positive regard or acceptance as "core conditions," see Carkhuff & Berenson, 1976, 1977; Mitchell et al., 1977; Truax & Mitchell, 1971).

Value conflicts and ethical dilemmas are inevitable when our professional values and ethics are applied in specific and concrete situations. These occur for a number of reasons. First, we need to apply values and ethics based on our own best judgments in ambiguous situations. As the National Association of Social Workers' (1980) code of ethics states in its introduction, "this code does not represent a set of rules that will prescribe all the behaviors of social workers in all the complexities of professional life. . . . Specific applications of ethical principles must be judged within the context in which they are being considered" (p. 1). For instance, the use of self-determination becomes more difficult in situations in which individuals are not sure what they want, or want the social worker to tell them what to do, or are so ambivalent about goals that they frequently change their mind.

Second, in another source (Anderson, 1981) I have identified the value dilemmas in situations in which our clients' rights seem in conflict with others' rights. All individuals in our society, not just our clients, must receive our respect for their dignity and worth and our protection of their rights for self-determination. An example of such a dilemma offered in that source is the following: "Where does the right of a parent who abuses his or her child end and the right of the child to physical security begin? Can one support the values of individual dignity, acceptance, and self-determination for *both* the abusing parent and abused child?" (Anderson, 1981, p. 17).

Third, values can be restricted by legal authority when the rights of others or one's own are violated. This situation can lead to decreased freedom and rights, such as in prisons, in mental health hospital placements, in child abuse and neglect situations, or in assessments of mental incompetence. In these situations, the person relinquishes the part of his or her self-determination that relates to the behavior that violates others' or one's own rights. The value conflict comes in establishing as much self-determination as possible within the mandated limits. This includes the social worker's determination of how authority will be exercised as well as the achievement of clarity about areas (in addition to the legal requirements) in which self-determination can be exercised.

The first step to facilitate coping with value conflicts and ethical dilemmas is to be aware of them. This requires awareness of our own interpretation of social work ethical principles and their relation to our own personal values. When we are aware of our own biases, prejudices, preferences, and aversions, we can "monitor the extent to which these factors are influencing, perhaps quite subtly, the decisions made and actions undertaken in the course of practice" (Simons & Aigner, 1985, p. 25). Especially important to monitor are our attractions and repulsions to those we encounter in our professional relationships. This awareness can prevent the seduction into sexual activities with clients—a very serious violation of the code of ethics—or into the authoritarian use of power with clients who might repulse us. Such relationships are not only unethical but can render the work dysfunctional and the encounter itself manipulative, sentimental, and generally frustrating and destructive for all involved.

We must also be aware of our moral and religious commitments. For example, a social worker with particular religious beliefs could feel that abortion (or military service) is morally wrong. Such social workers can still be effective and practice within the values of the profession, although they could not work in certain settings, such as an abortion clinic. Also, these religious values may not be appropriate for work with some clients or groups of clients. The decision on whether these values might block the needed work should begin in the practitioner's awareness. Then the practitioner can discuss the potential conflict with the client or client system so that they can decide if they can work together.

PREFERRED STYLE

Another key area of our self-awareness is recognition of our preferred style of interacting with others. Our personal values and beliefs greatly influence this style. We prefer certain positions, functions, and roles to others because we perceive them as more consistent with our values and comfortable ways of relating. Awareness of this style can enable us to develop our strengths and work on areas where our idiosyncrasies obstruct our ability to help others.

A great deal of research in social work and the other helping professions indicates that one's personality style leads to particular theoretical approaches and behavior in practice (for reviews, see Goldmeier, 1968; Mullen, 1969; Rice et al., 1972). This research suggests that more introverted persons prefer less direct approaches and techniques, while more extroverted persons prefer more confrontative approaches and techniques. Some are more comfortable in providing support and others in providing challenge in problem-solving processes. Most balanced theories of practice, including the interactional approach of this text, identify both support and challenge as key ingredients of helping relationships.

Therefore we must be aware of how our own styles affect our preferences in the use of self in practice situations. This awareness requires that we identify our style's strengths for and obstacles to providing help, both in general and in particular situations. Where are we located on the support–challenge continuum? How is our style affected by particular personality characteristics of clients and others? Do we find it easier to support and/or challenge certain types of people than others? How do our theoretical preferences and techniques relate to our style? These are the questions that help increase our self-awareness about our preferred style. The answers to these provide direction for sensitizing us as we tune in to our reactions in interpersonal transactions. We are then more likely to develop our strengths and prevent parts of our idiosyncratic style from becoming obstacles to the helping relationship and process.

COMMITMENT AND RESPONSIBILITY

Commitment and responsibility are two major concepts in the existential position on helpful human encounters. In the work of existential helping professionals, special importance is placed on the helper's level of commitment and sense of responsibility. In these works, commitment refers to the underlying concern for the other and how this concern manifests itself in service. We need to be aware of the level of our commitment in our interpersonal relationships in practice.

The strength of our commitment to the other does not imply like or dislike. Although possibly difficult, we can keep our level of commitment high with those we might not particularly like. In fact, it is in these very situations that it is most important for us to be aware of the degree of concern we can maintain. When we find our level of commitment or degree of concern for the other waivering in practice situations, we have the responsibility to become aware of this quickly and to try harder to care about the other.

Responsibility is closely related to commitment. When we commit ourselves to helping another as fully as possible, we take responsibility for our decisions in making ourselves *present* for the other. We are more "response-able." We take our helping relationship seriously, thereby becoming more aware of what we are doing—our own decisions and choices in the interaction. This awareness includes our recognition of where we are responsible through our actions for offering ourselves and a helping process and where we overextend this responsibility by trying to be responsible for the other's life, decisions, choices, situation, and/or growth.

THEORIES-IN-USE

All professional practice involves both espoused theory and theory-in-use (Argyris & Schön, 1975). Our espoused theories are the formally stated principles and concepts about human behavior in the social environment and what we can best do to influence it. Theory-in-use consists of the less conscious assumptions about self, others, the situation, and the connections among our own and others' actions, consequences, and situations. Our theories-in-use derive from our life experiences, preferred style, "implicit personality theory" as this affects our perceptions and conceptions of people (Bullmer, 1970), and aspects of our intuition or "practice wisdom" (Imre, 1984). As Chris Argyris and Donald Schön (1975) note, we give explanations of why we do what we do in relation to our espoused theory, but the theory that actually governs much of our actions is our theory-in-use. And this theory-in-use may or may not be compatible with our espoused theory.

This theory-in-use is not so conscious for us. In fact, we cannot increase our awareness of our theory-in-use by trying to state it directly; we must construct it from our own and others' observations of our behavior. When we know what we did in any given situation, based on what we were trying to do and why, we know our theory-in-use. We know the goal we were seeking, the action we deemed appropriate to achieve that goal, and the assumptions we made about these goals, actions, and consequences.

In this sense, our theories-in-use are our psychology and sociology of everyday life. They are the assumptions we are inclined to make, most often unconsciously, about human motivation, needs, personality, and behavior. We reflect these theories in our identification of our own thoughts and feelings during particular communications with others. When we examine these interactions, attempting to identify our thoughts, feelings, and assumptions, we can increase our awareness of our theories-in-use. This awareness, in turn, can lead to developing more compatibility between our theories-in-use and our espoused theories—between our personal self and the demands on our professional self in practice.

CONCLUSION

This second prerequisite competence concerns the ability to develop self-awareness for effective social work practice. Specifically, this competence requires skills for analyzing one's own interactions in practice. The first suggested learning exercise below promotes this awareness of one's purpose, values, preferred style, level of commitment, and theories-in-use. This analysis can increase the awareness of the current level of congruence between aspects of one's personal, and one's use of the professional, self in practice.

SUGGESTED LEARNING EXERCISE 4-1: SELF-AWARENESS

This assignment, adapted from Argyris and Schön (1975, pp. 37–62), provides the opportunity to develop self-awareness of our purpose, our values, our preferred style, our commitment and responsibility, and our theories-in-use. The use of such an assignment can enhance the knowledge of the relation of our personal self to our professional self in our current level of competence for practice.

Describe a challenging intervention or interaction with one or more individuals that (1) you have already experienced or (2) you expect to experience in the future.

If you have difficulty with either of these conditions, try a hypothetical case in which you doubt your effectiveness.

Begin the description with a paragraph about the purpose of your intervention, the setting, the people involved, and any other important characteristics.

Next, write a few paragraphs regarding your strategy. What were your objectives, how did you intend to achieve them, and why did you select these goals and strategies (include reflection of your purpose, values, preferred style, and espoused theory)?

Next, write a few pages of the dialogue that actually occurred or that you expect to occur. Use the following format:

On the one side of the page write what was going on in your mind while each person in the dialogue (including yourself) is speaking.

On the other side of the page, write what each person actually said or what you expected him to say. Continue writing the dialogue until you believe your major points are illustrated. (The dialogue should be at least two pages long.)

Finally, after you reread your case, describe the underlying assumptions that you think you held about effective action. Then identify your purpose, values, style, and commitment in this interaction.

In the work of Argyris and Schön (1975) is an example of a social worker who used this assignment to identify her theory-in-use and increase her awareness in practice. The worker was trying to help a person who did not seem to be changing his behavior. She wrote, "I feel annoyed with him and pretty determined either to cut off our interaction, delve more deeply into his problem, or demonstrate to him that he is in fact not interested in changing at all. The last alternative is fine with me. I dislike wasting my time on futile activity." At this point, we see that the social worker: (1) has already decided the course the next session should take; (2) has attributed characteristics to the client without telling him so that he can confirm or deny them; (3) has decided that the responsibility for failure lies with him and therefore does not explore her own role in the apparent failure; (4) assumes that she is responsible for the client's behavior; and (5) denies responsibility for her sense of failure. (She states that she dislikes having her time wasted, but a more accurate statement might have been: "I dislike being with a client I cannot help because I feel that I have been partially responsible for wasting my time.")

Later the worker wrote, "I knew that I had to be very much on top of the situation so that we would not fall back into our old ways of interacting. I tried to keep my objectives in mind all the time and I tried to push myself to think and evaluate clearly because I knew he did not want to hear what I had to say, and I could slip backward in a weak moment." Here the worker assumed that she, rather than the client, was in control. However, the social worker's purpose is to promote growth and responsibility. Her dilemma was that she was faced with a person whom she felt unable to help unless she violated her principles.

Looking more closely at her theories-in-use, we find that although the social worker claimed to dislike people who are dependent, passive, and weak, she selected tactics that reinforce these characteristics. Perhaps she wanted people to exhibit such characteristics so she could accept her predisposition to control others. She may even have selected a theory-in-use that minimizes the probability of being confronted on this issue by either the client or herself. Her assumptions that the client was not going to grow could be a self-fulfilling prophecy. A concluding dialogue reflects these problems with her theories-in-use, values, and style as related to her espoused theory about the professional use of her self:

SOCIAL WORKER: You seem to want or expect personal change to be easy.

CLIENT: No, I don't. I expect it to be hard but I know it's for my own benefit. But you must understand I have to work within certain constraints . . . (cut off by social worker)

SOCIAL WORKER: Why? You're working within "certain constraints" now and you're not going anywhere. You're saying you must accept these constraints. That doesn't make any sense; you can't change yourself and not expect to challenge your environment.

CLIENT: Why not? I mean, it's me that has to change if I want this to happen. I can't expect the world to change for me.

SOCIAL WORKER: Yes, that's true, but as I have told you many times you can make the world change so that you can live more fully in it.

CLIENT: I guess you're right. I know I don't have much self-discipline. That's one of my real faults that I can't do anything about. But now that I see my father coming apart at the seams, I want to change before I get to be like that, too.

SOCIAL WORKER: How much do you want to change? Enough to commit yourself to a job? Enough to risk some arguments with your wife?

CLIENT: Well, I'd like to teach young people something in psychology or religion or history.

SOCIAL WORKER: How do you think you could go about getting what you need to be a teacher for those subjects?

CLIENT: I don't know. I guess I'd have to get a teaching certifcate, but that's impossible.

SOCIAL WORKER: Why?

CLIENT: I didn't even finish college.

SOCIAL WORKER: Well, so what? Go back to school.

CLIENT: I'm too old. I'd be laughed at.

SOCIAL WORKER: Now, you know that's not true. People go back to finish up all the time. As I've said before, if you really want to, you can do anything.

This social worker, having used this assignment, may be in a position to test how much her espoused theories, her theories-in-use, and her own idiosyncrasies may affect her service to this person (and surely to others, too). With increased awareness, she may choose among the options for achieving her objectives that are more congruent with the client's needs and her own professional knowledge. She can get more wise to herself and begin to discover how her own needs to control lead to a theory-in-use that prevents autonomy development (her espoused goal) in dependent clients.

SUGGESTED LEARNING EXERCISE 4-2: PREREQUISITE COMPETENCE 2

Given an interpersonal and interactional situation in which you are involved, write a report that identifies your own:

- purpose in the interaction;
- values or preferences and their sources as these affect or could affect the interaction;
- potential value conflicts and ethical dilemmas;
- preferred style of interaction in this situation;
- strengths and obstacles to achieving the purpose of this interaction in this preferred style;
- responsibility for what occurs in terms of the choices made during the interaction;
- levels of commitment to others in the situation;
- assumptions regarding the others' behavior during the interaction;
- thoughts and feelings during each communication sequence of the interaction and the directness and clarity of communication throughout the interaction;
- current knowledge of the relation of the personal self to the demands of the use of the professional self in interactional situations such as this one.

II | Generic Social Work Process Competencies

5 Competence #1: Preliminary Phase: Tuning-In

The venerable teacher Confucius saw skill as the art of concentration on the task at hand. He taught his disciples to practice focused awareness and avoid the distractions of the "ten thousand things."

For instance, when Confucius was traveling with his disciples he passed through a forest where he saw a hunchback catching cicadas with a sticky pole. He used the pole as readily as if he were grabbing the cicadas with his hands.

Confucius said, "What skill you have! Is there a special way to this?"

"I have a way," said the hunchback. "For the first five or six months, I practice balancing two balls on top of each other on the end of the pole and, if they don't fall off, I know I will lose very few cicadas. Then I balance three balls and, if they don't fall off, I know I'll lose only one cicada in ten. Then I balance five balls and, if they don't fall off, I know it will be easy grabbing them with my hand. I hold my body like a stiff tree trunk and use my arm like an old dry limb. No matter how huge heaven and earth, or how numerous the ten thousand things, I'm aware of nothing but cicada wings. Not wavering, not tipping, not letting any of the other ten thousand things take the place of those cicada wings—how can I help but succeed?"

Confucius turned to his disciples and said, "He keeps his will undivided and concentrates his spirit—that would serve to describe our hunchback gentleman here, would it not?"

On another occasion, Yen Yuan said to Confucius, "I once crossed a gulf at Goblet Deep and the ferryman handled the boat with supernatural skill. I asked him, 'Can a person like me—not used to being on water—learn how to handle a boat so well?' and he replied, 'Certainly. A good swimmer has acquired his ability through repeated practice.

And if a man can swim under water, he may never have seen a boat before and still he'll know how to handle it!' I asked him what he meant by that, but he wouldn't tell me. May I venture to ask you what it means?"

Confucius said, "A good swimmer has acquired his ability through repeated practice—that means he's forgotten the water. If a man can swim under water, he may never have seen a boat before and still know how to handle it—that's because he sees the water as so much dry land and regards the capsizing of a boat as he would the overturning of a cart. The ten thousand things may all be capsizing and turning over at the same time right in front of him and it can't get at him and affect what's inside—so where could he go and not be at ease? Your practiced skill is the same in face of ten thousand things—as long as you don't look too hard on the outside and get clumsy on the inside."

The preliminary phase of social work process involves tuning-in skills. Tuning-in is the skill of bringing ourselves to the potential service of another. It entails a concentrated focus to prepare us "inside" for beginning the work in the face of the potential "ten thousand things" that might seem to be occuring "outside" in initial contacts. Three separate skills constitute this preliminary phase: tuning-in to self; tuning-in to client (other); and tuning-in to client's (other's) situation.

William Schwartz (1971) originally termed this skill "preliminary empathy." It involves our effort to get in touch with the potential feelings and concerns that a person may bring to the helping encounter. It also includes getting in touch with where we are in relation to beginning this work. The purpose of tuning-in is to increase our sensitivity to the meaning of the client's communications, however subtle and indirect, in our first contacts. It enables us to respond directly and with initial empathy to the indirect feelings and concerns that clients often initially communicate. When we tune-in, we prepare inside to respond with empathy outside.

TUNING-IN TO SELF

Tuning-in to self is a special case of self-awareness. This tuning-in is an affective rather than an intellectual or analytical process. We need to get in touch with our own feelings and values and to experience them as much as possible. The awareness and experience of these feelings and values through tuning-in helps to prevent them from becoming obstacles to our concentrating on the client's communication.

Alfred Benjamin (1974) sees tuning-in as an essential internal factor of every helping interview. He suggests that the first principle of helping interviews is bringing ourselves, especially our desire to help. To bring ourselves, we need to address the question: "What do we bring with us, inside us, about us, that may help or hinder or not affect [the other] one way or another?" (p. 4). We especially must try to establish two internal conditions: (1) bringing as much of our own selves as we possibly can, while separating our responsibility from the other's; and (2) feeling that we are concerned about the other, wishing to help, and having nothing at the moment more important to us than the other and his or her situation.

The assumption, supported by research (Carkhuff, 1969; Shulman, 1977), is that clients will sense early on the attitude and feelings we bring to the first contact—at least through the "truth" of our nonverbal behavior, which may speak louder than our words. Initial trust and contact seem to come not so much from our bringing perfect concentration and concern as from the other sensing we have tuned-in and are trying to do our best in this direction.

This attitude, of course, requires that we be honest with ourselves. Then we can admit first to ourselves and perhaps later to our clients some of these human imperfections. When we can accept our own infallibility, we can tune-in to those parts of ourselves that might prevent the way we "bring ourselves." We might, for instance, become more aware that we tend to cease listening because we are preoccupied with formulating our own response—a common tendency in early practice. Or we withhold responses because we are looking for that "right thing to say." As we tune-in to these parts of ourselves, we can begin to trust ourselves more. Rather than waiting for the perfect response, we can even risk responding with what arises in us at the moment and trust that it has evolved from our concern for the other. And to our surprise, we may learn more what research (Carkhuff, 1969; Shulman, 1984) suggests—most clients feel more helped by those they experience as human beings with failings who are working at understanding them and enabling them to understand their own potential for coping and growth.

If we are to help others cope more effectively with their psychosocial realities rather than defend against these experiences, we need to exemplify the same strengths in our tuning-in. We must especially avoid becoming like the fox who came across the luscious-looking grapes in Aesop's fable. When the fox discovered that the grapes were too high to reach, he decided they were sour. When we face our doubts or potential inadequacies in tuning-in, we can avoid defending against these current feelings by "sour graping" the client, the helping situation, and/or our commitment to competence as a social worker. Instead, we need to find ways of coping with these feelings.

Robert Carkhuff (1983) conceives tuning-in to self as part of the attending skill. Attending is the necessary precondition of helping whereby we posture ourselves emotionally, intellectually, and physically to concentrate on the other, to see and hear the other, and to convey our interest in the other. The first step in attending is tuning-in to our self, or what Carkhuff calls "preparing for helping." This self-preparation requires reviewing information, reviewing purpose, and relaxing. As we review information, we get in touch with what this means to us—the responses it generates in us and the bases for our potential empathy with the client and his or her situation. When we review our matching and enabling purpose, we can bring ourselves to first contacts with an openness to learn from clients and the goal of exploring their experiences of their situation. Relaxing can result from various methods: we might relax our minds through reflecting upon pleasant, soothing experiences; we might relax our bodies through deep breathing or brief meditation exercises.

For instance, you might work at an agency that has contracted with a local industry to offer employee-assistance services. The company has asked you to provide employee-assistance counseling for Arnold Swartz in an emergency appointment this afternoon. Arnold is described as a tall, broad-shouldered, well-muscled 23-year-old who has worked with the company for a year. He is basically a good worker but is easily agitated and provoked to anger, especially when corrected about mistakes. This morning he was suspended for 2 weeks because he hit his foreman. You have 10 minutes before Arnold is due for his appointment. How might you tune-in to your self in preparation for this initial contact?

Carkhuff suggests that you face your feelings about working with an angry and potentially violent Arnold Swartz. What feelings does this generate in you? Fear? Anger? Cautiousness? If he expresses hostility early about being with you, what might you do? Freeze? Snap back at him? Get firm? This information prepares you to face the meaning of his anger to you, which may help you begin to attend to its meaning for him.

You also have information that he is a good worker. What does that mean to you? That he is motivated to keep his job? That he may be motivated to use your help, or to control his temper?

How do you see and what do you state as your purpose for working with him and your goal for this first contact? To help him control his temper? To find out what is wrong with him? To explore with him his perception of the demands of his work situation and his reactions to them and what he wants to work on? Such reflection may prepare you to begin in a less threatening way that might defuse some of his anger or at least keep it from being totally projected onto you. It may also demonstrate the respect and empathy that are necessary for him to begin to trust your interest in and concern for him.

How relaxed are you? Butterflies in your stomach? Throat dry? Shoulders tense? Thinking catastrophic thoughts—like your saying something that provokes his anger and a physical attack on you? Try to clear your mind and relax your body. Picture yourself lying on the beach or hiking in the mountains. Take 10 deep breaths with your eyes closed and the beach or mountain scene in your mind's eye. Get as ready as you can and prepare to get to know what you do not know about Arnold Swartz.

Tuning-In to Our Feelings

We need to tune-in to our ambivalences. Most beginnings for us, as well as for those with whom we work, are marked by both wishes and fears, or pushes toward and pulls away from getting involved. We all tend to have general patterns to these ambivalences. Some of us tend to begin new experiences with "positive" feelings—high hopes and expectations—while our "negative" feelings—fear, anger, resentment—trickle into our consciousness later. Others may experience the fears more strongly than the hopes in beginnings. This general pattern is often affected by the nature of the experience we are about to enter and its perceived meaning for us.

If we perceive that the demands of the situation may outweigh our capacities to meet them, our feelings of inadequacy can be particularly stressful and overwhelm our excitement about confronting the challenge. It does us and those we serve little good to deny these feelings of inadequacy as a defense to cope with our stress. Only through facing and experiencing this negative side of our ambivalence do we seem to be able to move toward owning the positive feelings on the other side—our motivation of concern for the client and our desire to help as best we are able. We may find, for instance, that we block our realistic capabilities with an expectation of perfection and its concomitant fears of failure. With self-awareness, we can challenge these obstacles in ourselves.

Another set of feelings comes from our anticipated difference from the client. The client may be old; we may be young. The client may be black; we may be white. The client may be from a large urban area; we may be from a small rural community. The client may be married and have five children; we may be single. The client may be physically handicapped; we may not be. These differences are often first experienced with some discomfort. We may fear that we cannot bridge these differences. We may jump quickly to judging our own and/or the client's difference and feel some resentment about the potential work. It is important that we tune-in to the feelings that our sense of difference generates in us.

On the other hand, we may experience feelings about anticipated similarities to the client. We may feel relieved and expect that the beginning will be easy and smooth. If we do not tune-in to these feelings and remain aware of them, we might miss the inevitable differences that clients will communicate in our initial contacts.

Our anxieties, whatever their source, demand special attention in our tuning-in. Anxieties and fears decrease our awareness. The Greek word for anxiety is *angst*, which literally means "to choke, or to narrow." Anxiety chokes our consciousness of our own inside experience and narrows our awareness of what is actually happening outside of us. We most often draw in to ourselves to protect ourselves from anticipated pain. When we tune-in to these anxieties, which often precede and accompany our initial contacts with those we serve, we can develop ways to relieve some of their power and to prevent their becoming "ten thousand things" that weaken our concentration.

The ability to tune-in to our anxiety, or to any of the feelings we may have in the preliminary phase, requires our finding ways to experience these feelings more fully. This premise of experiencing our feelings in tuning-in evolves from a particular theoretical perspective on the place of emotions in human behavior—one that is existential (May, 1958) and interactional (Denzin, 1984). In this theory, feelings are embedded in the body and always experienced in a body–mind gestalt that is in an interactional process with the environment. Our emotions reflect our existence as *bodily felt* in experience, even before we can put words to it. This experience of existence as bodily feeling is always based on a human being-in-the-world. Feelings are interactional. Experiencing feelings, therefore, is not "subjective," but interactional; not intrapsychic, but interactional. It is not inside, but inside–outside. Our feelings are the encounterings in the world and with others. They are interacting-*with*, a fearing-*of*, a hoping-*for*, an angry-*at*, a trying-*for*, an avoiding-*of*. How we feel is not some response coming on top of what happens in our interactional experience; it *is* what happens, our *experience* of this happening.

The experience of our feelings is not only based on the unity of our body and mind as well as of person and environment, it is also a unity of process—of past, present, and future. We experience our existence in bodily feelings, in situations with others, and in the past and future. When we tune-in to present feelings, we can experience our past and projected future. This temporality of our feelings, when we open ourselves to experiencing the *felt* present, brings on the future-oriented process of their purposeful seeking of value and meaning. By experiencing our bodily felt continuity, our current feelings change toward a process of carrying us foward to potential alternatives, choices, and feelings. Experiencing of our feelings, first in body and then in symbols of meaning for us, implies a sense of direction for further environmental interaction.

In other words, a clear focus and more *whole* feel of now can change the quality and nature of our feelings and generate a clearer sense of new direction. For example, experiencing our anger at another more fully and wholly in the present may release us from the fragmented experience of internal anger and provide further steps toward interacting with the other. This directional process may carry our feelings forward to the hurt and love we experience in this relationship and imply an altogether different, yet continuous, interaction with the other.

In this perspective, then, feelings are sensations that express intentions and seek the meaning of interactional events. Anxiety, for instance, is the bodily sensation we experience when we face an opportunity to be true to ourselves and bear this freedom to choose. Thus anxiety is not the cause but the symptom of choosing too much security over growth in the events in our lives. As Søren Kierkegaard (1968) originally conceived *angst*, it is a "narrowing" or "shrinking" of our consciousness of choice through self-deception in the face of the "dizziness of freedom." We dam up our process of becoming as we shrink from our more authentic being. However, when faced and experienced, this anxiety is, in his words, "the reality of freedom as a potentiality before this freedom has materialized" (p. 55). Thus the fear of this freedom implies a future choice in the reality of freedom—one with the potential of greater consciousness, risk, vitality, authenticity, and responsibility to actualize our potential. At the heart of our anxiety is the possibility of growth.

Guilt, like anxiety, can speak. It calls forth the potentialities we have chosen to lock up in ourselves. When we open ourselves to the experience of our guilt, we can discover these forfeited potentialities, missed opportunities, avoided life challenges, and escaped authentic relationships to others. We may find the evolution of feelings of forgiveness; acceptance of our own human imperfections; humility; concern for others; and commitment to developing our own human-ness—all so necessary to working with others to promote a world where this being and becoming is more possible.

This theoretical side trip brings us to the destination of the need to find ways of experiencing our feelings in tuning-in to ourselves in social work practice. One way of tuning-in when we are alone with ourselves is through "focusing" (Gendlin, 1969). Focusing is a technique to attend to concretely felt bodily sensation and to ex-perience these feelings in their directional process and meaning. When one is vaguely aware of feelings about a particular potential client or others prior to first contact, the focusing exercise can be very useful.

Focusing Exercise

1. Take about 5 seconds to relax.

2. Now, pay attention to a very special part of yourself. Take about 5 seconds and pay attention to that part where you usually feel sad, glad, or scared.

3. Pay more attention to that area of yourself and see how you are now. See what comes to you when you ask yourself, "How am I now?" "How do I feel?" "What is the main thing for me right now?" Close your eyes, take about 30 seconds or less, and let it come to you in whatever way it comes to you, and see how it is.

4. If, among the things you have just thought of, there was a major anticipated problem with the person with whom you will work, and it felt important, continue with it. Otherwise, select a potential problem in work with this person and think about it. Make sure you have chosen a problem of real importance in your work with this person. Choose that problem that seems most meaningful to you and think about it, with eyes closed, for about 10 seconds.

5. Of course, there are many parts to the one thing you are thinking about—too many to *think* of each one alone. But you can *feel* all of these things together. Pay attention there where you usually feel things, and in there you can get a sense of what *all of this problem* feels like. Close your eyes for 30 seconds or less, and let yourself feel *all of that*.

6. As you pay attention to the whole feeling of it, you may find that one special feeling comes up. Close your eyes again, and for one minute let yourself pay attention to that one feeling.

7. Now, for another minute, close your eyes and keep following that one feeling. Don't let it be *just* words and/or pictures—wait and let words or pictures come from the feeling.

8. If this one feeling changes, or moves, let it do that. Reclose your eyes and take a minute to follow the feeling and pay attention to it—whatever it does.

9. Next, take what is fresh, or new, in the feel of it *now*. Go very easily. Just as you feel it, try to find some new words or pictures to capture what your new feeling is all about. There does not have to be anything that you did not know before. New words are best, but old words might fit just as well. Just take one minute, with eyes closed, to pay attention to what is fresh or new in your feeling and find the words or pictures to say what is fresh to you now.

10. If the words or pictures that you now have make some fresh difference, see what that difference is. Close your eyes and for a minute let the words or pictures change until they feel just right in capturing your feelings.

11. Now, take a little while to use in any way you want and to bring this exercise to a close for yourself.

Another way of tuning-in to your own feelings is through a simulated dialogue. This dialogue can take place with the potential client in your own head—through fantasy—or with a consultant, supervisor, or colleague—through role-playing. However this dialogue occurs, it is important that you attempt to express your own feelings as discriminatively and fully as possible and get reactions to these feelings from the other as if the other were the client. To express feelings fully and with discrimination, it is helpful to attempt to state your feelings, positive and negative, through several different words that might reflect both their category (kind) and their intensity more accurately for yourself and the other. The feeling list in Table 5-1 is an example of these different categories and intensities. You can add words to these lists that describe your feelings more accurately and more meaningfully to you. If in a fantasized or role-played dialogue with a potential client you choose words for your feelings from this list that do not quite feel right to you, you likely have a better word to use and to add to this list. As you begin to tune-in to your own feelings, you will likely learn to trust them more—including the trust in your own feelings about your feelings.

The purpose of tuning-in to one's own feelings is to bring one's self, one's concentration and presence unencumbered by the "ten thousand things," into service in behalf of the client. However, this tuning-in can also open us to the possibility of our experiencing the feelings of clients

TABLE 5-1 Categories of Feelings

"Positive"			
Levels of intensity	Excited	Surprised	Happy	Satisfied
---	---	---	---	---
High	Delerious	Astonished	Ecstatic	Delighted
	Intoxicated	Staggered	Exuberant	Enchanted
	Exhilarated	Stupefied	Triumphant	Satiated
Medium	Animated	Amazed	Exalted	Charmed
	Charged	Awed	Fantastic	Gratified
	Thrilled	Jolted	Tickled	Full
Low	Alive	Overcome	Great	Agreeable
	Great	Rocked	Lively	Glad
	Stirred	Startled	Super	Nice

"Negative"			
Levels of intensity	Distressed	Frightened	Anxious	Sad
---	---	---	---	---
High	Agony	Frantic	Baffled	Despair
	Crushed	Terrified	Perplexed	Devastated
	Tormented	Petrified	Tangled	Pitiful
Medium	Afflicted	Aghast	Blocked	Awful
	Pained	Dread	Confounded	Gloomy
	Troubled	Threatened	Stressed	Sullen
Low	Bad	Cautious	Careful	Down
	Ill at ease	Hesitant	Muddled	Low
	Upset	Shaky	Uncertain	Unhappy

more fully. The heart of this participation is our shared feelings and their intentionality, their meaning in our helping relationship. We and the client will feel together whether or not we are tuned-in to this aspect of the encounter. When we are tuned-in, we can more readily feel with and enable the client's process. As Rollo May (1969) has stated: "[Feeling] . . . starts in the present and points toward the future. . . . Our feelings not only take in consideration the other person but are in a real sense *formed by the feelings of the other persons present*. We feel in a magnetic field. . . . Every successful lover knows this by 'instinct.' It is an essential—if not the essential—quality of the good therapist" (italics added) (p. 91).

This presence, then, can enable the relationship with the client to be a real one. We will not be merely a shadowy reflector or transference screen, but a living human being who is concerned not with self but

"Positive"			
Appreciative	Affectionate	Relieved	Calm
Cherish	Loving	Consoled	Pacified
Revere	Infatuated	Freed	Sedated
Treasure	Rapturous	Solaced	Serene
Adore	Affectionate	Allayed	Collected
Esteem	Revered	Comforted	Mellow
Prize	Endeared	Unburdened	Restful
Admire	Close	At ease	Bland
Regard	Like	Helped	Quiet
Value	Warm	Rested	Undisturbed
"Negative"			
Angry	Disgusted	Ashamed	Embarrassed
Enraged	Abhorred	Humiliated	Demeaned
Infuriated	Abominated	Mortified	Flustered
Livid	Repugnant	Sinful	Stupid
Bristling	Evil	Chagrined	Disconcerted
Fuming	Nauseated	Criminal	Dumb
Indignant	Vile	Derelict	Rattled
Annoyed	Averse	Contrite	Awkward
Crabby	Gross	Regretful	Foolish
Sore	Rotten	Shameful	Silly

with understanding and experiencing the client's problems as much as possible. We can prevent the indictment attributed to Karl Jaspers: "What we are missing! What opportunities we let pass by because at a single decisive moment we were, with all our knowledge, lacking in the simple virtue of a full human presence" (Sonnemann, 1954, p. 343, cited in May, 1958).

Tuning-In to Our Values

The second aspect of the skill of tuning-in to self is tuning-in to our own values. Much of this skill was generally covered in Chapter 4, as part of the prerequisite competence of self-awareness. Here, the skill refers more specifically to awareness of values in particular anticipated client contacts.

Students of social work often struggle with value differences. At first, they may not even recognize their own values. Self-awareness can lead to accepting their own and the client's values, understanding the sources of these values, finding the areas of commonality as well as difference, and respecting others' right to be different. The student can then move toward acceptance of, and away from judging, differences in all client situations, especially when the other's identity is related closely to a different ethnic, cultural, or racial background or to a different sexual orientation or preference.

Also at first, students may experience, without clearly demonstrated awareness, a discrepancy between their personal values and professional social work values and ethics. Over time and with work, this awareness can increase and lead to more consistent use of the professional values of each individual's dignity, worth, and capacity for self-determination, as well as the ideal of social justice. They can become more aware of how professional values inform their sense of purpose, their conceptions of practice, their theories-in-use, their perceptions of the client and of their own helping tasks, and their own strengths and limitations.

Tuning-in to one's own values prior to first contacts contributes to the development of self-awareness. More directly, this tuning-in to values, as tuning-in to one's own feelings, prepares us to eliminate distortion from our concentration on the client's themes and values. We can be more present for the other and more ready to respond directly to indirect communications—especially in situations where these values can distort what we see and hear and the direction we take in our help.

When we tune-in to our values, we are more open to accepting different values and exploring the client's questions and dilemmas. When we do not tune-in to our potential value questions and dilemmas, we may unwittingly judge our clients, avoid raising pertinent value questions, or shut off discussion of values even when the client initiates them.

Consider, the following five situations and tune-in to what personal values and potential value dilemmas you might bring to these first contacts:

1. You work at a family-planning clinic and are about to see a 15-year-old girl for the first time. The referral information states that she is sexually active and fearful of the possibility of becoming pregnant. She wants help in getting contraceptive pills but does not want her parents to know about it.

2. You work at a daycare center and are about to see a 23-year-old woman who gave birth to twins a week ago. She is coming to see you for the first time because she wants help in obtaining daycare of some kind for the children so she can return to her job as a secretary in an insurance company. Her husband has called you before this first meeting to tell you that he is the owner of a thriving computer software company, does not need her income, and wants her to stay home with the children.

3. You work in a nursing home and have been asked by the director of nursing to meet with a 79-year-old man and a 78-year-old woman to discuss changing their room assignments so they can room together. They have been visiting each other in their current rooms for the purpose of having sex and would now like to room together.

4. You work in a crisis intervention program and are about to meet a client who is requesting help in resolving conflicts between himself and the person he has been living with in an intimate relationship for the past 2 years. Until recently, they have gotten along very well together and the relationship has been very personally and sexually satisfactory. Your client, a 25-year-old, is gay and lives with another 25-year-old man.

5. You work at a public adoption agency and are about to meet a black couple who have applied and been approved for adoption. You have a child available for adoption whose mother was white and whose father was black. The child is very light-complexioned, with Caucasian features. A white couple has also been approved for adoption, but having applied only recently, they are lower on the waiting list than the black couple.

All of these standard situations are fraught with potential value conflicts and dilemmas. How do you balance your professional concern for the adolescent and for parents' rights with your values regarding sexual morality and collusion against informing the parents? How do your values regarding money and/or women's liberation affect your perceptions and judgments about the young mother's request for daycare services? How can you weigh your service to the wife in this situation against your values regarding her relationship with her husband? What are your values regarding sexuality and morality that might affect your work with the couple in their 70s who want to room together? Where do you stand if this decision creates pain and conflict within their respective families? How do your own sexual preferences affect your aceptance in working with the gay couple? What are your primary values in matching children to parents in adoption—physical characteristics, record of ethnic similarity, intellectual capacity, motivation, and so on?

The following steps are often very helpful in tuning-in to our own values in anticipated first contacts:

1. Be aware of our stereotypes and the judgments we make—both good and bad—on the basis of the early stereotypes we form about a particular other. Especially consider how we anticipate a certain individual on the basis of "theys." This is the generalized "they" found in such statements as "they" are trying to beat the system; "they" always wear loud colors and yell too loudly; "they" are lazy—and so on.

2. Strive to evaluate ourselves and our values objectively and rationally. Look at the origins of those values we are aware we bring to particular helping situations. Consider the purpose they serve for us and whether they would also serve this purpose for these particular others.

3. Differentiate among those values that dictate a personal style of living for us and those that this particular client or other may find better meet his or her needs and style of living.

4. Review the values of our professional philosophy and what living this philosophy requires from us. Consider the strengths of beliefs about the following statements:

a. Human beings, by the very fact of their existence, have an inherent dignity and worth. This calls for respectful, nonjudgmental acceptance of their being.

b. Human beings have the inherent capacity to develop in more fully human ways. This calls for understanding and accepting their autonomy, including their self-direction and self-determination in choosing their values and finding ways to live them.

c. Human beings develop within a set of complex social environments. This calls for understanding, accepting, and promoting their interdependence.

d. The professional relationship is the medium through which growth, or positive change, can occur in both the individual and social spheres. This calls for the use of self to enable individuals and environments to discover and develop their own potential.

The nonjudgmental nature of these principles does not mean not having values. We are walking compilations of values and biases. All of us have grown up with a whole set of values—a way of interpreting our interactions in society. We cannot avoid making these judgments in evaluating clients. All human relationships are based on values. In social relationships we are constantly making judgments—good or bad, like or dislike, useful or not useful. The more we are involved with others, the more we bring our values to the relationship. Thus we will confront value differences in any relationship we face in social work practice.

Whenever we meet with another in social work practice, we are insinuating or attempting to influence values. Whether we indirectly reinforce certain values by well-placed "uhum's," whether we make a direct statement, or whether we give advice, we are presenting a particular model of values to the client. We are suggesting or insinuating some kind of social value. When we ask about feelings we are promoting a communication value—one that may or may not differ with the values of the client. At this fundamental level, all social work practice involves socializing processes. This includes some form of teaching social values.

All models of practice are based on particular values that are inherent in the means and ends of the approach. The "medium" of our help, the practice models we use, is a "message" of values in all of our practice relationships. In brief, we cannot work value-free. The question, therefore, is: How do we use our awareness of our values, our tuning-in to them, in behalf of those we serve?

First, we do not judge others severely because they do not fit our values. Our social agencies have sometimes been notorious for this. For instance, they may be established to deal with individuals and confront a Hispanic client who brings his or her entire family of eight children to meet with the worker in a small cubicle. They may label clients who are nonverbal and do not share their feelings as uncooperative or unmotivated and not find ways of serving them. We could do the same as individual practitioners. Thus, we need to tune-in to the consequences of our values and suspend judgment when we confront strong differences in people we meet in practice.

When we confront these discrepancies between our own values and those we serve in practice, we can use these incongruencies to mediate social values. Then these discrepancies in values can become a major dynamic in our helping process.

Our lives—our own and our clients'—are in a continuous process of negotiating with environmental interactions to determine our identity and values. All relationships are dynamic processes where people are potentially influencing each other. All social work practice has this dynamic and becomes a process for negotiating values. When we are aware of our own values and biases and open to those of the other—

which may change ours—we can be truthful and responsible about our own social and professional values in practice.

From taking responsibility for our own values comes recognition of and respect for others' differences. Then, too, we can accept the effect that those with whom we work have on us. They can, and will, influence us. We become partners in this negotiating process and together seek those values that work best for each. This perspective helps us increase our awareness of values and biases that is so basic to helping others explore the meaning of both current and potential behaviors and choices.

Therefore, we can work with value differences that might even repulse us at first—if we can take responsibility for our own values in our tuning-in and open ourselves to understanding the other's values in a negotiating process. We should be very careful not to deny the repulsion and our reactions to the value difference. This denial would cut off our humanness. This humanness and our potential to be concerned about and try to understand others is the very basis on which we can understand and respond effectively to the other. Our understanding and response, evolving from our concern and from our wanting to see the world from the other's eyes and beliefs, initiates the very negotiating process in which both we and the client can grow. Confronting differences with respect and understanding, then, produces one of the most challenging, exciting, and self-actualizing experiences of being a social worker. Tuning-in to our own values consistently benefits both ourselves and those we serve.

TUNING-IN TO THE CLIENT

Tuning-in to the client is the third skill of this preliminary-phase competency. Lawrence Shulman (1984) defines this tuning-in skill as "an exercise in which the worker, either alone or with supervisors or colleagues, attempts to develop preliminary empathy with the client" (p. 22). Thus tuning-in involves anticipating clients' needs, feelings, and concerns by putting ourselves in their shoes. As with tuning-in to our own feelings, this anticipatory empathy requires an affective as well as intellectual process. We must try to experience their potential feelings and their meaning in ourselves.

This skill begins with our applying general knowledge to sensitize ourselves to a client's life in relation to developmental needs, culture-bound perception, and the potential experiencing of the current life situation. We use this general knowledge to answer the relevant parts of the question: What might this current situation and initial experience with me *mean* to the client?

For instance, students often begin anticipating clients' needs and behavior on the basis of stereotypes born of experience (or lack of experience) with similar people. In tuning-in, students can begin to use their generalized ideas to sensitize themselves to the client's range of potential feelings and concerns and to be prepared to respond to them. The first step in this tuning-in is to seek from one's current knowledge base the major themes the client may bring because of a particular stage in life-cycle development, particular sociocultural contexts, and the current life and helping situation.

For example, assume you are providing intake services at a residential center for adolescent boys. The juvenile court has sent a 16-year-old youth who has violated his probation on three occasions. You may have learned through your studies that an important theme for adolescents is identity (Erikson, 1963). Thus you may anticipate that at one level this boy is like most adolescents—trying to discover who he is and who he wants to be while sorting out society's conflicting messages about what makes one an adult or a "real man." Perhaps you have read J. D. Salinger's *Catcher in the Rye*, or Claude Brown's *Manchild in the Promised Land*, and also "know" that this identity theme is often related to differentiating oneself from the adult world and the world of one's family, to wanting to be important in the eyes of one's peers, and to searching ambivalently for autonomy and independence while wishing to maintain some sort of relationship with family and others. Maybe, in addition, you tap your own experiences as an adolescent and remember how painful it was to feel left out, how important it was to be good at something (anything), and how difficult it was to control your own impulses and to be the kind of person you wanted to be. All of these generalizations can help you to begin to tune-in to this boy's developmental needs and potential themes.

Then you can tune-in to the meaning of this situation within the sociocultural context. What do you know about youths such as this, who are in trouble with the law? Might he perceive himself as an outcast from family, the adult world, and society as a whole? Might he fear becoming an outlaw—that the only acceptance he is worthy of is from other outlaws? Might he fear he is a "loser" or will end up as one? Adolescents in trouble must be experiencing a number of mixed, and mixed-up, feelings from resentment to fear for self and future.

You know, then, that he is facing at least two significant beginnings in his life: a placement in the center and a potential working relationship with you. What do you "know" about beginnings? What are the feelings, questions, and concerns he may have about this new experience? He likely will be scared and trying to deny and hide these fears. He will wonder what the center's workers, including you, will be like, what you think of kids like him, how you treat them. He will also wonder what the other kids will be like and how he might fit in and find a place for himself. He will also possess the wishes and fears in some ambivalent combination that we all bring to beginnings. He may fear the new demands placed on him and be concerned about whether he can meet them. He will be using his own stereotypes, his own "theys"—about you, the staff, the system, the other kids—and these can intensify his fears and resistance. He will also have some wishes— that the place is not as bad as he thinks, that he might be accepted, that someone may be willing to get to know his mixed-up feelings and understand him. There also will likely be some sense of hope, however diminished, for more self-fulfilling change.

This more analytical tuning-in sensitizes one to the client's early concerns. Tuning-in to the client's *feelings* requires more experiential work. This exercise requires becoming the client for a while, stating one's feelings as this client, and attempting to experience more fully the meaning of these feelings for oneself.

The first basis we have for this tuning-in is our own experience, which may have been similar to the client's. What experiences have we had with first encounters with people in authority? What were our feelings and concerns? What were these experiences like for us when we were adolescents? How do we feel when we are meeting someone whose impression can greatly affect our lives? Or when we want help desperately and hope the other is willing to give it?

Use the adolescent boy in the above example and try this experiencing of the client's feelings in tuning-in. Become this youth as much as you can and state how you feel in this first contact with the worker. Be sure to state these feelings in "I" terms. Do this now before reading on.

Perhaps your tuning-in went something like this: "I resent adults controlling my life, pushing me around, telling me what to do, and here is another one. I hope this one is different, but I doubt it. I wonder what this worker expects from me and thinks of me? I'm scared and want to run away. I would—except I'm afraid of what they would do to me then. I hope it's not so bad here. Maybe this worker and these kids will accept me. I'm really troubled and terrified I may not get the help I need. What if I am a loser—how in the hell am I going to end up? I'm so confused about myself now. Maybe it's best that I sit back, not care too much what happens to me, and see what's going on here!"

This tuning-in gives us a better chance of responding with empathy to the real meaning of indirect communications. We are less likely to miss these communications or to respond defensively. When we respond directly to these indirect communications, we accurately recognize feelings in the client's early expressions. This response involves picking up and empathizing with expressed feelings, sensitivity to subtle or disguised expressions of feelings (e.g., the authority theme behind questions or anger), perceptiveness about nonverbal cues, ability to tune-in to probable feelings not quite expressed (e.g., the hurt beneath the anger), and perceptiveness about ambivalent feelings.

This tuning-in to the client, like the next skill of tuning-in to the client's situation, is always done in a tentative way. It must be clear that anticipatory empathy and preparation are useful only when they seem to help us follow the client's leads. Tuning-in must never be a self-fulfilling prophecy that dictates what we do. Tuning-in to both the client's feeling and your own should increase sensitivity to potential feelings, concerns, and responses and the chance that your spontaneous reactions to the client's communications will be on-target and helpful. If not handled in a tentative way, it can simply produce a new stereotype to crash against the stereotypes that clients bring to our first encounter. This result would be most deleterious to the purpose of the work. Paradoxically, then, the most critical aspect of tuning-in to the client is the very ability to disregard it when our hunches prove inaccurate, so that we may feel and experience and respond to the reality of our initial encounter. And if we tune-in fully but *tentatively*, we can find a reservoir of understanding in our responses to these early engagements.

TUNING-IN TO THE CLIENT'S SITUATION

The third skill of this preliminary-phase competency is tuning-in to the client's situation. This skill requires a preliminary ecological assessment. We apply the ecological perspective presented in Chapter 3 to the information we have on the client and his/her situation. This sensitizes us to the potential range of factors and systems interacting in the client's life. The factors may be (1) biological (e.g., physical health); (2) psychological (e.g., vulnerability to separations); (3) social (e.g., family or peer-group pressure); (4) cultural (e.g., values); (5) economic (e.g., unemployment or underemployment); or (6) political (e.g., legal recognition of rights). The systems may be family or household, friends, school, work, neighborhood, extended family, social welfare, health, court, recreation, religion, and so on.

As we begin practice, there is a tendency for us to emphasize one or a few of these factors and/or systems to the exclusion of others. We need to work on developing a sensitivity to and perceptiveness of all of these aspects and their transactions in clients' situations and an understanding of which of these are likely most relevant to a particular situation. We need to develop an ecological perspective and to apply such a framework to our tuning-in and ongoing work.

Tuning-in to a client's situation entails using ecomapping as a tool to identify how these factors and systems might influence the client's adaptive coping in potential areas of stress and as potential resources. (The use of ecomaps was described in detail in Chapter 3.) This preliminary ecomapping requires identifying the major systems likely transacting with the client in the particular situation and the possible nature of these interactions. This tuning-in—again, always tentative— assures the use of the ecological perspective for a more comprehensive gathering of data about the meaning of the client's transactions with the environment in initial assessment, generalist service planning, and mediation.

In situations involving a female or minority-group client, the "dual perspective" (also presented in Chapter 3) is an additional tool for this preliminary ecomapping. The dual perspective, when used in tuning-in, sensitizes us to the client's relationship to the immediate "nurturing" cultural environment and its systems and to the larger, dominant, "sustaining" one—as well as to the relationship between these two cultural worlds that influence the client. The use of the ecological perspective, ecomapping, and the dual perspective in tuning-in alerts us to potential client strengths and resources in the environment and to deficits, not in the client, but in those systems with which the client is interdependent.

CONCLUSION

This first competence of generic social work process concerns the preliminary phase. The competency is the *ability to tune-in to self, client, the client's life situation, and the helping situation consistent with the social work perspective*. The three skills that constitute this competency are (1) tuning-in to self, (2) tuning-in to the client, and (3) tuning-in to the client's situation.

Tuning-in to self is the basis for preliminary empathy and bringing ourselves to initial contacts. We need to tune-in to our own feelings and values. Tuning-in to our feelings entails awareness of our ambivalences and feelings regarding similarities and differences in preliminary contacts. These feelings are best experienced through specific exercises. Tuning-in to our values involves confronting differences in our values and those of a potential client, anticipating value conflicts and dilemmas, and separating our personal from our professional values.

Tuning-in to the client is both an analytical and experiential process. We use generalized ideas and our awareness of our stereotypes to sensitize ourselves to the client's potential developmental needs and life themes, culture-bound perceptions, and concerns and feelings about us and about the current situation. We can experience these feelings and their possible meanings to prepare ourselves for tentative responding to them when communicated—directly or indirectly—in initial contacts.

Tuning-in to the client's situation applies the ecological perspective to anticipate the range of factors and systems impinging on the client. Through preliminary ecomapping and use of the dual perspective, this tuning-in can assure that we understand the client and his or her situation more accurately and comprehensively, thus establishing the necessary base for generalist service planning and effective mediation through the ongoing use of social work process.

SUGGESTED LEARNING EXERCISE 5-1: TUNING-IN

Choose one of the following brief vignettes and use the three skills in this chapter to tune-in as fully as possible. That is, in relation to the vignette: (1) tune-in to your own feelings and values by using the exercises suggested in this chapter; (2) tune-in to the client developmentally, socioculturally, and with regard to potential feelings and concerns; and (3) tune-in to the client's situation by drafting a preliminary ecomap. In all of these situations, you are a member of a community service's intake screening unit.

1. An elderly white man has been referred to your office as the place to "get some help." He lives alone in poor housing, does not always have enough to eat, and seems confused at times.

2. A referral has been made by the Department of Human Resources of a 25-year-old white woman who has been unable to find work. This woman is a high school dropout who is functionally illiterate and has never worked except for a little "street hustling."

3. Head Start has referred a black mother who seems unable to discipline her child, an unruly 4-year-old. The child throws temper

tantrums, sasses adults, hits other children, and will not share. Conferences with the parent and Head Start have not produced any improvement in the child's behavior at school or at home.

4. A referral is made of a 27-year-old Puerto Rican male who is unemployed and living at home with his parents. He has very few social contacts except for occasional visits to a local gay bar in the neighborhood. The parents are worried and disapprove of the visits to the gay bar.

5. A referral is made on a 30-year-old white male ex-offender who has been seeking employment since release from state prison 8 months ago. He has no transportation and seldom keeps appointments.

6. A referral is made of a 28-year-old Japanese-American woman who stays at home with her parents and goes out very little. She has a part-time job at the YMCA. She has become more withdrawn as each year goes by. This problem began after her graduation from college and the death of her fiancé in a car accident. (The parents are much concerned and have set up many appointments, but she refuses to attend counseling sessions.) She has begun to hear all kinds of noises, and drugs have become an everyday thing.

7. A referral is made of a 16-year-old white mother of an infant. She is unmarried, has dropped out of school, and has difficulties caring for the baby. She does not keep appointments with the pediatrician at General Hospital.

8. A 22-year-old black, married college student who is having financial difficulties is referred to your unit. His stituation is complicated by his wife's possible pregnancy. While both came from Catholic families, he wants to discuss the possibility of an abortion (not yet discussed with his wife) because he fears he could otherwise not remain in school.

SUGGESTED LEARNING EXERCISE 5-2: TUNING-IN IN THE FIELD

Use these same tuning-in skills prior to an initial contact with a prospective client in the field. Write a brief report describing how you tuned-in and assess how this tuning-in affected your ability to respond directly and with understanding to the client's feelings and concerns in this first encounter.

6 Competence #2: Beginning Phase: Establishing Helping Relationships

Tom Technic was recently informed by his wife Martha that she was having an affair. Tom was shocked, pained, and very scared, because he seemed to have lost control over this relationship, and possibly his world as he understood it. He couldn't eat, sleep, work, or communicate with people. He knew he needed help.

So Tom bought the software package, "Solving Your Personal Problems," for his home computer. In his desperation for relief and understanding, Tom immediately plugged in the program and began his counseling.

"PLEASE STATE YOUR PROBLEM," the computer instructed.

"MY WIFE, MARTHA, IS HAVING AN AFFAIR," punched in Tom.

"HOW LONG HAVE YOU BEEN EXPERIENCING THIS PROBLEM?" the computer retorted.

"I'VE KNOWN FOR THREE DAYS," responded Tom.

With that information the computer asked Tom the ubiquitous question in helping: "HOW DO YOU FEEL ABOUT MARTHA'S AFFAIR?"

Tom thought for quite a while. There were so many mixed and complicated emotions welling up in him. He typed: "SICK, SCARED, HURT, CONFUSED, TIRED, AND VERY ANGRY."

The screen printed back: "YOU FEEL SICK, SCARED, HURT, CONFUSED, AND TIRED. WHY?"

Tom now felt more annoyed than anything else. He informed the computer: "NEVER MIND THE WHY. YOU MISSED MY ANGER."

101

Quickly the computer returned: "I'M SORRY. YOU FEEL ANGER. AT WHOM ARE YOU ANGRY?"

"RIGHT NOW AT YOU," answered Tom.

"YOU ARE ANGRY AT ME. WHY?" came the reply.

Furiously, Tom typed: "BECAUSE YOU DIDN'T HEAR ME, UNDERSTAND ME. YOU AREN'T WITH ME. HOW CAN I MAKE YOU UNDERSTAND?"

"I'M SORRY," the computer printed. "LET'S START OVER. PLEASE STATE YOUR PROBLEM. HOWEVER, THIS TIME STATE IT IN TERMS OF WHAT YOU WANT TO CHANGE ABOUT YOUR SITUATION."

Tom was really desperate. He stated, "MY WIFE, MARTHA, IS HAVING AN AFFAIR AND I DON'T KNOW WHAT I WANT TO DO ABOUT IT."

The computer reflected, "YOU ARE INDECISIVE. WHAT DO YOU THINK IS THE FIRST THING YOU SHOULD DO ABOUT MARTHA'S AFFAIR?"

With tears in his eyes, Tom typed, "I REALLY DON'T KNOW."

"YOU ARE RESISTING," admonished the computer. "HOW DO YOU FEEL ABOUT THE HELP I HAVE GIVEN YOU SO FAR?"

Tom punched the keys with a vengeance: "I FEEL LIKE BLOWING YOUR BRAINS OUT AND THEN MY OWN!"

"DOES NOT COMPUTE," flashed on the screen. "ARE YOU CONSIDERING TURNING ME OFF?"

"A great idea," thought Tom, as he pulled the plug.

Then he picked up the telephone book, finding the family service agency in his community in the Yellow Pages. "I do need help. I hope *someone* can understand," Tom said to himself as he dialed the number.

Tom Technic, in this story, takes a significant step toward help in his realization that people, not programs, make a difference. People need people. This fact of human existence is the basis of all social work process. In initial contacts, this need translates into attention to the nature of the interaction between the social worker and others. What the social worker brings to this interaction, a difference that no computer can duplicate, is a capacity to form a very special kind of human relationship—a helping relationship.

The first competence of the beginning phase is the ability to establish helping relationships. The establishment of helping relationships is, in reality, a foundation competence. All phases of social work process require a particular quality of interaction among the social worker and others that defines the helping relationship. This principle of the social work process makes the beginning phase so vital to the establishment of helping relationships. The quality of later interactions depends greatly on how they begin. The competence of establishing the beginning helping relationship demands the use of skills that are also fundamental to its further development. These three skills, covered in this chapter, are (1) using purpose and function, (2) balancing support and challenge, and (3) responding to and with feelings. This chapter defines social work helping relationships, reviews the models of "core conditions" of helping relationships, and presents the three central skills for establishing social work helping relationships consistent with the competence model of this text.

DEFINITION OF SOCIAL WORK HELPING RELATIONSHIPS

One of the primary values of social work is the special medium of the helping relationship. Yet, what constitutes the helping relationship has defied adequate definition. Webster's dictionary may be strangely accurate when it defines relationships as "persons connected by consanguinity or affinity" or a "type of kinship." The best relationships, such as those we establish in helping, seem to be shared in the blood and understood most from unspoken experience. They often appear as a uniting of souls—whether in the experience of a 2-minute interchange or from a lifetime of working to build it.

Helen Harris Perlman's (1979) book on relationships is subtitled "The Heart of Helping," and she is not one to be careless with her words. Perlman's "heart" is the one that Blaise Pascal wrote about in the *Pensées*: "The heart has its reasons which Reason does not know; a thousand things declare it" (1965, p. 343). The heart of relationship is our potential for compassion, for feeling, for giving and taking sustenance and nurturance in an emotional bond with another.

Perlman traced the central place of the relationship in human growth and development from the original emotional bonding of mother and infant to the central and peripheral meanings of human relationships throughout the life cycle. Her unifying theme of these relationships, developed in her conception of the professional helping relationship, is that relationship is central to the change *process*. Relationships *move* us. They *motivate* us. They *emote* us. The heart of the helping relationship, then, is an *emotional* experience. This experience builds a bridge between the helper and others through which the first steps of change and growth can be taken toward coping, adapting, challenging, and changing obstacles to one's goal attainment and development. The helping relationship is, therefore, a necessary—although not totally sufficient—condition of all effective help. In Perlman's (1979) words the professional relationship is necessarily based on the following fact: "The emotional bond that unites two (or more) people around some common concern is charged with enabling facilitative powers toward both problem solving and goal attainment. Thus relationship is vital in the conveyance and utilization of any service given by one human being to another" (p. 2).

The helping relationship is a special case of this professional relationship. The phrase "*the* helping relationship" refers, in fact, to two general aspects about it: its purpose and its processes that appear to promote that purpose. These are the two major similarities in helping relationships for most people in most situations for most problems. In reality, *the* helping relationship for all seasons, for all situations, does not exist. The actualities of helping relationships—their quality, quantity, emphasis, centrality, length, and so on—depend upon their conscious, individualized use by the helper as based upon assessments of the client's needs and goals, the purposes and functions of the specific service, and the ecological and phenomenological understanding of the particular person–environment interactions. Nevertheless, all helping relationships have the central purpose of supporting and enabling the client's work on the problem situation for which help is proferred and are based in the processes that establish the emotional bond that enhances this work.

The distinguishing mark of the *social work* relationship is precisely maintaining this *combination* of focus on the problem and its emotional understanding by the helper. The helping relationship is not a prelude to the help. One does not establish a relationship and then focus in on the problem. Neither is the helping relationship an aftermath of focus on the problem. One does not base a helping relationship on tumbling ahead to "fix" things for the other without exploring *and empathically understanding* the other's concerns, feelings, wants, and goals. Helping relationships are based on the simultaneous, interwoven focus on the problem and empathic understanding of its personal and emotional meaning for the other. It develops out of this interchange in which the helper seeks to understand both the pressing problem and what propels the other to need and/or seek help. Social work helping relationships, then, begin from "starting where the other is."

It is this very combination of simultaneous attention to the other's problem and emotional being that actualizes the helping relationship in social work. It *enables*. It empowers. It moves. It motivates. It creates the conditions and the underlying reciprocal processes that make work on the problem a partnership. Establishing social work helping relationships, then, is defined as the *practitioner's conscious, reliable, and creative use of purpose and function, support and challenge, and response to and with feelings to enable the client's active engagement in using personal social services for more effective coping with aspects of his or her life situation.*

The basic premise of this chapter and its early placement in this book lies in the view that the helping relationship in social work is a necessary tool for providing effective service. In this sense, the helping relationship is not an end in itself but a means to the end of the work that brings practitioner and client together. This position does not deny the fact that the qualities of the helping relationship can themselves meet major needs for many clients. And this dynamic is apt to become even more significant in future practice. As Perlman (1979) suggested, in our growing technological and impersonal society, one seeks *humanizing* relationships whenever they can be found. Another comprehensive book, entitled *Relationships in Social Service Practice* (Keefe & Maypole, 1983), concluded: "The forces shaping human relationships and thus practice relationships will continue to reflect tension, change, and crisis. Rigid, impersonal formal organizations and mindless regressive social and political protest will sit like threatening giants on each side of the narrow gate to a humane social future. The humane values, skills, and practice relationships of dedicated caring professionals are partial keys to that future" (p. 241).

A somewhat more optimistic prediction comes from *Megatrends* (Naisbett, 1984). He predicted that one of the major directions of the remainder of this century is the interrelated "high tech/high touch" need in our society. The more high tech is forced upon us, the more high touch, or a counterbalancing human response, we need. The more we interact in a technological physical world and are pulled to treat ourselves and others as machines, the more we are counterpulled by a spiritual world of human touch, of relationships. Some even suggest that this megatrend will establish a special domain for social work: the delivery of *personal* social services, for which this technology will create a need among all members of our society (CSWE, 1985). However much the helping relationship is best conceived as a means rather than an end of the social worker's services, we must be sensitive to the fact that in today's and tomorrow's world, this relationship may more and more serve to fulfill the need for human ties so desperately sought by many. And it may well be that these very human ties are among the building blocks for social change. For now, as we establish effective helping relationships with those needing our help, we may be preserving and repairing those human ties that promote individual and social growth and can create a responsive and humane society. In the interdependent world of those we serve, our small pebbles could ripple widely across the waters of life. Reality or dream—it is a hope worth keeping.

CORE CONDITIONS OF HELPING RELATIONSHIPS

Various models of helping relationships have identified a configuration of "core conditions" for establishing them. A brief, chronological review of some of these models from diverse disciplines reveals a remarkable resemblance among those helper elements deemed essential in establishing effective relationships.

Fred Fiedler (1950) questioned therapists from divergent theoretical backgrounds on the elements of an "ideal therapeutic relationship." From his pool of 119 statements describing patient–therapist relationships, respondents significantly selected 14 items, the top 4 of which were (1) empathy, (2) a tolerant atmosphere, (3) permitting "patient" choice, and (4) attempts at understanding "patient's" feelings.

In a speech delivered in 1954 and later published in *On Becoming a Person* (1961), Carl Rogers first postulated what he considered essential conditions of establishing a helpful relationship. (For further development of these concepts, see Rogers, 1957, 1966, 1975; Rogers et al., 1967.) Rogers's general hypothesis of what he termed the "facilitative relationship" is as follows: If one can provide a certain type of relationship, the other will discover within the self the capacity to use that relationship for growth, and change and personal development will occur. The three core facilitative conditions the helper brings to this relationship are genuineness, acceptance, and empathic understanding.

First, the more genuine the helper can be in the relationship, the more helpful it will be. Genuineness brings *reality* to the relationship. To Rogers, this reality is the deeply important first core condition; only if the other experiences reality in the helper can he or she successfully seek reality in him- or herself. This genuineness means that the helper is as consistently aware as possible of his or her "positive" and "negative" feelings and expresses them through words and behavior. The helper risks such expression rather than presenting an outward façade while holding in such feelings and attitudes.

Second, the more acceptance the helper feels toward the other, the more the helper creates a relationship the other can use. To Rogers, this acceptance means a warm regard for the other as a person of unconditional self-worth—of value no matter what the other's condition, behavior, or feelings. It is a respect that can grow to liking or "prizing" the other and create a base for the other to possess his or her own feelings in his or her own way. Acceptance particularly means respect for the other's feelings and attitudes of the moment—no matter how negative or positive, or how irrational or contradictory to those of the past or those that the helper wishes existed. This acceptance of each fluctuating aspect of the person is how the other experiences warmth and safety in the relationship. The safety of being acepted, liked, and prized as a person provides a highly important element of the helping relationship.

Third, the more the helper empathically understands the accepted feelings and communications of the other, the more the relationship is a significant medium for help. Acceptance *per se* means little without an empathic *understanding* of the other's feelings and communications. This empathy provides the *freedom* for self-understanding and responsible choice. As Rogers (1961) puts this condition: "It is only as I *understand* the feelings and thoughts which seem so horrible to you, or so weak, or so sentimental, or so bizarre—it is only as I see them as you see them, and accept them and you, that you can feel really free to explore all the hidden nooks and frightening crannies of the inner and often buried experience" (p. 34). The freedom established through empathic understanding, then, is Rogers's final core condition of the helping relationship.

Thus, conceptualizing from his experience, Rogers found the facilitative helping relationship to be characterized by a transparency on the helper's part in which the helper's real feelings are present; by an acceptance of the other person as a separate person with value in his or her own right; and by a deep empathic understanding that enables the helper to see the private world of the other through the other's eyes. When the helper achieves these conditions, the client experiences a companion who can accompany him or her in the search for solutions to problems. The relationship promotes the feeling of freedom to undertake such a search. This hypothesis for help has been tested and supported by numerous research studies (for comprehensive reviews of this research, see Carkhuff, 1969, 1983; Carkhuff & Berenson, 1976, 1977; Truax & Mitchell, 1971). The centrality of this hypothesis, which the research to date seems to support, was first stated by Rogers (1960) in the following terms:

I am by no means always able to achieve this kind of relationship with another and sometimes, even when I feel I have achieved it in myself, [the other] might be too frightened to perceive what is being offered to [him or her]. But I would say that when I hold in myself the kind of attitudes I have described, and when the other person can to some degree experience these attitudes, then I believe that change and constructive personal development will *invariably* occur—and I include the word "invariably" only after long and careful consideration. (pp. 34–35)

In 1957, Felix Biestek introduced his book, *The Casework Relationship*, to the social work literature. Apparently unaware of Rogers's budding work, Biestek developed the essence of the helping relationship in seven principles that together meet the client's needs through the response of the worker and the client's awareness of this response. These principles are (1) *individualization*, or recognizing, understanding, and actively responding to each client as an unique human being; (2) *purposeful expression of feelings*, or accepting all of the client's feelings—positive and, especially, negative; (3) *controlled emotional involvement*, or empathic understanding of the client's feelings; (4) *acceptance*, or valuing the client's innate dignity and personal worth and letting the client be as he or she really is in the moment; (5) *nonjudgmental attitude*, or not judging the guilt or innocence of the client as a person while evaluating behavior; (6) *client self-determination*, or respecting the client's freedom and degree of constituted right to make his or her own choices and decisions; and (7) *confidentiality*, or preserving secret information concerning the client within clarified and/or constituted rights.

These principles, with the possible exception of confidentiality, are core elements of helping relationships formulated by Fiedler (1950) and Rogers (1961). They fit into Rogers's three facilitative conditions and help to elaborate them.

For the most part, all subsequent models have included such helper attributes as genuineness, empathic understanding, and acceptance— whether packaged in such words as *authenticity, reality, warmth, respect, support, concern, confrontation, immediacy*, and/or *concreteness*. Outside of social work, Robert Carkhuff (1969), for instance, translated these attributes into a set of helper skills. The skills for establishing, or initiating, helping relationships are empathy, warmth, respect, genuineness, concreteness, and self-disclosure, followed by such skills for initiating action on the client's part as confrontation and immediacy. Gerard Egan (1975) similarly conceived the skills for initiating helping relationships in such a way to enable client self-exploration as primary-level accurate empathy, genuineness, respect, and concreteness. Later problem-solving relationship skills demand advanced accurate empathy, helper self-disclosure, confrontation, and immediacy.

Within social work, Alan Keith-Lucas (1972) postulated that the helping factors in all phases of the helping relationship come from the combined sequence of three elements: reality, empathy, and support. This helping factor requires the helper to express over and over again in various forms and with relevant content the following statements:

"This is it." (Reality)
"I know it must hurt." (Empathy)
"I am here with you; you don't have to face this alone." (Support)

D. Coryden Hammond and colleagues (1977) proposed four "effective elements" of the "facilitative conditions" of the helping relationship. These are, in sequence, empathic communication, respect, authenticity, and confrontation. For helping relationships to achieve their purpose in the human services, Helen Harris Perlman (1979) presented five necessary attributes. This purpose is to "meet human needs in ways that deepen and fulfill the sense of social caring and responsibility between fellow human beings" (p. 54) and requires the helper to bring to service relationships warmth, acceptance, empathy, caring/concern, and genuineness. In Thomas Keefe's and Donald Maypole's (1983) most recent book on practice relationships in the social services, the primary characteristics were developed under the concepts of empathy, acceptance, and authenticity.

Therefore subsequent work, both in theory and in research, substantially concurs with Rogers's original necessary conditions of genuineness, acceptance, and empathic understanding as the essential conditions of establishing helping relationships. However, the differences from Rogers's original hypothesis, however subtle, are most informative for the skills selected in this chapter. In his classic presentation of these "core conditions," Rogers (1957) referred to them in the article's title as "the necessary and sufficient conditions of therapeutic personality change." While many representatives of the helping professions appear to agree that Rogers has winnowed out "necessary" qualities in beneficent relationships, several in social work do not consider them "sufficient" (Keefe & Maypole, 1983; Perlman, 1979; Pippin, 1980). For the many tasks other than therapy carried out and services rendered by social workers, other problem-solving skills need to be added to these conditions. Even within the therapeutic models, we find additions to these skills in the later action phase of helping relationships: for example, Carkhuff's (1969) and Egan's (1975) skills of advanced level empathy, immediacy, and confrontation; and Hammond and colleagues' (1977) confrontation.

More subtly, Rogers's genuineness has been redefined as everything from total authenticity and transparency on the part of the helper to a specific, purposeful, and sincere expression of feelings within the boundaries of the relationship's purpose and function. Acceptance has been conceived as falling on a spectrum from unconditional positive regard to separating acceptance of feelings from acceptance of behavior that is destructive to the self and/or others. Empathic understanding has been conceived on two levels—primary and advanced—and has been viewed as conditioned by its accuracy. Accurate primary-level empathy, then, provides the support of understanding the surface feelings and meanings of the other's communication from the other's frame of reference. Accurate advanced-level empathy was mentioned by Rogers (1975) in later development of this model; it involves "sensing meanings of which he/she is scarcely aware, but not trying to uncover feelings of which the person is totally unaware, since this would be too threatening" (p. 4). In addition to the support of surface understanding, which may reflect or even parrot the client's feelings, advanced-level accurate empathy in such models as Carkhuff's (1969, 1983) and Egan's (1975) require challenging the client to deeper understanding. This involves communicating an understanding not only of what the other says but also of what the other implies, hints at, and communicates nonverbally, as well as connecting seemingly isolated aspects of experience and awareness to understanding the other's life. While reaching for what the client sees only dimly and connecting seemingly isolated feelings and content around meaningful themes, the helper provides both support and challenge—when this empathic understanding is on-target; that is, when the helper invents nothing and is accurate.

Rogers captured many of the necessary, and almost sufficient, skills needed for initiating helping relationships. This holds regardless of whether this relationship is established with an individual client, another service provider, a family, a group, or any other professional contact in behalf of the service. However, these conditions interweave with the reality of the work. The work's focus, its structure, and the engagement of the other demand skills in using oneself in relationships within the realities of its purpose and its function. In addition, all helping relationships demand an intricate balance of support and challenge, of acceptance and expectation or "encouragement." Acceptance and understanding are fruitless without work and the ability to engage the other in this work. It is the work that this relationship enables and not the relationship itself that determines its success. Finally, all three of the core conditions—genuineness, acceptance, and empathic understanding—are dimensions of a single significant process—the process of shared feelings. The remainder of this chapter presents these three implied skills for establishing helping relationships: the use of purpose and function, the balance of support and challenge, and responding to and with feelings.

USE OF PURPOSE AND FUNCTION

The purpose of the relationship permeates all aspects of social work practice. In direct service with clients, students initially may perceive the relationship as an end in itself, as in friendships. Or they may see the relationship as based on what they can do for the client and jump in to "fix" the situation by offering solutions without exploring the client's concerns, perception of needs and goals, and life situation. This orientation to process, or to task, takes on balance as students identify with and use the social work process for enabling adaptive growth in both clients and their impinging environments through the mediating function. Then their relationship to clients provides both the support of empathic understanding and acceptance and the challenge of the reality of the client's situation and the specific purpose of their *work* together.

This clarity of purpose and function and its consistent use free the student to relate authentically and genuinely. With clear recognition that the relationship is totally for the client and that it demands consistent concern (not necessarily liking) for the client and for others involved in his or her life situation, the student can begin to trust bringing more and more parts of him- or herself to the encounter. Thus more spontaneous and genuine responses are focused.

The use of purpose and function is marked by this ability to focus the work together with clients. A clear sense of purpose and direction maintains this focus and keeps the client on track. In focusing the work, students may show a beginning awkwardness or a need to establish a friendly relationship before getting down to business, thus promoting aimless discussion. Eventually, they may begin to bring the discussion back to focus, to why they are really together. If the client is uncomfortable or avoiding the issues, students develop some ability to discuss the client's discomfort or pain and to risk facing, or even creating, necessary unpleasantness. A consistent sense of purpose, first for the student and then for the client or other, should emerge very early in the interaction. The other skills for establishing helping relationships flow from this common purpose.

In establishing effective helping relationships, students move from jumping too quickly to provide a concrete service, or having difficulty explaining their purpose and function without ambiguous jargon, to a clear early statement of purpose and function and a negotiating style that seeks a common, understood purpose. This negotiation comes from exploring the client's, or other's, concerns and wishes and explaining what the agency and they can do. They make a tentative plan in partnership with the client, consistently checking out, evaluating, and renegotiating the mutual understanding of the purpose; the goals; their respective functions, roles, responsibilities, and tasks; and the process (or the way they can work together).

From early successes in establishing warm, positive relationships, students move to tuning-in and using the self in different ways as responses to the fluctuating needs of various clients at different times. They begin to tune-in more sensitively to the client's mood, become more comfortable with quietness, join their moments of enthusiasm, and understand and accept their distorted images of and feelings (positive and negative) toward the student without premature explanations or defensiveness. They learn to empathize with that part of the client that resists work and change as well as that part that strives for growth. They begin to see that working relationships are truly based on understanding, concern, and a shared sense of purpose, not on the pleasantries of friendship.

Recent attempts to define professional helping relationships in social work are careful to distinguish that we establish such relationships with a variety of others for a variety of purposes (Keefe & Maypole, 1983; Perlman, 1979; Proctor, 1982; Specht, 1985). Enola Proctor (1982), for instance, defined the worker–client relationship according to how it achieves its purpose as this purpose is translated into specific outcomes. In her view, the purpose of the relationship lies in its conscious attempt to contribute to an individualized treatment plan. She proposed that the relationship can be defined more clearly and more effectively for particular client situations by considering the following three questions:

1. Given the client's problem, situation, and the larger purposes of intervention, what kind of relationship is most helpful at a particular point of time?

2. What outcomes in the client–situation transaction is the relationship to accomplish?

3. What must the practitioner do in the interaction with the client to accomplish the desired outcomes of the relationship?

Harry Specht (1985) developed a matrix of helping relationships that are dependent upon the variety of others with whom we interact. These others can include clients, intimates of clients, trainees, supervisors, consultants, colleagues, and community resource people. The nature of these others and our purpose for our interacting with them require our ability to establish a variety of helping relationships: clinical, collateral, collegial, and sociopolitical. Specht raised an important concern when he reconceptualized these relationships as interpersonal interactions and suggested we pay more attention to the knowledge and skills needed for "managing" professional interpersonal interactions for collateral, collegial, and sociopolitical purposes. These relationships call forth different qualities than do clinical relationships. They may be shorter in duration; less intense emotionally; less positive or negative in underlying positions and feelings; and less, or more, demanding of particular skills. Yet the skills discussed in this chapter are applicable to all of these helping relationships. This is why I have interchangeably used the terms *client* and *other*. These skills are generic because they concern the common threads of all professional relationships in social work—the interweaving of attention to the person and the problem at hand. When adapted to the situational elements of the interaction, they serve the purpose of the work that brings us and the other together. Client or colleague, we stand on the common ground of our purpose and connect through the human ties of how we clarify and use this purpose and function, balance support and challenge, and respond to and with feelings.

Take time to consider how you would state your purpose and function in each of the following situations. Try to state clearly your purpose and the mediating aspects of your function.

1. You are a social worker in Protective Services. You are following up a complaint of child abuse of Tracy, a 7-year-old girl, and are about to meet Tracy's mother and two younger children in her apartment.

2. You are a social worker in a men's prison. You are meeting with a prison inmate for the first time. He was sent to prison for the second time 3 days ago, and you will be working with him while he is placed in his current cell block.

3. You are a social worker in a rape crisis clinic. You are meeting with an adolescent who was raped last evening by a neighbor.

4. You are a social worker in an employee assistance program of a local industry. You are meeting with a young childless couple who have come because of marriage problems.

5. You are a social worker in juvenile probation. You are meeting with a group of seven adolescents, three girls and four boys, who are chronic school truants.

6. You are a social worker in a community hospital. You are meeting with the oldest son of a 72-year-old man who has been living alone and needs constant nursing attention upon release from the hospital.

7. You are a social worker in a public school system. You are meeting with a school teacher with whom your client, a 10-year-old boy, seems to be in constant trouble.

8. You are a social worker in a public housing project. You are meeting with an income maintenance worker with the AFDC program who has decided that a family with whom you work and whom you judge to be eligible for financial assistance is not eligible.

If you have tried to state a clear purpose and your mediating function in each of these situations, you have likely discovered that this task is difficult. You may have found yourself seeking more information on the particular agency's purpose and function in order to determine what you might say about your own. This information, of course, is often helpful, but the helping relationship is primarily established in your giving the other a sense of how you will work for and with him or her. Let us take each of these situations and look at examples—only *examples* among a variety of alternatives—of how you might *begin* to clarify your purpose and function.

In the first situation—the potential abusing parent—you might say something like this: "I am———. I am a social worker at———. I am here because we have received information that Tracy might be getting hurt in your home. You probably don't really want to see someone like me, but I want to learn more about your situation in your family and, if there are problems between Tracy and you, or anyone else, to help things work out better for you and Tracy. Do you have any questions about what I have just said?"

In the second situation—the prison inmate—you might try: "I'm ———. I'm a social worker whose job while you're in B Block is to help you and this place work to get you ready for returning to the community and staying out of places like this. You're probably wondering what I can do for you and how I can help you and this prison to work for you. [Remember the tuning-in skill!] Well, we can explore your current cell placement, your ideas about school or training, and your concerns about your current placement and see what might be best for our accomplishing this task of getting you and this place to work for your return in the best possible way. What's your reaction to what I've just said?"

In the third situation—the teenager who was raped—you might consider: "I am———. I'm a social worker here at Rape Crisis. We work to help you sift out the meaning for you in all that's happened in this difficult period and to help you decide what you want to do to cope with this situation. I imagine you are experiencing a lot of confusing feelings about yourself, your attacker, and your future. I'd find it helpful if you could begin to talk about these. Then, we can discover together what these mean, about what you want to do and can do to get through this difficult time in a way that's best for you. Where would you like to begin?"

In the fourth situation—the couple with marital problems—you might state your purpose and mediating function as follows: "I'm ———, a social worker. I understand you've come for help to work on your relationship with each other. I see our purpose together as coming to understand what each of you sees as problems in your current relationship. I see my role as helping you express your concerns and feelings about the relationship and helping you talk to each other to discover ways of making it more what you want it to be. How does this fit with your ideas about what you wanted from being here?"

In the fifth situation—the adolescent group: "I'm———. I'm a social worker for———. We believe this group can be useful to you and to us. You are all people who have had trouble staying in school. You seem to be experiencing some difficulty in making a go of it there. We know that staying in school and using it isn't always very easy. That's why we organized this group. We believe this group can be a chance for you to help each other. As you listen to each other, share some of your feelings and concerns, and try to help each other, we think you will learn a great deal that may be helpful in your own situation. That, then, is the purpose of this group. My role has a couple of jobs. First, I will try to help you talk to and listen to each other, as this isn't always easy, especially with people in the group who may seem like strangers to you at first. Second, I will share some of my own ideas along the way—those that I think may be useful to you. What do you think about this purpose and your roles and mine?"

In the sixth situation—the son of the father in the hospital: "I'm ———, a social worker here at———. I've been informed by Dr.———

that your father will be released in 2 weeks and will need constant nursing care for an undetermined amount of time. I've talked to your father, and he wants to return to his own apartment. I want to help him and the family plan what's best and possible for him when he is released. There could be a number of alternatives, such as a private nurse or nursing home, but these depend on what the family and he want and can manage. I wanted to meet with you now to begin to explore what we might be able to do together that's best for him. What questions or concerns do you have about this need to plan for his release?"

In the seventh situation—the teacher: "As you know, I've been working with————. I wanted to meet with you to talk more about your concerns and feelings about him in your class and to explore how I might be of help in improving the current relationship between you. I know it must be hard for you to have to work with him every day when he seems to be causing so much trouble in your class, but perhaps we can figure out ways together to help him improve his behavior. What do you think?"

In the eighth and last situation—the AFDC worker: "I'm————, a social worker with————, who has been working with the———— family and referred them for AFDC. They've told me that you decided they were not eligible. From all that I know about their situation and your requirements, I thought they were eligible and that's why I referred them to you. Can we review their situation together so that I might understand more why you don't think they qualify for this assistance?"

Not all of these statements would be made as the first content of the interaction. In fact, in many cases the first content will likely come from the client or other. Nevertheless, these statements are made early in the exchange to clarify purpose and function and thus help establish a working helping relationship. In all of these situations, we note a common pattern to the initial use of this skill. The worker states who he or she is, as a name and as a professional; suggests how the work may begin and toward what enabling purpose; suggests a go-between, or mediating function, for him- or herself; and reaches for feedback, or reactions, which might begin the negotiating process of clarifying purpose and function. While the use of this skill comes in consistent attempts to assure the purpose and focus of the work, this initial clarification is most significant. It begins the contracting process, covered in the next chapter, and assures a simultaneous concern for the person and the problem situation. It initiates the work.

BALANCING SUPPORT AND CHALLENGE

The work itself begins through a balancing of support and challenge and a responding to and with feelings. This section presents the skill of balancing support and challenge in the initial establishment of a help-ing relationship. The final section of this chapter considers the skill of responding to and with feelings.

Implied throughout this chapter, but directly relevant to the sup-port/challenge skill, is the social worker's basic stance in helping relationships. This stance implements the mediating function. No bet-ter word describes the social worker's basic stance in all helping relationships than *enabler*. The enabler makes able, capacitates, em-powers, benefits. The social worker empowers others through en-abling the helping process and others' development toward their po-tentials. In enabling there is an element of facilitating, which implies assisting in progress by easing and accelerating. However, facilitation does not mean "doing for" or pushing others past their own process of development. Facilitation comes from enabling others to use the power of their own choices and actions to confront their situations and work toward adaptive growth in both themselves and their environ-ment. It comes from *empowering*.

The functions and tasks for enabling are related to, but different from, the client's functions and tasks. The helping relationship and its process, then, is a *parallel process*. The parallel process implies that the tasks of the helper and of those using help are not only different, but must be clearly distinguished from each other. When one takes over the tasks of the other—as with the worker who states the goal for the individual, family, or group using help—the typical result is confusion. The other has the task of determining goals and committing to work on goals (and the additional task of determining and committing to *common* goals in families and groups). The social worker's task is to enable goal determi-nation and to confront others with what they are doing to determine goals and how they are working, or not working, to accomplish them. The principle of parallel process clarifies the different yet interdepen-dent tasks of the social worker and others in the helping relationship. Any obliteration of the differences between these two sets of processes, this division of labor, renders the work dysfunctional and the encounter itself manipulative, sentimental, and generally frustrating for all in-volved—others as well as the practitioner. The important enabling work—and it is work for both the other and us—will not get done.

A number of studies of work with individuals, families, and groups attempt to identify the significant functions and tasks of the helper in this parallel process (Anderson, 1984a; Carkhuff, 1969; Lieberman et al., 1973; Olson, 1980; Shulman, 1984). In general, the helper's tasks fall into four basic functions that implement the enabling stance. In effective helping relationships, helpers assume all four of these functions to some degree. These are:

1. *Providing*: This is the function of caring, which provides the basis for establishing the relationship and setting the climate through expressed support, affection, praise, protection, warmth, acceptance, genuineness, and concern.
2. *Processing*: This is the function of meaning, which encourages change and growth through expressed challenge, reflection, interpretation, clarification, and confrontation.
3. *Catalyzing*: This is the function of stimulating, which sparks feeling expression through reaching for the other's feelings and expressing one's own.
4. *Directing*: This is the structuring function, which provides direction for the work through establishing and clarifying limits and roles.

The research suggests that these four helping functions have a striking relationship to outcomes. *Providing* and *processing* have a linear relationship to positive outcomes: *the greater the providing and the greater the processing, the greater the positive outcome*. The other two functions, *catalyzing* and *directing*, have a curvilinear relationship to outcomes—that is, the rule of the golden mean: *too much or too little catalyzing and directing results in lesser positive outcome*. Too little catalyzing can lead to an unenergetic, devitalized process; too much, to a painful, nonintegrated experience. Too little directing can lead to a bewildered, floundering process; too much, to a highly structured authoritarian relationship where the interactional process will be arrhythmic and not free-flowing.

Therefore the effective helper functions moderately as a catalyst and director and strongly as provider and processor. Both providing and processing are critical; neither alone appears sufficient to ensure success. Providing, or actively caring, establishes the climate and support for enabling change and growth, but this change takes work. Enabling this work requires the challenge of processing and some catalyzing and directing. The balance of support and challenge, initially and throughout, is a necessary skill for establishing the helping relationship.

This skill embraces what Paul Tillich (1962) asserted as a fundamental value of social work: a form of love or caring called *caritas*, which is not only accepting, but is also critical and able to transform what it loves. *Caritas* demands both support and challenge. This acceptance of another's being and the expectation for the other's becoming—this *caritas*—when combined with use of purpose and function and responding to and with feelings, is the essence of direct help.

In relationships with clients, students need first to learn to accept the client and then to begin to challenge—providing support along with the challenge. Some students go through periods of being too heavy on the support side or too heavy on the challenge side, perhaps achieving the integration with some clients but not with others. Eventually they develop a consistent style that incorporates both the support of acceptance and the challenge of expectation in their relationship with clients (and systems people) with a reliable sense of tact and timing.

In addition, this skill requires the ability to move back and forth across the subjectivity–objectivity line with clients (and others, such as systems people). This involves the capacity to empathize with others and the ability to step back and look objectively at the other, the self, and the interaction between them. In a self-reflexive manner, students learn to "stand back to get close." This aspect of the support/challenge skill evolves and becomes particularly critical when the student shares the client's pain and encourages the client (other) to take action on his or her own behalf.

Finally, this skill includes the ability to maintain an active–passive balance. This combines passivity (or "contained activity"), letting the client struggle with his or her own themes, and activity, the ability to speak up, suggest, advise, confront, or do for the client. Students may go through phases of being too active in giving suggestions, advice, or referrals and in doing for the client. Or they may be too passive, hesitant about making suggestions, giving opinions or information, and unwilling to do some things for some clients at some times. Eventually, they learn to be comfortable with both activity and passivity, as based on an integrated style of both support and challenge and a clear sense of professional purpose and tasks.

In the use of the support/challenge skill, two useful principles are to provide support before challenge and to challenge the client to make a half step rather than a quantum leap forward. Take, for instance, the following interchange between a social worker and client; determine what might be a supporting, and then a challenging, response (the challenging response should suggest a next small step for this client):

Jane Gross is a 31-year-old woman. She has been married for 12 years and has two girls, aged 12 and 10. Jane had come to a crisis-intervention center the previous day with her two children, carrying a large suitcase. She had several bruises on her arms and one on her face, accompanied by a recent gash over her left eye. One of her daughters had recently had a bloody nose, and one of her eyes was bruised. Jane came to the center because she and her children had left home due to her husband's physical and emotional abuse. She was placed in a battered women's shelter overnight and has returned to the center this morning without her children to talk with *you*, a social worker at the center. She begins with, "It got so bad I had to take the kids and leave. At first Hal just shouted. Then he started hitting me. Then he hit the kids also. It was happening more and more often." (crying) "I don't know what it is I do that sets him off. I've tried, but I always do something wrong."

How might you respond to Jane in a way that first offers support and then initiates some challenge for her in this situation?

One possible response is: "Things are really bad for you and your kids now and have been getting worse for some time. You seem scared and even a little guilty because for some reason you believe this is your fault. It might also seem like you're all alone now in having to figure this situation out and to make decisions about it. I want to help you with this—to try to understand more what it's like for you and what we may be able to do together to change this." (All of these statements provide support—and then comes an initial, slight challenge.) "You must be furious at Hal, as well, for his violence and wondering where you want to and might go from here. Tell me more about what it's like for you and your kids now with Hal."

Whatever response you created, the key is to seek and express understanding of the person, the problem situation, and of the nature of the *work* together. When these three points are understood, support and challenge is present. This initial balance of support and challenge fuels the work. As the relationship develops, this balance of support in acceptance of the other and his or her situation and of challenge in expecting work might just be the most crucial skill of all. To be accepted as one is and expected to become the best one can become in a meaningful relationship with another is the essence of experiencing love and care. This balance of support and challenge, then, may be the most profound way we can begin to care actively for another. The other's trust of us and the helping process derives from this experienced reality: This social worker cares about me.

RESPONDING TO AND WITH FEELINGS

Feelings, our subjective experience of emotions, are vital to all relationships. Relationships are emotional bonds, and we experience these bonds through shared feelings. Therefore, the meaning of all significant relationships, and especially the helping relationship, derives from the experience and communication of our feelings.

Feelings bind relationships. Feelings also ground and direct our experiences with reality. They are a vital center of all of our transactions with our world. As such, how clients see and feel their problems in living determines much of what they want to do about them. This third skill for establishing helping relationships—responding to and with feelings—is significant both for its role in initiating the helping relationship and its role in the client's problem-solving process. As e. e. cummings has written:

> since feeling is first
> who pays more attention
> to the syntax of things
> will never wholly kiss you.

Great poets, novelists, playwrights, musicians, and artists master the language, communication, and meaning of feelings. Most theoretical discussions of feelings pale before a Shakespeare soliloquy, an Emily Dickinson poem, a Brontë or Dostoevsky novel, a Van Gogh painting, or a Mozart concerto. Like the physical sense of feeling, these *touch* us.

Theory (Denzin, 1984; Gaylin, 1979; Viscott, 1976) paints feelings as both our angels and our devils. They are our sixth sense. They interpret, arrange, direct, and integrate the other five. They evolve from our perception of the world and ourselves and in turn color and define what we perceive. Feelings *are* our experience and a large part of the world we live in. They speak—loudly, softly, or in disguised tones—to tell us whether what we experience is threatening, painful, regretful, sad, or joyous. Because so much of what we know depends on our feelings, we can be "possessed" or set awash in confusion by dimly perceived or understood feelings and overwhelmed by a confusing inside–outside world.

Feelings, all feelings, are the power that drives us and are as an inevitable part of our living with reality and finding the fullest meaning in life as our problem-solving intelligence and our organized will. Feelings are the physical form in which we experience our estimate of the beneficial or harmful relationship of aspects of reality to self. They are our intuitive values and our energy. They are, when integrated with our rational thinking, like the engine, drive shaft, and back wheels of a car that get us going and keep us going. The direction they take us depends upon other aspects of our steering mechanisms and needs the front wheels as the rational problem-solving thought to keep us in the desired direction. More specifically, feelings are felt values, both positive and negative, which become conscious when there is a break, voluntary or enforced, between our needs and the objects of our needs. They are our awareness of where we are and what we need, demanding to be *experienced* and *acknowledged* and driving us toward action to meet these needs.

In social work, we, through both our model and our response, help others to bear, accept, and own their feelings and to use this awareness as a basis for choice. The difference between developed emotion and simple emotion is like that between a sense of purpose and crude impulse. Crude impulse slips over into action with little consciousness—it just happens and is neither accepted nor rejected. Here is where children begin. The anger of the young child is normally momentary, has not much body, and passes quickly from a sense of being thwarted into explosive, irrelevant action—a scream, a kick, a blow, a temper tantrum. The child does not experience him- or herself as angry but experiences the object as bad. Unless the child is allowed to be angry, even though he or she is not allowed to hurt someone else, he or she will never learn where the feeling belongs. Like the parent with the child, our task is not to stop the emotion, but to help the other be responsible for it, accept it, and make it his or her own.

Clients need to experience not only their own feelings but also the emotional reactions that they arouse in us. In other words, if we respect our own feelings and are willing to express the anger as well as the care, then the client, too, will find it easier to express the hurt or the fear or the sense of injustice that otherwise would tend to be hidden, even from the self. This does not mean to govern with anger or smother with love—but to admit and accept, without guilt, the feelings in relationship with the client that, by their very depth and reality, exposes us to periods of pain and defeat.

Shared feelings resonate with the emotional timbre of relationships. They are the music underneath the words of communication. For instance, think of your own friends and the way you find any two of them unalike. What may come to mind is that one is more attractive than the other, more talented, or more intelligent. But if you really pin yourself down to the most discriminative analysis of difference, you will likely find that it lies in the quality, depth, completeness, and spontaneity of the emotional life—not fundamentally in the appearance, behavior, or intellect. Beauty can lose its charm, exemplary behavior leave us cold, and an able mind bore us—if not related to the feelings that are at the core of the integrated, conscious personality and give it the coloring to which we respond. These feelings ground the relationship in emotional truth—to which we respond consciously and with a gut-level acceptance or rejection. When combined with a clear sense of purpose, these shared feelings—the emotional ties that bind the helping relationship—touch us at the core of our individuality and our common humanness. We are not only more of what we feel but we "become" more that which we want to be.

The helping relationship, then, is what the existentialists term an "encounter" or "primary meeting" (Buber, 1970; May, 1958, 1969). The heart of the encounter is shared feelings and their intentionality, their communication of the meaning of one's being and becoming, in relationship with another. This shared feeling always reverberates from person-to-person encounter ("I-Thou") in the moment of one's interactional field and promotes the integration of our basic autonomy and interdependence. As Rollo May (1969) expressed this aspect of helping relationships: "[Feeling] . . . starts in the present and points toward the future. . . . Our feelings not only take into consideration the other person, but are in a real sense partially *formed by the feelings of the other person present*. We feel in a magnetic field. . . . Every successful love knows this by 'instinct.' It is an essential—if not the essential—quality of the good therapist" (p. 91).

In the moment of encounter, the relationship between the social worker and client is a real one. The practitioner is not merely a shadowy reflection or transference screen but a living human being who happens, in relationship with the other, to be concerned not with his or her own problems in living but with understanding and experiencing the other as much as possible.

The concept of encounter implies aspects of the helping relationship we have not previously addressed in social work. First, this encounter is a total relationship. While marked by a sense of purpose and parallel processes, the encounter involves all levels of relationships for those experiencing it. These levels include real persons; friends; *agape*, or self-transcending concern for another's welfare; as well as the frankly erotic and the obstacles to attraction, passion, and compassion. When we are open to encounter, we need to be open to all of these possibilities in ourselves and others in our transactional feeling and communication field. Then we can use all these parts of our own feelings to understand and promote the possibility of change for and/or in the other.

Second, the potential for encounter is always to a greater or lesser extent anxiety-creating as well as joy-creating for those involved. Encounter is always a risk for both the social worker and the client. We risk confronting the fears of our own feelings, perceptions, and intentions and changing ourselves. Taking this risk in our helping relationship can result in some of the greatest pain and greatest joy of being a social worker. The payoff for us in risking the sharing of our feelings is authentic, yet functional, relationships with others in personal learning and growth. The payoff for the client, or other, is adaptive growth in transactions with the environment. The helping relationship, when based on shared feelings, becomes the major medium for change and growth.

Helping relationships thus are grounded in the reality of feelings as much as in purpose and content. Students need to learn to develop empathic understanding of the other's feelings, to respond to these, and to share their own feelings in encounters with clients. Early in their learning, students may tend to reassure clients prematurely or change the subject because of their discomfort in experiencing too much of the client's pain, anger, or fearfulness—or because of their uncertainty about how to respond. From this the student may move toward the ability to express empathy, put unexpressed feelings into words, and explore both sides of ambivalence. The abilities to accept and deal with hostility, to tolerate anxiety, to stay with and reach for other's pain, and, in group and family situations, to draw upon the cues or feelings of other members also develop. Students stop fearing feelings as irrational components of the client's behavior and stop struggling against these by means of logic and debate. Rather, they appreciate the purposive nature of irrational feelings and seek to understand and address them.

For instance, students will move from giving up when faced with resistance from a client, or pushing, confronting, exhorting, advising, or getting into a battle with the client. Instead, they become able to discuss the client's resistance, the meaning to the client of the helping process, and the fear and resentment inherent in change. They recognize the need for defenses in the face of perceived threat and for periodic avoidance of stressful content. In other words, students learn to respect the integrity of the human being and to see how feelings behind resistance reflect the client's efforts to maintain self-esteem in patterned approaches to interpersonal relationships and social demands.

Finally, students can share their own feelings about the client, the client's situation, and their relationship process together. As students move from inhibition to spontaneity, their feelings often are first conveyed awkwardly—both bodily and verbally. At times students will assume the client would feel as they do. Or they will share personal experiences that interrupt the flow of affect and the focus on the client's experience. Then, students can develop more sensitivity to the client's reaction to his or her own feelings and the ability to sense when the client is embarrassed, fearful of closeness, or resentful of the interruption. Eventually, the student can share the positive and negative feelings involved in the relationship and current aspects of the encounter.

INITIATING HELPING RELATIONSHIPS WITH RESISTANT CLIENTS

Three special uses of the skills of this chapter, particularly responding to and with feelings, deal with working with resistant clients, the use of authority, and establishing helping relationships with socially diverse clients. All clients will resist work and/or change to some degree. Even those who come for help out of their felt need (the voluntary client) will encounter fears and resistances in the face of giving up old patterns and considering new ones. Resistance, however, is most often strongest in those who do not come for help out of their own volition. These include involuntary and nonvoluntary clients.

Involuntary clients are those who are required by law or policy to be offered help. These include probationers and parolees, those suspected of child abuse and/or neglect, the elderly in need of protective services, and so on. We have long lacked an accepted name for those clients who tend to fall between the voluntary and involuntary. The "nonvoluntary" label has been suggested recently to describe such clients, those who have been forced to come for help without choosing it for themselves (Garvin & Seabury, 1984). These include the child who is brought by the parent, the spouse who comes at the partner's threat to leave the relationship otherwise, the father who attends the first family counseling session based on a family problem that the mother brought to the worker, the parent who is asked to come for what was presented as a problem with the child, and so on. Much of the theory of helping in social work and other disciplines assumes work with voluntary clients. In practice, however, we may find that a significant part of our work takes place with involuntary and/or nonvoluntary clients.

The social work models for establishing helping relationships with resistant clients promote the primary skills of reaching for and sharing feelings about the experience of the resistance and negotiating an understanding of mutual purpose (for a review, see Gitterman, 1983). These skills require movement from labeling resistance as a personality characteristic of the client to viewing it in an interactional perspective. The interactional helping process is a reciprocal one, with each person affecting the other and being influenced by many systems impinging on the encounter. Resistance, then, is understood as a way all clients, and especially involuntary and nonvoluntary ones, cope with a variety of distrusts and fears born of their transactions with their environmental systems.

Resistance is an ambivalent coping—a mistrust seeking trust. To confront resistance requires initial trust in the helper, a feeling of initial safety, and shared purposes. Resistance seeks honesty and acceptance, support and challenge. The movement from resisting to accepting help occurs by reaching for and touching the other's feelings, by sharing one's own purposes and feelings, and by creating emotionally charged currents that make an alliance seem safe and potentially useful.

Those resisting help usually seethe with feelings that are situationally created. These can often include fears, resentments, embarrassments, guilt, shame, and despair that one has, or *is*, a problem or that one will be rejected, or *is* rejected, by the would-be helper and those systems that are the agents for help. Pleasant evasion through small talk, when perceived through the coloring of these feelings, most often serves to arouse more uneasiness and suspicion. The feelings of resistance need to be faced and accepted to accept the other. To start where the other is, the first problem to be understood and worked on is the person's feelings and perceptions about this intrusive person, place, and purpose.

Confronting resistance requires speaking to the feelings and, through them, to the client. Tuning-in to potential resistance can help us begin with such understanding statements as "You probably resent having to see me"; "You must not like having to see someone like me"; "You must think this is none of anyone's business"; "You probably wish I'd go away"; and so on.

Quickly following such momentary comments, which may convey initial acceptance, comes clarifying your purpose. This includes why you are there. "Your wife suggested I see you because your boss referred you to me" ("because I am required by law to be here"; "because you are required by law to be here," and so on). It also includes your broader purpose of help: "You seem to have troubles, or be *in* trouble"; "I need to hear from you how you see and feel about this situation"; "I know there are at least two sides to every trouble story and I want to hear yours"; and so on.

Then, it is important to help the other begin where he or she is, how he or she sees and feels the situation, what he or she considers the problem and needs to be. The other seeks acceptance of the story as *his* or *hers*. This does not imply agreement with the reality presented but an understanding that this is the way the other sees and feels the situation. And feeling and seeing the situation as such, what might the other want to do about it? Here the social worker reaches for ambivalences—accepting the negative feelings expressed first and then reaching for the positives; or accepting the positives first, then reaching for the negatives. These ambivalences concern feelings about both the helping situation and the problems themselves—wherever the client is, or whatever he or she is willing to share. Understanding these feelings, as they continuously interweave with the facts, possibilities, and limits of what the other wants and what the social worker agrees to do, is the major dynamic for moving one who needs help to one who actively seeks and uses it. Thus the relationship of the helper and the resistant client is grounded in both emotion and purpose.

THE USE OF AUTHORITY IN HELPING RELATIONSHIPS

The use of authority is a second important factor requiring special use of the skills for establishing helping relationships. The many authors who have focused on the use of authority concur that it is an essential part of all practice and the central part of establishing helping relationships with involuntary and nonvoluntary clients (for a review, see Palmer, 1983). Social workers often denounce their authority out of the misconception that it is synonymous with power and control and therefore a hindrance to effective helping relationships. But authority, like resistance, is an interactional concept that depends upon negotiated and committed consents on the right to make decisions on pertinent issues within the helping relationship. In practice, this initial authority derives from one or several overlapping bases: (1) legally constituted authority, as in corrections and child protection; (2) institutionally constituted authority, as in adoption or income-maintenance programs; (3) positional authority, as in hospitals and family services; (4) expert authority, as in any social worker's recognized competence; and (5) personal authority, as in the social worker's perceived life skills. This authority, whatever its sources, can impede or enable the development of trust. The constructive and positive use of authority—

by stating one's purpose and function clearly up front, by the *caritas* of support and challenge, and by reaching for and expressing feelings—can provide the client with a feeling of confidence that the worker knows what he or she is about, is secure in his or her position, intends the best both for the person and society, and merits attention and respect. Such experience and perception engender trust. This includes a trust that the worker is not afraid to face the reality of the situation with the client and to deal with it.

With involuntary clients, the skill of reaching for and sharing feelings about power and authority in the relationship is crucial. This use of skills brings into the open and elicits understanding of the client's feelings, distortions, and misapprehensions that impede the development of trust. Discussing the realities and issues of power and authority at the first contact and encouraging the client to express fear and/or anger about this reality can help the client recognize the naturalness of these feelings and thus accept them. This can help establish a more trusting relationship and free the client's emotional energy for constructive action in the face of the uncomfortable realities in the situation.

In this initial contact and throughout the process, power and authority are negotiated. The boundaries for negotiation relate to the purpose and function of the helping relationship. The client always has the self-determined right and power to refuse to use the help, but may not have the authority to control the consequences of this refusal or the actions the practitioner may take. All of the specifics of these choices and their bases in power and authority need to be clearly communicated from the first. In child protective services, this means the worker in an investigation can note that the parent might not want to talk and might find it difficult, but that the worker is required to determine how the child was injured and can recommend removal of the child from the home if abuse is found and the parent refuses help for this situation. The negotiation should provide choice for the other as the service's function and legal and institutional base permits: "I know this is very hard for you to talk about, but I am required to get this information. Would you prefer to rest a minute before we go on?" As clients face and begin to grant this authority of the worker, the worker must remain attuned to what clients are feeling. This increases the potential for deeper trust vested in the position, expertise, and personal authority granted the worker. The client's pull of hope can arise from the push of discomfort. Then the helping relationship can accomplish what it is designed to do: It can *empower* the client to cope more effectively with interactional problems in living.

INITIATING HELPING RELATIONSHIPS WITH
SOCIALLY DIVERSE CLIENTS

Social diversity is the third important factor requiring special use of the skills for establishing helping relationships. Ideally, the bond of the helping relationship is a very human one that transcends all kinds of differences. This tie is possible even when working with clients who differ culturally and racially. But in reality, we are all touched by a society that stands for human dignity, equality, and mutuality while it heaps disrespect, injustice, and segregated practices for minorities on all of us. To the extent that those attitudes, however hidden or denied, imply a superordinate–subordinate social relationship among people of different races, each of us is racist. As Leon Chestang (1970) proposed: "The indisputable fact is that race is an issue in [social work] practice. It is the intervening variable no matter the presenting problem; it is an integral part of, if not *the* problem to be worked when the race of the [worker] and the client differ" (p. 114). Neither we nor our clients can initiate, although we may work toward, a helping relationship based on "color blindness." This would be a relationship initiated in deception, not in trust. Instead, we must accept and confront this difference directly and respect it in our relationship with others.

This factor of racial, ethnic, and/or cultural difference in helping relationships requires a special perspective in understanding the other—the dual perspective presented in Chapter 3—and a special use of the skills presented in this chapter. The use of the dual perspective heightens our sensitivity to feelings and perceptions that negatively influence establishing helping relationships with minorities and women. Clients from groups that have been systematically restricted from the dominant white society have developed ways to cope with its representatives in instrumental, pragmatic interactions for their survival and sustenance, while meeting relationship needs within their own nurturing environment of family, friends, and cultural community. They come with a group and individual history and a world of reasons to mistrust relationships with representatives of the dominant society. They often bring an intensified need for respect, emotional support, and empowering that such a trusting relationship can provide.

The inherent differences that become socially patterned, such as race, create stereotyped perceptions, expectations, and particular feelings for both workers and clients in initial contacts. Differences in race, social class, ethnicity, sex, and age are all potential obstacles to establishing helping relationships. Besides an acute sensitivity to, and the ability to use the dual perspective to understand, the strengths and adaptive behavior and communication of these differences, the strategies for establishing helping relationships in the literature (see, for instance, *Social Work*, 1970) crystallize into the same skills developed in this chapter. Initial trust evolves from a clarity of purpose and function and a specificity of focus; the emotional support of acceptance and the respect for strength in challenge; and the reaching for, responding to, and sharing of the feelings that these differences arouse in the immediate helping situation. To the other's unexpressed or skillfully camouflaged statement that "I don't trust you; you cannot understand what it's like for me and will treat me as a stereotype rather than as a culturally evolved person as well as a unique person in my own right," the social worker using these skills will find a way to say: "I imagine it is difficult to trust me. I don't know what it's like for you and I likely have some problems in trying to understand this. But I want to understand, will try to learn and understand, need to understand, if you will let me. Tell me how you feel and see this difference between us, as well as what you feel and see in this situation we will work on together."

Social diversity, like resistance and authority, affects the content and intensifies the need for effective use of these three skills for establishing initial helping relationships: using purpose and function, balancing support and challenge, and responding to and with feelings. These skills, taken together, begin the interaction. They interweave concern for the person and attention to the situation and establish an important basis for future negotiation, interaction, and work. They provide the resisting, authority-sensitive, and/or socially different client a glimpse of potential trust. This means sharing together of the fact that although it will be difficult, client and practitioner can work together in certain ways for particular purposes. This is the source from which successful social work flows.

The following situation, taken from an article on social work counseling from a "black perspective" (Ward, 1983), concerns a client who is socially diverse, likely to begin with resistance, and ambivalent about authority. Consider how you might respond to and with feelings toward establishing a helping relationship in initial contacts with Todd, about whom you have the following information from his mother, Mrs. Shott.

Todd Shott, a 12-year-old black child who lived with his 29-year-old divorced mother, was referred for counseling by juvenile court to a delinquency prevention program under the auspices of a family agency in a large metropolitan area. The prevention program was located in a low-income black community with a high incidence of juvenile delinquency.

The manager of a suburban shopping center drug store had filed a juvenile court petition against Todd, alleging theft; Todd was accused of taking candy from the drug store at 11:00 A.M. on a school day. As a first-time offender, Todd was referred for counseling, which met with his mother's approval. According to Mrs. Shott, the store manager indicated that Todd was frequently in the store during school hours and he surmised that Todd was a "school dropout like most of the black boys." The manager was suspicious that Todd would "rob him"; Mrs. Shott agreed with his suspicions because "children are so bad."

Mrs. Shott expressed disgust with Todd because he was not to be trusted and because during the past year his teachers had sent notes to her about his disruptive behavior in school. Mrs. Shott said that she did not know what was wrong with Todd and expected counseling to straighten him out. She worked hard, provided Todd with more than adequate food, clothing, games, and toys. He attended a "good school." Her future expectations were that Todd would get a job and become independent.

Todd, a small-framed, frightened-looking youngster, expressed dislike for school because the teachers "seem like they forget me—they don't call on me" and because the "other children don't play with me." He had no explanation for taking the candy and admitted frequent visits to the drug store because he did not like school. He feared what would happen at the agency.

Todd's parents divorced when he was seven, about 16 months after Mr. Shott returned from the service. Although Mr. Shott graduated from high school and completed one year of technical school, he experienced 12 months of unsteady employment and he fluctuated between dejection and anger. Mrs. Shott saw her dream of owning a house slowly disappearing, which she attributed to her husband's sporadic employment. Mounting tensions in the marriage soon led to divorce. Mr. Shott moved in with a brother who lived in another state. He secured employment for minimum wage in a garment factory. He visits Todd periodically, and Todd visits him during the summer.

Mrs. Shott had an associate business degree and had worked in a secretarial position with an insurance company for 11 years. She worked primarily with whites and provided on-the-job clerical training for several white women, one of whom became her supervisor at a salary exceeding Mrs. Shott's own. Two other former trainees' salaries paralleled her salary. Mrs. Shott was aware of the inequities but rationalized the company's need for more clerical staff; she was proud of her knowledge of the company, her training ability, and her social relationships that extended beyond work.

Three years ago, Mrs. Shott purchased a house in a white suburban community that had only two other black families. Mrs. Shott and Todd were the only black family on the street, and Todd attended a predominantly white school.

Todd's teachers were white, and he was the only black in his seventh-grade class. Over the telephone, the teacher had discussed with Mrs. Shott Todd's need for special education because of his "below-level math and reading skills." Also, by telephone and notes, Mrs. Shott had been advised of Todd's "hyperactive behavior," which she responded to by whipping him. She visited the school twice and verbalized her embarrassment over Todd's "bad behavior." She was concerned that Todd did not associate with any of the other boys in the school. Todd was not permitted to ride the school bus after cutting a two-inch slit in a seat.

Todd spent most of his time in the house when at home. This resulted from a neighbor's complaint that he had pushed her 9-year-old daughter. Mrs. Shott's response was a harsh lecture to Todd. Todd always enjoyed visits to his maternal grandmother and 18-year-old uncle, who remained in the black community where the Shott family formerly lived. Mrs. Shott preferred Todd to have minimum contact with the former community, except for relatives, because of possible negative influences.

However you find a way to start where Todd is and wherever you go with planning your work to address the various environmental systems impinging on Todd's current situation, it is important to negotiate with him where each of you stand and what you might do together regarding a number of immediate relationship issues. These include his nonvoluntariness, his feelings and yours about your authority, and his feelings and yours about his blackness. You need to confront and address these issues while you are clarifying with him the purpose and respective functions of your work together and helping him to share with you, and to understand how he sees and feels the current situation. If Todd is to trust you and work with you in his own behalf, he will need to experience your difference from other "authorities" he has faced in his young life. This difference comes from your perspective, your person, and your skills, as he discovers them in this initial contact.

CONCLUSION

The first competence of the beginning phase of social work process is the ability to establish helping relationships. Social work helping relationships emerge from simultaneous focus on the client and his/her definition of the situation that has brought the two of you together. They entail core conditions of genuineness, acceptance, and empathic understanding, as well as the generic skills of using purpose and function, balancing support and challenge, and responding to and with feelings. These skills initiate the work process for which the relationship is established. They enable and empower the client and increase trust in and hope for beneficial outcomes—even in the face of such potential obstacles as resistance, authority, and social and cultural diversity. They forge the emotional bonds and the sense of purpose necessary for any effective working relationship.

SUGGESTED LEARNING EXERCISE 6-1: SELF-HELP

Choose a problematic area of your life that is relevant to your interpersonal style and your competence as a social worker. Write about two to four pages of a dialogue with yourself in which one side of yourself shares this problem and another responds. When responding, use the three skills for establishing a helping relationship: clarify the purpose of your helping yourself, balance support and challenge to yourself, and respond to and with feelings. When you have finished this dialogue, identify each response in terms of one of these three skills and use the scale for evaluating these skills under Competence #2 in the Educational Outcome Competence Rating form found in the Appendix of this book.

SUGGESTED LEARNING EXERCISE 6-2: INITIATING HELPING RELATIONSHIPS IN THE FIELD

Record a dialogue that represents your first meeting with an involuntary, nonvoluntary, or otherwise resisting individual, family, or group. Describe your assessment of the quality of this relationship at this point. Then use the scales under Competence #2 on the Educational Outcome Competence Rating form in the Appendix.

7

Competence #3:
Beginning Phase II:
Competence and Skills

Barney Bright was a boilermaker who was hired to fix a huge steamship boiler system that was not working well. Barney listened to the engineer's description of the problems and asked a few questions. Then he went to the boiler room. He studied the maze of twisting pipes, listened to the thump of the boiler and the hiss of escaping steam for a few minutes, and felt some of the pipes with his hands. Next, he hummed softly to himself, reached into his overalls, and took out a small hammer. Finally, he gave one soft tap to a bright red valve. Immediately, the entire system began working perfectly, and Barney went home.

When the steamship owner received Barney's bill for $1,000, he complained that Barney had only been in the engine room for about 15 minutes and requested an itemized bill. The itemized bill that Barney sent him read:

For tapping with hammer	$ .50
For knowing where to tap	999.50
Total	$1,000.00

The primary competence of the beginning phase of social work process is "knowing where to tap." The three skills for this competence are contracting, initial assessment, and service planning. Like Barney Bright's skills, these skills require gathering information, defining and studying systemic problems, and determining the goals and targets for addressing these problems. This beginning assures on-target intervention in the work phase and increases the potential for effective service. It engages the client in service use. As partners, we know what to tap and where to tap for more effective functioning in person–environment interactions.

All three of these skills—contracting, initial assessment, and service planning—are both a process and a product. Contracting is a negotiating process that leads to a working agreement, or contract. Assessing is a process of defining and studying problems and strengths in person-environment interactions for a formal statement of these understandings. The formal statement constitutes a written assessment. Service planning is establishing goals and targets to address assessed problematic interactions through a formal service plan.

CONTRACTING

The helping relationship covered in the last chapter and the three skills of this one (especially contracting) promote the client's engagement in the social work process. Engagement, by dictionary definition, refers to an inducement to participate. To engage another is to involve, to attract, to mesh, to bind. Contracting sets the service process into gear, with the client, the problematic situation, the agency's service, and the helping process meshing in behalf of the client and inducing his or her initial participation. This involvement of the client assures that the purpose of the help is to enable a better match between the client and his or her environmental systems. Also, it begins the enabling itself through encouraging, empowering, and energizing.

Contracting is the skill of negotiating the purpose, problem, and process of work. It involves clarifying purpose; defining functions and roles; encouraging client's feedback on purpose; agreeing on the initial problem(s) for work; prioritizing concerns, goals, targets, and tasks; and displaying belief in the potential of the work. Contracting requires a clear and direct statement of mutual demands and expectations. This clarity of expectations increases trust and decreases fears. It also provides the concrete realities of the helping process in which the client can responsibly choose to engage in the use of the service.

Many research studies in social work suggest that contracting in the first contact is a crucial skill. It contributes greatly to whether the client will continue or discontinue using the service (Blizinsky & Reid, 1980; Hollis, 1980; Knapp, 1980; Levinger, 1960; Maluccio & Marlow, 1974; Mayer & Timms, 1969; Perlman, 1968; Reid, 1970, 1978; Reid & Shyne, 1969; Rhodes, 1977; Ripple et al., 1964; Schmidt, 1969; Shulman, 1977; Stein et al., 1974; Wood, 1978). The earlier studies discovered a relationship between the clarity and mutuality of purpose and expectations and continuance in social work process. For instance, Julia Schmidt (1969) found a substantial number of discontinuing clients reporting that they were unclear about the social worker's purpose of the service and help. Florence Hollis (1968), Joel Mayer and Noel Timms (1969), and Lillian Ripple and colleagues (1964) discovered a "clash in perspectives" between social workers and clients in initial contacts and therefore a lack of agreement on the definition of the problem. Clients who found practitioners not staying with their definition of the problem and clarifying how they might help with it stopped short of engagement in the use of the service. Helen Harris Perlman (1968) conducted a pilot study with 26 clients. She and two other social workers were able to lower the dropout rate of clients during the intake process by concentrating on eliciting clients' conceptions and expectations of the helping process and by clarifying discrepancies between expectations and what could be offered realistically. The clarification of roles and expectations, when mutual agreement was achieved, was a potent determinant of continuance in the process.

The more recent studies have examined the systematic skills used in contracting and their relationship to service continuance and use. Sonya Rhodes (1977), following others (Maluccio & Marlow, 1974), observed that "ambiguities about the contract and its unsystematic application as a principle of practice may account for a consistently higher percentage of unplanned client withdrawal" (p. 125). In her study in a Veterans Administration hospital, she found that contracting failed to define clients' roles adequately and to establish full mutuality (Rhodes, 1977). William Reid (1970, 1978) and colleagues (Blizinsky & Reid, 1980; Reid & Shyne, 1969) related clarifying and prioritizing of the client's view of problems and establishing time limits and client and worker tasks to promote positive outcomes. Their research blazed a trail for use of the written contract and its contribution to client engagement and work in a number of fields of practice (Harris, 1978; Hosch, 1973; Knapp, 1980; Stein et al., 1974; Stein & Gambrill, 1977). Katherine Wood (1978) reviewed numerous outcome studies in social work direct practice and found the systematic use of contracting and contracts related significantly to outcomes. Lawrence Shulman (1977) found contracting as a systematic skill that was among the most critical, especially in clarifying purpose and roles, for establishing the beginning helping relationship.

Beyond the empirical rationale for contracting, ethical reasons abound in the literature (Anderson, 1981; Compton & Gallaway, 1984; Garvin & Seabury, 1984; Hepworth & Larsen, 1986; Middleman & Goldberg, 1974; Pincus & Minahan, 1973; Simons & Aigner, 1985). This position has promoted the use of the contract as a basic instrumental value of social work practice. For instance, the most recent curriculum policy statement of the Council on Social Work Education (CSWE, 1982) noted in the section on values that "social workers' professional relationships . . . are furthered by mutual participation . . . social workers respect people's rights to choose, to contract for services" (p. 7).

Effective contracting practices the principles of accountability to the client, respect for human dignity and worth, and self-determination. It is a tool for enabling empowerment. The open negotiation and agreement of a contract permits the client, at least in theory, to hold the social worker accountable for his or her actions. Even though clients often feel powerless (and frequently may be) to confront the social worker about not upholding the terms of the contract, its use does show respect for the individual's rights and encourages partnership, or a balance of power, in the work together. It can reduce dependence and generate self-determined choice. In contracting, clients are not expected to enter into a relationship with an unknown social worker based on blind trust that their interests will be capably served. They can choose their commitment to the relationship and the helping process based on clear mutual expectations and the agenda for work. This honesty, or the absence of a hidden agenda, reflects another central ethical principle of social work practice. Effective contracting, then, is not just a fact of effective practice but also an ethical prescription.

Effective contracting as a process requires learning to define the purpose and nature of the work. Students at first may struggle to clarify the specific purpose of service and be vague or too jargon-dependent in this statement of purpose. Similarly, they may not be able to give clients a clear idea of how they might help. Later they may state their purpose and function without getting clients' reactions. Students learn to negotiate with clients an initial contract that focuses on their work together. Contracting involves (1) clarifying purpose through a simple statement; (2) clarifying function and mutual roles and responsibilities through giving the clients a beginning idea of how they might help; (3) reaching for clients' feedback, or reaction to and ideas about this purpose, function, and the nature of their work together (with special attention to the authority theme); (4) exploring the clients' most immediate concerns for which service was initiated; (5) prioritizing these concerns with clients to determine the most immediate concerns, goals, targets, and tasks; and (6) encouraging clients in the belief that there are possibilities for change, no matter how small at first, in the situation. In sum, this skill includes the ability to enable problem exploration, to translate client wants and needs into target problems, and to establish relevant and feasible tasks for enabling the client to divide and work on specific target problems.

Clarifying Purpose

Clarifying purpose requires a simple, nonjargonized statement by the social worker of the general area of work. This statement begins to define and establish the demands on and expectations of the client. It should also clarify the agency's and social worker's stake in providing the service. If the social worker has a specific agenda, or reason for the contact, the statement puts this agenda clearly on the table. For instance, in the first contact with a husband whose wife has placed the children in the custody of a child welfare agency: "Your wife has signed forms to place your children under the care of our agency. I wanted to meet with you to have you sign the agreements, but before that, to discuss what this means to you and your children. We know that you, as their parent, are very important to them now and in the future, and they to you. I know it can be an upsetting time for you as well as them, and I thought you might also have things on your mind you want to discuss."

Clarifying Roles

Clarifying roles entails making statements that give clients a beginning idea of how a social worker (you) might help and what they can do in their own behalf. In the above example: "I want to help you achieve your plans for what is best for you and your children, and I need to know what your hopes are for your and their future." Or, in a group context: "You all have many concerns in common. We formed this group because we think you can really help each other with these common concerns. My job will be to help you share them with each other and to help each other come up with ideas that may help. I'll also share my own ideas, when I think they will help."

Reaching for Feedback

Reaching for the client's feedback means requesting the client's response to the opening statement ("How does this idea about our work strike you?") and soliciting the client's sense of the specific work to be done ("What are some of the things most concerning you right now?"). Time needs to be taken through waiting out silences, reframing questions ("How does this statement of how I can help fit with what you expected?"), and emphasizing the importance of clarity about the work ("I want to take the time to be sure we understand how we might try to work together. What are your ideas about this at this time?"). Also, the authority theme, a taboo area not easily initiated by the client but seething in how the client sees and feels this contact, often needs to be addressed: "I imagine you have some resentment about working with me when you know I'll be making a recommendation about your children returning to live with you in the future. What are your reactions to this part of my job?"

Prioritizing Concerns

Exploring clients' most immediate concerns is the first step in putting the client's agenda on the table. The underlying question is: What do you see now that I might be able to help you with? This question can be asked in many forms: "What are some of the concerns you have at this point?"; "I'm sure you have a number of things you want to discuss; what concerns you most right now?"; "Where would you like to start?"; "You seem to be wondering where to start; what seems most in your mind right now?" This exploration is designed to establish agreement on the target problems for work. Target problems are those problems the client knows about, cares about, and wants to do something about as they relate to the purpose and function of the service. Those concerns that the client puts on the agenda are explored initially in relation to how much they hurt and bother him or her and whether the social worker and agency can help or find help for them. They become target problems when they are determined to be strong concerns that fall into the agency's purview. Then they are further explored in relation to priorities, details about their occurrence, and ways of addressing them.

This prioritizing of concerns to determine the target problems, goals, and tasks begins to move contracting as a process to the formal contract as a product. All models for formal, written contracts (Epstein, 1985; Garvin & Seabury, 1984; Hepworth & Larsen, 1986; Reid, 1978; Stein & Gambrill, 1977) suggest contract terms on the following subjects:

1. Specification of major priority problems
2. Statement of goals (objectives); that is, the desired outcomes in each problem area
3. Targets (people and resources) to be influenced

4. Tasks, or activities, the client will undertake
5. Tasks, or activities, the practitioner will undertake
6. Time expected to accomplish tasks
7. Scheduling of interviews and other contacts

This aspect of contracting requires much questioning, listening, and negotiating. The example that concludes this section demonstrates many of the ways that the social worker can engage the client in the process of prioritizing concerns and focusing the contract on target problems, goals, and tasks.

Instilling Hope

Encouraging clients about the possibility of change is the part of contracting that directly instills hope. The agreement to work together itself often dispels the client's fears of facing troubling situations alone and instills some hope. Often, however, the social worker's commitment to the contract displays a belief in the potential of the work that can energize the client's hopes and work in the face of what seems like an overwhelming and immobilizing situation. This encouragement requires statements designed to convey to the client the idea that there is always a next step, no matter how small at first, in the situation. For example: "Things may seem impossible to you right now, but if we start to tackle them one at a time, I think you can get somewhere." It is vitally important that this statement not be given lightly and establish a false hope. The practitioner must base such a statement on a vision of how the situation can be divided and approached—as the other is seeing and feeling it and as the strengths and resources in the person and environment interact in relation to it.

Example

The following example (adapted from Epstein, 1985) presents a client with several possible target problems who may prefer help in a way that the social worker cannot provide it. Thus the example reinforces the two most basic principles of contracting: (1) contracting starts where the client is, and (2) contracting is negotiating. In this vignette, assume that you are the social worker at a community mental health clinic. Mr. Steele has been referred to you through intake as a person who appears situationally depressed because of unemployment and who is concerned about his interpersonal problems. Assume also that you have begun to clarify your purpose and his and your roles in your initial statement and that he has shared his current concerns with your help. The following is a summary of these concerns, which you now need to help him prioritize into target problems, goals, and tasks.

Mr. Steele is a 35-year-old man, overly tied to his mother. He has just been laid off from his steelworker's job. In the interview thus far he has emphasized that he has been rejected by his girlfriend, Ms. Over. He acts unconcerned about being unemployed. He does not want to discuss job prospects. He says he wants help to improve his relationship with Ms. Over.

Mr. Steele is a union steward and an expert on the employment situation in his trade. The stress of his unemployment has brought him to confront the fact that at age 35 he ought to emancipate himself from his mother and get married. He cannot understand why his girlfriend has lost faith in him and become cool and distant. He has increased his attention to her without the desired results. The problem is identified as conflict with the girlfriend. Mr. Steele specifies the problem as Ms. Over's drawing away from him, not accepting dates, and refusing to talk about marriage.

Ms. Over seems to be drawing away from involvement with a jobless man. Mr. Steele may have been keeping up his courage by making light of the unemployment problem. He might want her closer so she can help him keep up his courage. You are not sure if you want to examine more carefully whether Mr. Steele ought to consider his joblessness as a problem.

Where and how might you proceed to explore Mr. Steele's problematic situation? However you proceed, you need more details about his view. You may, for instance, respond in one of the following ways:

"So you see the problem as your needing help with your girlfriend's coldness."
"Tell me the details about how she shows this coldness."
"How is her attitude different now from earlier?"
"What is she doing all this for, do you suppose?"

In order to get more useful details, your statements have to be definite and clear in order to encourage Mr. Steele to be specific:

"Am I hearing you right?"
"Is your job situation under control?"
"You know what to do?"

"But your girlfriend is a mystery to you?"
"Give me an example."
"Another example, please?"
"What did she say?"
"What did you say?"
"Then what happened?"
"How did that make you feel?"
"Can you put yourself in her place?"
"How might she have felt?"
"What do you suppose she is afraid of?"
"Have you discussed all this with your mother?"
"What does she tell you?"

Clarifying summary statements to determine target problems are very important:

"So—the essential thing is that you want to get married, and she wants to have less to do with you?"
"Until you lost your job she was interested in you as a date, but never allowed you to get really close? Now she is more distant?"
"Because you are worried about your job future you would like very much to have the support of closeness with her? And she says no?"

There are several ways to prioritize (Epstein, 1985):

1. Priority may be assigned to the problem that is identified by the client as being of highest interest.

2. Priority may be assigned to the problem as it is identified by professional judgment. Professional recommendation is especially needed when the client is unable to develop appropriate and feasible ideas about priorities. Professional recommendation may also be needed where legal or police authorities require that the client work on a particular problem. Without some degree of client agreement, however, it is not likely that much progress can be made.

3. Setting priorities may be postponed for a short or long time, during which the participants explore questions from a number of different perspectives. A tentative posture on priorities is appropriate when an issue is obscure. The client's commitment may be ambiguous, or the client may be perceived as needing more time to become secure in the helping situation.

In Mr. Steele's case, he wanted two priorities arranged in this order:

1. You should talk to Ms. Over to appeal to her to change her attitude.
2. You should show Mr. Steele how to talk and behave to have more influence with Ms. Over.

This is an example of a common occurrence when priorities are discussed. The first priority (that you talk to Ms. Over) may be impossible for you to do. The second priority is possible, but you might disagree with it because the idea is too narrow and oversimplified. This means that you must take issue with Mr. Steele, knowing that he may be distressed by that disagreement. To put the refusal in a positive light you might say: "You and I could talk with Ms. Over together, provided she is willing to come here for such a conference."

Mr. Steele should be told the reason for your inability to comply with the request: it is not out of unwillingness to help but out of your knowledge that there is no way to call in Ms. Over for a talk without violating her self-determination. It is fairly certain that she will respond negatively to such a call, making things worse for Mr. Steele. However, if he wants to ask Ms. Over to come and she agrees, you would discuss the interpersonal problems they have together.

How he should go about asking her to come might then be discussed and/or rehearsed. Mr. Steele and you can discuss and/or rehearse when and where to broach the subject, what should be said, what attitude should be projected, what should be done if she says no, and what should be done if she perhaps says yes. If all this seems too difficult to Mr. Steele, you could propose that the second priority— helping Mr. Steel learn some interpersonal skills that might be more effective—should be made first priority.

You may even choose to explain that you have reservations about both these priorities. The problem is composed of more complicated factors that are not directly touched on by Mr. Steele's suggestions. It is not clear what the couple mean to one another or what Ms. Over's reservations are. They could have something to do with Mr. Steele's personality and unemployment, or with Ms. Over's hang-ups about marriage, or maybe even with her desire to marry someone else.

When the priorities have been decided with Mr. Steele, you need to establish the goals. You can elicit from him an image of what the results of your work together should be, what they should look like or feel like. Mr. Steele needs to describe his idea of a successful ending: what he should be able to do, to have, or to feel.

CASE MANAGEMENT

The other two skills discussed in this chapter—initial assessment and service planning—evolve from the growing conception of foundation-level practice as performing the critical function of case management. Case management has become the practice model, primarily developed in practice itself, for direct-service generalist practice. As now developed, the concept of case management combines the best ideas of direct-service practice with the best ideas of community practice in behalf of a particular population-at-risk. Research on what social workers actually do in practice suggests that mediating through this case-management function is the most distinguishing element of the tasks of those who are educated for foundation-level social work (Attinson & Glassberg, 1983; Biggerstaff & Kolevson, 1980; Cummings & Arkava, 1979; Kolevson & Biggerstaff, 1983; Lamont & Miller, 1983; Mahler, 1982). A few studies further imply that foundation-level social workers are uniquely effective as case managers (Cummings & Arkava, 1979; Olsen & Holmes, 1982; Wattenberg & O'Rourke, 1978). When compared with advanced-level social workers and ones untrained in social work, these practitioners are "the most effective in performing what has become known as the 'social broker' role" (Olsen & Holmes, 1982, p. 100).

Several fields of practice define social work via the case-management function. These include *aging* (Abrahams & Lantz, 1983; National Conference of Social Welfare, 1981; Steinberg & Carter, 1981), *child welfare* (Case Management Research Project, 1980; Wells, 1980), *mental health* (Altschuler & Forward, 1978; Bagarozzi & Kurtz, 1983; Johnson & Rubin, 1983; Sanborn, 1983), and *health* (Grisham et al., 1983). This case-management function is very likely to expand in importance with expected increases in the elderly population; growing recognition of the prevalence of child neglect and abuse, including sexual abuse; the continued deinstitutionalization of the chronically mentally ill and disabled; and the growing predominance of chronic physical illness and disability over acute illness. This concept of case management from such central fields of social work practice will likely influence many other fields of practice.

As now developed, case management includes individual, family, and group counseling; management of environmental issues; linking clients to resources; providing social support through formal and informal resource systems; coordinating services; and, in general, assuring continuity of care. The emphases are on working with the strengths in both clients and their impinging environments, providing the social support of "being there" for clients in their problems of day-to-day living, and assuring their continued mutual adaptation in the community, in group homes, or in other types of care. The major skills for case management, gaining more consistency across models, are: (1) initial interviewing; (2) assessment; (3) service planning; (4) adaptive counseling with individuals, families, and small groups; (5) brokerage; (6) service monitoring and coordination; (7) community intervention; (8) advocacy; and (9) evaluation. The remainder of this chapter focuses on the initial assessment and service-planning skills as pertinent to case management and the theoretical perspectives of this text (ecological, phenomenological, interactional, and task-centered/problem-solving). Subsequent chapters focus on the remaining skills necessary for effective case-management practice.

INITIAL ASSESSMENT

Students at first are prone to view situations in simple cause-and-effect terms. They may believe that the situation would change if the client would only choose to act differently. Then, they may conceive the service as using their relationship with the client. As students begin to understand the complex transactions between clients and their environments as these affect life situations, they recognize the need for more ecological assessments and generalist practice. Students learn to start where clients are in concerns and in contracting for service. They begin to develop understanding of clients' life situations from an ecological perspective and assessment. This assessment includes ecomapping the transactions between clients' needs and capacities and perceived stresses and resources of their impinging environmental systems. There is determination of the client's, family's, other primary group's, organization's, and community's relation to the client's stressful life situation in terms of both strengths, or resources, and obstacles, or blocks, to meeting the client's service needs. The student uses the dual perspective for special consideration of these transactions and the goals and targets for intervention in behalf of clients whose cultural, racial, ethnic, and/or sex differences are subject to discrimination and oppression. In addition, students assess the client's needs–strengths–resources transactions and the meaning to the client in terms of specific life themes.

Assessment as Process

Assessment, like contracting, is both a process and a product. Social work assessment is distinctively a mutual process. Client and practitioner together seek to understand what is mismatching in the client's interactions with the impinging environment and to determine how best to enable more synergy. Assessment, then, is the ongoing mutual process and product of appraising the strengths and problem areas in the client's current environmental interactions and determining targets for intervention. This section focuses on initial assessment. However, the guidelines herein are applicable to the ongoing assessment enterprise throughout social work process.

Effective assessment is not only also based on the social work ethical principle of mutuality, but also on the principle of individualization. Mary Richmond first proposed formalized, individualized, person-in-situation assessment in social work practice in her classic, *Social Diagnosis* (1917). To Richmond, social diagnosis is an assessment of an individual or family that attempts "to arrive at an exact definition as possible of the social situation and the personality of a human being in some social need—in relation to other human beings upon whom he [or she] depends or who depend upon him [or her] and in relation to the social institutions of his [or her] community" (p. 357). This early version of a person–problem–situation systems model of assessment unique to social work has evolved into more recent models of *ecological* assessment (Germain, 1981; Siporin, 1975, 1980). Ecological assessments for generalist case-management practice view person–environment(s) interactions as a unique blending of individual autonomy and interdependence. Seeking the meaning of these interactions, informed by the phenomenological perspective, assures that assessment is a mutual, individualized process and product that increases the effectiveness of intervention in foundation-level, direct-service generalist practice.

Assessment, like social work practice itself, is both science and art. We understand people and their needs from an objective use of knowledge and from our empathic participation in their lives. We apply general theoretical models and principles to their social realities with a great deal of creative skill. We use both analytical and interactional skills, both rational analysis of information and our subjective experience with those we serve. Max Siporin (1975), who has contributed a great deal to the skills for the process and content of assessment in social work, wrote; "The social worker [in assessment] is concerned with gaining knowledge and making judgments, in terms of tested hypotheses and empirical facts, as well as in terms of creative discoveries, experiential meanings, and empathic transactions with the client" (p. 219). In effective assessment, we look from the outside and from the inside, with reason and with experience, with a dispassionate and compassionate understanding, to obtain an integrated objective and subjective appraisal. As Harriet Bartlett (1970) earlier noted, in social work we need to see the wholeness of person and situation to assess the multiple factors within this gestalt and to identify the crucial interactions calling for intervention. This comes from viewing person–environment interactions with empathy and considerable objectivity, in terms of their meaning for the self-realization and growth of the individuals involved, and with balanced concern for the relationship between the inner and outer factors that affect their current adaptive growth. In this sense, assessment is always a cyclical process of standing back to get close, standing back again to get closer, and so on—a continual knowing of the person–environment configuration as experienced by the client and in such a way that the intervention can contribute most to the client's needs. This increases the level of knowing in which we can dwell more fully in what we know. Hence our knowledge of another moves from observation to encounter.

The research on this process has been limited. Several generalist assessment models have been developed (Anderson, 1981; Compton & Galaway, 1984; Garvin & Seabury, 1984; Hepworth & Larsen, 1986; Siporin, 1975). However, rather than testing generalist models for differential assessment, the social work research (only some of it recent) has attended more narrowly to evaluating specific instruments for limited aspects of assessment or to studying the clinical judgment procedures in assessment. (See *Social Work Research and Abstracts*, 1981.)

An ecological/interactional framework for assessment currently cannot depend upon empirical guidelines but can be heuristically derived from theory. This would include the following: definition of situation, ecomap of areas of stress, analysis of ecological transactions, analysis of meaning, analysis of targets.

Definition of Situation

The concept of definition of the situation originally comes from the work of W. I. Thomas, an interactionist sociologist. Thomas (1938) proposed that social "facts" entail how social realities are defined. The basic principle is that if people define situations as real, these situations are real in their consequences. Hence, assessment begins with how the client and others define the situation and often entails its mutual redefining. The first step is ascertaining how the client sees and feels the current situation. In other words, how does the client define the problem? In an assessment of the client's definition of the situation (problem), we need to note the content for the client as well as the client's attribution of cause, blame, and/or responsibility for the situation. A useful typology for this definition evolves from the task-centered (Reid, 1978; Reid & Epstein, 1974) and life, or ecological (Germain & Gitterman, 1980), models for social practice. Potential target problems are defined and classified as follows:

1. *Interpersonal conflict*: A problem between two individuals where at least one is behaving in a way the other finds objectionable. ("We fight all the time"; "We don't get along.")

2. *Maladaptive interpersonal patterns*: A problem in certain aspects of one individual's interpersonal relations. ("I don't have enough friends"; "Other kids pick on me.")

3. *Life transition*: A problem in movement from one social position, role, or situation to another, often including making decisions in relationship to the change. ("We have to decide about having children"; "I don't know whether to stay in school or not.")

4. *Difficulties in role performance*: A gap between how an individual performs a social role (parent, spouse, student, employer, patient) and how that person would like to. ("I can't control my children"; "I can't hack math.")

5. *Reactive emotional distress*: An emotional problem in response to a specific set of circumstances (death of a family member, loss of status, financial difficulties) in which the individual's major concern is the feelings themselves rather than the situation. ("I'm down because I've lost my job"; "I'm worried about my health.")

6. *Habit disorders*: A problem in addictive behavior, phobic reaction, concern about self-image, or thought disturbances. ("I can't get through the day without a drink"; "I'm so depressed all the time, and I don't know why.")

7. *Formal organization*: A problem in an individual's relationship with an organization other than another individual. ("The court is on my back"; "They won't let me return to school.")

8. *Inadequate resources*: A lack of specific resources (money, housing, food, child care, health care, transportation, a job). ("We have been evicted and have no place to stay tonight"; "I'm sick and I can't get to the hospital.")

The use of this typology can augment the client's definition of the content of the situation. Each problem can be categorized to determine its distinguishing nature. Such specification is a first step in the definition of the situation with the client.

Once the problem content is defined by the client in a way the social worker can understand, the definition of the situation expands to how the client perceives the cause of this current problematic situation: within self? within another? within particular interactions? in organizational conditions? in community conditions? in societal conditions?

The second part of this definition of the situation often requires negotiating a new definition. This redefining, called "reframing" in the family therapy literature (Minuchin & Fishman, 1981), provides an interactional perspective on the problem that is often a prerequisite to change. The goal is a mutual definition of the problem as inside-outside, as a *mismatch* that derives in part from the client and in part from the environment, as well as mutual identification of potential resources within both the person and the situation for enabling a better match. This reframing can relabel disasters as challenges, hopelessness as choice, fears as wishes, and individual blame as interactional reciprocity. Because how one defines a situation is one side of the same coin of how one acts in the situation, this redefining in assessment can be a critical aspect of change. In this reframing, it is vitally important that we retain the client's definition and emphasize those slight differences in our definition calling for small next action steps that the client cannot perceive: "Your wife left you and you are lost; you now face the challenge of replacing that relationship to meet your needs at this time"; "You've lost your job because you struck back at a boss you've always considered unfair; you now face the challenge of finding a job without a good reference and preventing any future confrontations like this"; and in the earlier example of contracting with Mr. Steele, "You wish you could control Ms. Over's feelings and behavior toward you and fear what might happen if you can't. I believe you know that you can't really control her and that's difficult to face, but you can control yourself. That is, you can try some ways to let her know what she means to you and what you'd like to happen in your relationship with her and take the chance that she might share these wants."

Ecological Assessment

The definition of the situation for focus constitutes the "target problem(s)." Target problems need further analysis in their ecological context. Therefore, the next step in assessment is to ecomap the areas of stress, strengths, and potential targets for intervention in problematic transactions. The basic format for this ecomap was presented in Chapter 3. Here, the ecomap is applied to Mr. Steele, whose situation was presented earlier in this chapter.

Mr. Steele notes three specific problems: his interpersonal conflict with Ms. Over; his question about getting married; and his potential inadequate resource from losing his job as a steelworker. His major concern is his relationship with Ms. Over. Currently this interaction appears to flow one way, from Mr. Steele to Ms. Over, and is very stressful for him. However, in his decision to attempt to influence Ms. Over to marry him, he hints at a strong two-way but stressful relationship with his mother. We do not know how the family (he and his mother) relate to potential resources for adapting to stress (especially in the extended family). We do know that he is still a member of his union, which may ameliorate the financial concern from his job loss, and that he has begun to establish a connection with our agency. A current ecomap of this situation might then be as shown in Figure 7-1.

This ecomap places Mr. Steele in a particular niche regarding his impinging ecological systems. We gain an initial picture of stressful transactions and potential strengths and resources in the environment for his adaptive growth. We also discover some direction for gaining further information on his current situation in our assessment. The unknowns suggest that we delve more into the nature of his interpersonal patterns with Ms. Over (and perhaps friends), his relationship with his mother, Ms. Over's relationship to him and his mother, and other social support systems (extended family, friends, neighbors, religion).

Needs and Resources

The next step in assessment is the analysis of needs, strengths, and resources. In the ecological context, adaptive growth in the interactions between people and environments requires balance among three critical exchanges: individual needs and environmental resources; individual wants and environmental opportunities; and individual capacities and environmental demands and expectations (Garvin & Seabury, 1984). Individual needs are both basic human ones (Maslow, 1970) and life-cycle ones (Erikson, 1963).

Abraham Maslow (1970) placed basic human needs on a hierarchical continuum. These needs are "instinctoid" in nature. That is, they are biopsychosocial, and their frustration leads to ill health and stunted development. The basic needs with which the human being is born include: (1) physiological or survival needs (air, water, food, shelter, sleep, sex, contact); (2) safety and security needs (predictability, control, structure); (3) belongingness (participation, fidelity, validation) and love (closeness, caring); (4) esteem (respect, competence, effi-

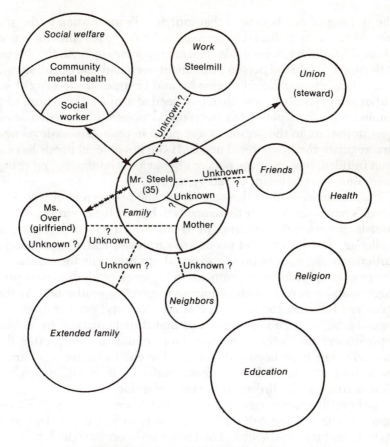

FIGURE 7-1 Ecomap for Mr. Steele.

cacy); and (5) self-actualization (realization of unique potentialities). Needs must be satisfied according to this sequence. In other words, individuals are not concerned with esteem—nor can social work directed to this goal appeal to them—until they have a minimum and consistent satisfaction of their survival, safety, belongingness, and love needs.

At any given moment, all five needs are present for the individual but one need is dominant in terms of the individual's motivation. The individual's first unsatisfied need in order of priority is that person's dominant need. Lower-level needs must be satisfied before higher-level needs dominate. Any change in the person, the environment, or both may shift the individual's dominant need along the continuum.

The shifting of needs creates that individual's motivation in the situation. Motivation is based on needs, actions, goals, and the energy released to achieve these goals. The energy increases with the intensity of the need. While the person's dominant need may shift from situation to situation, the individual's behavior and energies are seeking at least partial satisfaction of more than one need at a time. The nature of the dominant needs explains the people and objects in the environment most important to the person at any point in time. Higher-level needs then regulate the lower-level needs. If the lower-level needs have not been fulfilled, however, the person's behavior is immature and energy-consuming in an attempt to satisfy them.

The resources to meet these needs are the people and objects in the person's environment. For these needs to be met the environment must furnish the essential nutrients of freedom, justice, orderliness, and challenge. The lower-level needs are survival-oriented and therefore particularly dependent on the external environment for satisfaction. The newborn, for instance, comes into the world with dominant physiological and survival needs requiring responsive mothering. As these needs are fulfilled, the needs for safety, security, predictability, and control arise, requiring an environmental climate marked by stability, dependency, protection, and freedom from fear. Only after these survival needs have been satisfied can the child's higher-level growth needs (belongingness, love, esteem, self-actualization), which were present from birth, directly influence behavior.

Maslow, therefore, conceptualizes the lower-level needs as deficiency needs that are culture-bound and therefore dependent on the environment for satisfaction. The higher-level needs (which have integrated and subordinated lower-level ones) are, in his view, growth or "being" needs that often transcend cultural constraints in their fulfillment. The environmental vitamins and nutrients essential for both survival and growth led Maslow to the concept of synergy as an ideal environmental situation. In a synergistic environment one's own selfish satisfaction of needs is connected with others in the mutual aid of human relations. Therefore, the good of others is the same as the good of the self. (See Figure 7-2.)

Erik Erikson (1963) placed life-cycle needs into a series of age-related tasks that require social resources to promote development. His theory, like Maslow's, is hierarchical and epigenetic (based on the emergent biological growth of the organism). At each of the eight stages of growth, the individual experiences a psychosocial crisis brought on by a physiological transition. These crises are resolved through the successful completion of tasks that result in a favorable

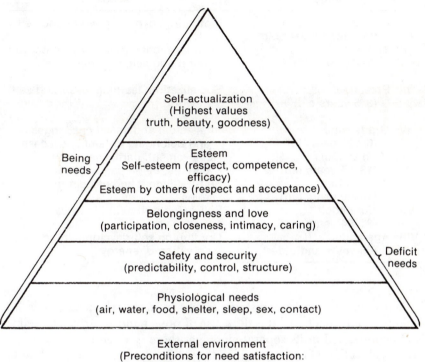

External environment
(Preconditions for need satisfaction:
freedom, justice, order, challenge)

FIGURE 7-2 Maslow's hierarchy of needs.

ratio of the positive sense of the self's growth over the negative sense of self that persists throughout a lifetime. This positive sense of self at each stage is the basis for the resolution of later developmental tasks. Table 7-1 summarizes Erikson's eight stages of psychosocial development.

In the first stage the infant is developing trust in the self, its own capacities, and the selves of others. The infant's needs are "to get" and "to give in return." As one is weaned, one experiences more of a self—separate physically and emotionally from mother and others. While trusting the self and others, the infant still has enough mistrust of having every wish satisfied to seek increased self-support (autonomy).

TABLE 7-1 Erikson's Stages of Psychosocial Development

Stage	Needs
I: Infancy (less than 1 year old)	Mothering, exploring world and self
II: Toddler (1–2 years old)	Learning, fantasizing, play perceiving world and self, security
III: Preschool (3–5 years old)	Socialization, learning, asserting self in world
IV: Grade school (6–12 years old)	Intellectual and social challenges and belonging in family, success
V: High school (13–17 years old)	Achievement, partial separation from parents, belonging with peers
VI: Young adult (18–20 years old)	Self-fulfillment and esteem in adult roles
VII: Mature adult (21–64 years old)	Self-actualization in life roles
VIII: Aged adult (65 years and older)	Continuing self-development, conservation of energy

Autonomy, in the second stage, comes from the sphincter needs "to hold on" and "to let go." It is the sense of power and control. The self is still experienced in its separateness, yet there is a need to yield one's own will to the will of others, leading to acceptance of a developing interdependence. A healthy level of shame and doubt makes the assertion of the self more interdependent and less willful in the assumption of interpersonal initiative.

The third stage involves a balance of initiative and guilt. The self becomes more convinced of its separateness and seeks its own direction. The consciousness of self and others in relationship is heightened. Others are more assertively extended beyond the mother—to the father, grandparents, neighbors, playmates. The guilt experienced when one does not comply with one's own or others' standards for behavior brings on a search for competence through industry.

In school, in the fourth stage, the child experiences a fresh opportunity to compare the self with others—to appraise one's own difference without loss of self-esteem (inferiority) or loss of the capacity for human relations with peers, teachers, and others. Intellectual, physical, and interpersonal skills expand in cooperative teaching-learning experiences with others. One learns to cooperate with others,

Crisis	Tasks	Purpose
Basic trust vs. mistrust	Trusting self and others	Sense of hope
Autonomy vs. shame and doubt	Interdependent separation of self from others	Sense of self-control
Initiative vs. guilt	Purposeful and conscious relating to others	Sense of self-direction
Industry vs. inferiority	Purposeful cooperation with others	Sense of competence
Identity vs. identity diffusion	Commitment of self to others	Sense of fidelity
Intimacy vs. isolation	Loving self and others	Sense of love
Generativity vs. stagnation	Caring for self and others	Sense of care
Integrity vs. despair	Being self with others	Sense of wisdom

follow the rules of the game, and develop close friendships in which both the purposes of self and the relationship can be furthered. The child seeks more of this sense of self that will lead to a personal identity.

The fifth stage in development is adolescence. While seeking an identity within one's peer group, separate from the family, and in the wider world in which one is to become an adult, the adolescent finds new energy, increased powers, and wider opportunities (with less identity diffusion) for personal identity in human relations, in work, in sports, and in other interests. There is an increased sense of fidelity—a disciplined devotion to shaping one's world and developing relationships based on intimacy.

The sixth stage of young adulthood continues to emphasize the needs of self-esteem, self-fulfillment, and intimacy through home and work roles and the prevention of isolation. The dreams of childhood are weighed against the realities of one's situation in an attempt to make life choices that increase self-actualizing human relations. Loving extends to others in a deepening sense of generativity to prevent stagnation.

Mature adulthood, the seventh stage, brings a more consistent, less fluid sense of self, and the self extends to giving more in human relations in the family, at work, and in the community. The sense of responsibility for self, others, and the world deepens. Changes are not as swift unless earlier developmental tasks demand attention. In this case, earlier unresolved crises evolve and need to be resolved in a movement toward integrity.

The last stage is the aged adult whose diminishing physical energy begins to cause disengagement from the wider world to conserve integrity with friends and family. One's life course is rerun in memory, with resultant satisfaction or despair. Death, as the end of life, can stand as an affirmation of the journey. The wisdom gleaned on this journey can be left for those who continue the life process on their own varied paths.

Many services function primarily to meet specific developmental needs through the provision of specific resources. These resources can play a great role in the successful completion of life-cycle tasks. They can assist the family and its members, for example, as they negotiate the complex institutions on which they depend for meeting their needs. For instance, the baby's needs for the responsive mothering that engenders development of basic trust depends on the mother's resources in such areas as health, income, and parenting skills. Income maintenance, prenatal care, hospital services, and well-baby clinic services are among the significant resources available to ameliorate or prevent such problems as inadequate parenting, unwanted children, and child neglect and abuse—problems that make the infant's task of developing basic trust difficult indeed. The social worker is in a key position to help mothers who need these resources.

Thus each developmental stage can be examined in terms of how our specific social services enhance the accomplishment of crucial tasks—both in ameliorating problems that obstruct growth and in preventing problems through the provision of basic resources. For instance, children and youth in Stages II through V require a great many resources, including social services, to enable their basic socialization in developing an autonomous, self-initiating, and industrious sense of self. Without this sense of self-identity, they will be unable in adolescence to make healthy decisions about values, sex, career, and so on. Services are often needed to help the family and other agents of socialization provide the required resources. Moreover, backup formal resources from child welfare services, homemakers, group and foster homes, and so on are needed when the family and other natural resources break down and such problems as behavior reactions, inadequate socialization, and social and learning failures result. Often, then, our function is to mediate between the individual's developmental needs and society's resources. Assessment centers on these developmental needs and necessary resources as strengths.

Wants and Opportunities

The analysis of needs, strengths, and resources leads to an analysis of wants and opportunities. Needs are reflected in wants, but wants do not carry the same imperative as needs. Nevertheless, a great deal of an individual's behavior and motivation relates more to wants than to needs. You likely do not *need* to be in a social work education program, but your wanting to be in one influences much of what you do. In fact, wants can supersede needs; our desire to succeed, achieve, and learn can dominate some of our most basic needs—at the same time perhaps contributing to meeting our higher-level self-esteem and self-actualization needs.

Wants need environmental opportunities for their realization. In assessment, we should trace our knowledge of client's (or other's) aspirations to the opportunity structure that exists in the environment. Often opportunities can be blocked or underdeveloped by "isms." Sexism, racism, classism, and ageism, for instance, limit opportunity structures and must be addressed to enable interactions that allow realistic wants to be achieved. Unrealistic wants need to be reconsidered in reaction to both the individual's capacities and the environment's opportunities.

Capacities and Demands

The final ecological interaction occurs between an individual's capacities and the environment's demands and expectations. A mismatch between capacities and demands causes stress. Developmentally and individually, we possess particular skills and lack others. When we meet environmental demands that tax our skills to meet our needs and achieve our wants, we need to increase our skills, change the environmental or our own expectations, or do all of these. Assessment should focus on how individual capacities and environmental demands and expectations match and mismatch and what causes such a match or mismatch in these ecological transactions.

For example, Mr. Steele seems motivated primarily by his belongingness and love needs. He is seeking a closer and potentially permanent relationship with Ms. Over. This need is consistent with the developmental task of young adults (intimacy vs. isolation) and is perhaps strengthened by his movement toward generativity, or developing his potential to care for himself and others out of more mature love. However, his wants of such a relationship seem thwarted by Ms. Over's withdrawal of opportunity and his own periodically more dominant need to control the relationship. His current insecurities prevent his risking open communication about where he stands with Ms. Over and what she needs and wants in this relationship. This current mismatch, the basis for his greatest concern and stress, lies in his use of skills to meet the environmental demands of her withdrawal from him. More assessment is needed about the strengths of Mr. Steele's need for love, as it can outweigh his need to control, and his actual skills, if motivated, to influence the blocks in his opportunities. In brief, we need to know if he has the skills to confront Ms. Over with what he wants, or if we need to help him with these—assuming he has sufficiently strong motivation to do the best he can to influence this situation.

In sum, the assessment step following ecomapping is to examine the ecological interactions in three potential areas of matching and mismatching. This analysis seeks the strengths and problematic areas in these transactions. These interactions, in constant adaptive or maladaptive change, are shown in Figure 7-3.

Meaning Assessment

The analysis of meaning requires an assessment of life processes. We seek the major life themes reflected in the other's patterns of perceptions, thoughts, feelings, and behavior. A life theme is a central pattern that often weaves its haphazard way through the fabric of our lives. These themes exist in the present, while they are spun from our past and pull us toward our future. Our life themes bring meaning to our experience of our worlds.

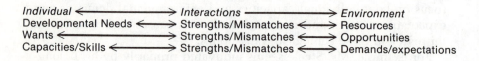

FIGURE 7-3 Ecological interactions.

In assessment, we need to follow the definition of the situation, the ecomap, and the analysis of the ecological interactions of needs and resources in the context of the client's search for meaning in terms of his or her life themes. We need to ask: What are the major life themes experienced here? What do these themes mean to our work? How do these themes affect what we can do together on behalf of the client? These questions assure our phenomenological focus in assessment. Only as we discover the significant meanings symbolized in the patterned themes that tie together the other's perceptions, thoughts, feelings, and behaviors—the other as a *whole* person in the experience of his or her world—can we determine targets for intervention on behalf of the other.

This life process, like all process, is dialectic. Each theme has a positive and negative counterpart—a thesis and antithesis—from which the client seeks a synthesis. The synthesis is the creative integration of these two seemingly opposing parts in our lives. Among the major life themes are developmental ones, such as Erikson's (1963) trust/mistrust, autonomy/shame and doubt, initiative/guilt, industry/inferiority, identity/role diffusion, intimacy/isolation, generativity/stagnation, and integration/despair. We also experience the interpersonal themes of autonomy/interdependence, separation/union, love/will, security/growth, and commitment/detachment (Anderson, 1984a). To help others with their life themes, we need to listen to the music as well as the words of what they seem to be working on.

For instance, we cannot help another gain interdependence without an underlying autonomy. If the major life theme is autonomy/interdependence and the other has underdeveloped autonomy (such as strong resistance and rebellion toward others), we need to enable the development of positive autonomy (more responsibility to self and to others) first. If autonomy has developed more positively (the other experiences self-responsibility) we need to enable more interdependence (caring about and for others). Similarly, one needs to develop one's separateness for union, one's will for love, one's detachment for commitment, and one's security for growth.

Therefore, we need to assess not only the major life themes but also to interpret the particular nature of these themes in the person's current interactions. This task involves the empathic answers to the following questions: What side of the dialectic is developed most? What side is developed least? Where is the other in this current point of development? What are the resources in the person and in his/her impinging environment that can provide opportunities for progressing toward the integration of this dialectic? How can I use myself to enable initial steps in this integration?

SERVICE PLANNING

As students move from defining problems as the need for change in clients to understanding person–environment matches and mis-matches, they establish goals, targets, strategies, and methods for delivering service in more generalist service plans. These plans include when, why, and toward what goals they will work with (1) clients themselves in their own behalf and through which method; (2) client groups and family groups and through which methods; (3) organizations in behalf of individual or groups of clients and through which methods; and (4) communities in behalf of groups of clients and through which methods. The plan includes the identification of specific theoretical models to direct the interventions. Often, the assessment and service plan is presented to clients in a written contract that specifies goals and client and practitioner tasks to achieve these.

This skill includes the ability to question and think critically about programs, theories, alternative approaches, and the effectiveness of interventions. This critical thinking, based on knowledge of approaches, should lead to ideas about changes and strategies to bring about change. The planning entails the ability to formulate ideas about the social work process and the steps involved in moving from initial contracting through termination. Initially, students often question the purpose and the process and cannot be expected to have a clear idea of what is helpful or why. They begin by seeing one useful step and move toward seeing a range of approaches. In the planning, students move toward working partnerships with clients in establishing clear goals and articulating first steps. They help clients select goals that maximize their motivation, capacity, and opportunity—moving from being too protective or too ambitious in the goals decided upon in the service plan.

This skill also includes the ability to explicate the rationale for their service planning and intervention. This rationale entails identification of the agency policies, procedures, and programs; the practice theories that influence specific service planning and intervention; and the critical assessment of these influences as they relate to effective service in specific situations as well as to services to clients in general.

Goal-Setting

The first step in service planning is goal-setting. The authors and researchers who have focused on goal-planning promote a number of useful principles for its effective use in service planning (for reviews, see Garvin & Seabury, 1984; Hepworth & Larsen, 1986; Wood, 1978). Goals translate assessed needs into desired outcomes, identified targets, and strategies for service planning and intervention. Goals specify what clients (or others) wish to accomplish—needs turned into wants—in their *common* venture with us. Goals are established in a preliminary fashion as we assess clients' needs and wants. Desired changes in the clients' life situations correspond to this mutual assessment of needs and wants. The process of assessment helps assure the partnership of specifically shared goals on which the work is based. Formalizing these goals is the first step in planning effective service. Therefore, the principles of goal-planning, developed by the various authors cited above, are a vital part of direct-service practice. Dean Hepworth and Jo Ann Larsen (1983), for instance, suggested that the first step in good planning is clarity about the type of goals we are setting. These types include discrete, continuous, individual change and shared, reciprocal goals. Discrete goals occur often in practice. These are one-time actions or changes to resolve or ameliorate concrete aspects of problems or concerns. Examples include obtaining a needed resource such as income assistance, housing, or medical care; making a major decision, such as deciding to place an unborn infant for adoption; or making a specific change in one's environment, such as moving from one's parents' house to an apartment.

Continuous goals contrast with discrete ones but may be closely related to them in much of our work. Continuous goals are those that reflect ongoing, most often incremental, steps of accomplishment in progress toward ultimate desired outcomes. These would include ongoing accomplishments in such desired outcomes as expressing feelings openly, managing conflict effectively, asserting one's rights, controlling one's impulsive behavior, participating in group discussions, handling stress effectively, and so on.

Individual goals target the individual. The expectation is that the person will think, feel, and/or do something different to change parts of the self and/or the environment. The changes in the person tend to include cognitive (thinking), emotional (feeling), and/or behavioral (doing) changes. These include such cognitive changes as increasing the number of positive thoughts about one's self and decreasing the number of self-deprecating ones; such emotional changes as learning to express tender feelings or expressing anger more constructively; and such behavioral changes as using relaxation exercises to control stressful reactions or reducing or eliminating drug or alcohol consumption. Individual goals can also focus on interpersonal or environmental changes but will be limited to what the person can do to influence these changes (asking another for a date, initiating a conversation, moving to another neighborhood, and so on).

When individual, interpersonal, or environmental change in desired outcomes depends on changes in others, then shared and reciprocal goals must evolve. Much of our direct-service practice demands that we target the family, group, and other interpersonal systems to meet the needs and wants of those we serve. In these situations, we have multiple clients. In fact, the family or group itself becomes our client system. Then, the system's change goals need to be held in common by members (shared) or involve agreed-upon exchanges of different behavior (reciprocal). The distinguishing feature of shared goals is the members' commitment to change their interactions toward similar desired outcomes: two marital partners agree to listen to one another without fighting; family members agree to use feedback to clarify the intentions of each other rather than jumping to conclusions; group members agree to pursue a goal of hearing from every other member before making a decision that affects them all.

Reciprocal goals tend to be *quid pro quo*—a "this" for "that." In others words, each person in an interactional system agrees to modify aspects of personal behavior *only if* others change *different* (not the *same*, as in shared goals) aspects of their behavior. An example of a reciprocal goal is the agreement of one partner in a marriage to work on listening more attentively if the other agrees to share more verbally—leading to the ultimate shared goal of better communication. Environmental changes, particularly at the organization and community level, often require work on reciprocal goals to achieve shared goals. For instance, achieving the shared (by consumers and the organization) goal of better service delivery may require mediation in which consumers and the organization identify reciprocal goals (e.g., if consumers guarantee that the waiting room will not become a hangout for youth gangs, the health clinic will move into the neighborhood where it is needed most).

Clarifying the type of goal enhances the ability to select and define goals with care. A number of principles serve this careful use of goals. First, goals should be relevant. That is, goals motivate clients when they believe that accomplishing them will make a significant difference in their lives. Relevant goals are the clients' goals—based on their own choices and invested with an underlying emotional commitment.

Second, whenever possible, goals should be concrete. Concrete goals are specific, explicit, and measurable rather than general, abstract, and untestable. When goals are concrete, their achievement can be monitored and evaluated similarly by both client and practitioner.

For instance, such nonconcrete goals as "improving social relations" or "enhancing the social environment" become concrete when stated in such specific terms as "initiating and maintaining conversations with others" and "obtaining living arrangements in a center for elderly people that provides social activities." The specifying of concrete behavioral changes prevents "drift" (Reid, 1970), or wandering in the helping process that practitioners note and that clients report (Schmidt, 1969). Concrete goals lead to clearer subgoals as "way stations" along the journey to effective help: "Initiate a conversation with at least three strangers in the next week"; "Contact the admissions director at two separate centers for the elderly and make appointments to discuss their service."

In family and groups, these goals are either shared or reciprocal. Establishing concrete goals in these situations requires specifying essential behavioral changes for all members in the target system (the family, family subsystem, or group). Concrete common goals assure that all members are clear about the part they play together in accomplishing changes in their system. For instance, if the ultimate goal in work with a family is to reduce conflict and to achieve closer and more harmonious family relationships, members must be clear about concrete individual goals whose accomplishment can contribute to achieving the system's goals. This same principle applies to small groups and family subsystems (parent–child, marital couple, siblings, and so on).

Third, goals should be feasible. Several authors (Garvin & Seabury, 1984: Hepworth & Larsen, 1986; Reid, 1970; Wood, 1978) admonish practitioners to avoid formulating over ambitious or unrealistic goals. We need to help clients assess the achievability of their goals in relation to both personal strengths and limitations and environmental potentials and constraints. This principle requires a delicate balance between challenging others to achieve the best possible and preventing devastating discouragement, disillusionment, and defeat.

Fourth, whenever possible goals should be stated in positive rather than in negative terms. Clients' motivations for self-actualization and adaptive growth increase with commitment to what can be gained rather than in attention to what they must give up. Reducing or eliminating the frequency of drinking binges is better formulated as achieving ever-increasing periods of sobriety, one day at a time. Reducing blaming in family systems is better stated as increasing family members' awareness of each others' strengths and frequency of statements of appreciation of these strengths. Eliminating low levels of participation in a small group is more motivating when stated in terms of tapping the group's potential for mutual aid by reaching for each other's participation.

Fifth, goals should be consistent with the function of the agency and the resources of the practitioner. When the practitioner is open to the prioritized goals of the client, he or she can know whether the client has come to the right place and the right person to accomplish them. The relationship of the client's goals to the agency's functions and services and the practitioner's knowledge and skills needs specific attention and clarity in goal-planning. When parts of the client's goals fall beyond the scope of the agency, the practitioner needs to formulate a discrete immediate goal of securing needed services through referral or other mediation. Similarly, when the client's goals demand knowledge and skills beyond yours as a practitioner, you have an ethical obligation to clarify this limitation and seek the person who can best help. Those wanting help for severe depression and suicidal tendencies require particular medical and controlled environmental resources. So would those with a long history of violent behavior. Even in rural settings, where you and the client may face the choice between no service or your less-than-optimal service, if the problem and goals exceed your knowledge and skills, you need to explain your limitations and allow the client to choose.

When we follow these guidelines, we translate needs and targets into useful goals through a reciprocal negotiating process. Starting with the client's wants, we establish a mutual, explicit end and steps to accomplish that end. We establish priorities on which to plan service delivery. When we and the client know what it is we want to accomplish together in the client's behalf, we are in a position to decide with the client how best to achieve these goals in our service planning. This achievement comes from our selecting appropriate intervention systems, methods, and strategies for the work.

Selecting Intervention Systems

The first step in selecting intervention systems is determining what needs to be influenced to bring about our relevant, concrete, feasible, and functional goals. The questions become when, why, and how we will address individuals, groups, families, organizations, and/or communities to enable the accomplishment of these goals. In other words, we need to be clear on when we will work with (1) clients themselves in their own behalf; (2) client groups and family groups in behalf of individual clients and others; (3) organizations in behalf of an individual or groups of clients; and (4) communities in behalf of groups of clients. These inter-

vention systems, in turn, determine what methods we should use (casework or individual counseling; group work; family counseling; organizational development; or community organization) and, within methods,
which practice models provide us with informed strategies to influence
these target systems. Figure 7-4 summarizes these alternatives in the
service-planning process and provides guidelines for such planning.

Effective generalist service plans evolve from placing the goals we
have negotiated with the client into such a matrix. In direct service,
most early goals fall into Quadrant A, including the goals of negotiating service goals with clients. This requires effective use of such
casework skills as starting where the client is, interviewing, problem
identification, and contracting. Such casework models as the problem-
solving and task-centered ones can usefully inform this work to

Intervention system

	Individual	Others
Individual	**A** Work with individual in own behalf Target: Individual change and development Methods: Casework or individual counseling and problem solving	**B** Work with families and groups in behalf of individuals and others Target: Family and/or group change and development Methods: Family-centered groupwork, counseling or problem solving and group-work, group counseling, or group problem solving
Others	**C** Work with organization and resource systems in behalf of individual client Target: Organization and/or informal resource systems change and development Methods: Consultation; linkage; case advocacy	**D** Work with communities in behalf of individual and others Target: Community change and development Methods: Community organization or development; policy or program development; cause advocacy

Client system (label at left spanning rows)

FIGURE 7-4 Generalist service-planning framework.

achieve this early goal of goal planning. As some service goals reflect needed changes in interpersonal behavior or family systems, the potential for planning work with small groups and family systems evolves. Similarly, at points in providing the service the goals often indicate a need to influence aspects of the service network: our own agency, other organizations, or less formal resource systems (e.g., extended family, neighbors, and so on). Here, consultation, linkage, and/or case advocacy need to be considered. Finally, some goals may evolve that call for work in conjunction with and in behalf of a number of others, including our individual clients, to influence change in the community at large. Then, we would accomplish community development or change goals through such methods as community organization, policy or program development, and/or cause advocacy.

If we take Mr. Steele's situation, presented earlier in this chapter, a planning matrix may read something like Figure 7-5.

Approach Selection

This skill of service planning requires a knowledge of and at least a beginning ability to use the approaches, or theoretical models, for practice that inform the work. The prevailing models in social work are too extensive to cover here and have been presented in another source (Anderson, 1981). Whether the models for practice and their concomitant strategies and techniques to accomplish stated goals come from these espoused theories or one's "theories-in-use" (see Chapter 4), the plan should include a clear identification of the theory base for what we are trying to do. This theory constitutes our rationale for the plan. This rationale is tested in how we apply our plan, including its theory base, in our formal evaluation of the work. In the ongoing work, the goals and our plan for achieving them can be constantly monitored, evaluated, and made more effective only if we are clear about what we are trying to accomplish (and how). This effectiveness comes from the clarity of the goals, targets, methods, and approaches (practice models) we have selected and used in our part of the work.

CONCLUSION

The second competence of the beginning phase of social work process is the ability to engage clients through initial contracting, assessment,

Intervention system

A *Individual*	B *Group/Family*
Goal 1: Enhancement of Mr. S's contact with Ms. Over Method: Casework Approach: Task-centered casework	Goal 1: Development of Mr. S's autonomy (initiative) in relationship with his mother Method: Family groupwork Approach: Family counseling: reciprocal goal
Goal 2: Increase in Mr. S's skills for relating more openly with others Method: Casework Approach: Counseling	Goal 2: Increase in Mr. S's skills for relating more openly with others Method: Group work Approach: Mutual aid group with others who share goal
C *Organization*	D *Community*
Goal 1: Mr. S's employment Method: Consultation/brokerage Approach: Referral Goal 2: Same as 2A Method: Consultation Approach: Group-work plan for agency to offer group service	Goal 1: Establish premarital and dating counseling for couples in community Method: Community organization Approach: Community planning

Client system: Mr. Steele

FIGURE 7-5 Goals-intervention planning matrix.

and service planning. These three skills refer both to a mutual negotiating process and a product in the beginning phase of work. Contracting entails a mutual agreement on the purpose, tasks, problems, and goals for the work together. Assessment and service planning are central to case management in direct-service generalist practice. Initial assessment requires defining problems in their ecological context and gaining an objective and empathic understanding of the interactions that are resources for or obstacles to achieving the goals of the contract. Service planning specifies these goals and relates them to the assessed targets that need to be influenced to accomplish the goals and the methods and approaches that will be used for this influencing of targets. Assessment and service planning especially address the individual, family, group, organization, and community needs and resources for the work. The use of these skills, based on the principles in this chapter, contributes to effective generalist direct-service practice.

SUGGESTED LEARNING EXERCISE 7-1: BEGINNING

Select a problematic situation in your own life and/or in a field assignment. Draft a written contract for enabling change in this situation for yourself or in behalf of the person you work with in the field. If with yourself, clarify what you want to accomplish and what you would try to have different parts of your self do to bring this about (for example, you may have some of your "hurting" self talk about the hurt, some of your "supporting" self tell you you're OK, and some of your critical self challenge you to behave differently). If a field assignment, use the principles for contracting in this chapter in your written contract.

Next, assess the situation. Define the target problems in more detail; draw an ecomap; identify needs and resources, including wants and opportunities, capacities, and expectations. Try to identify the meaning of this situation to the person experiencing it in terms of what seems like a central life theme (or themes). Write this assessment. Finally, develop a service plan. Specify concrete, relevant, feasible goals and draw a matrix using the four quadrants—A, B, C, and D. Place goals within the relevant intervention systems on the matrix. Then, identify what methods and possible approaches (or strategies) you might use for these interventions to achieve each of these goals. Conclude by assessing your current level of mastering this competence and these skills by rating this sample of your work. Use the scales under Competence #3 on the Educational Outcome Competence Rating form in the Appendix of this book for this rating.

8 Competence #4: Work Phase: Direct Intervention

Jill Addams, a social worker who has spent her last 25 years at the local children and youth agency, recently announced her retirement. Two days after the announcement she received a telephone call from Pam Press, who was recently hired by the local newspaper. Pam wanted to visit Jill and interview her about her life. Jill wasn't sure she had much to say that might interest Pam, but she agreed to the interview.

While waiting for Pam to arrive, Jill began reflecting on her life and career. She remembered the zeal with which she had left her social work education and begun her practice. Oh, how she wanted to change the world! How early in her career in another children and youth agency she had faced the limitation of this course and begun to identify with her function of helping people cope more effectively with what seemed to be an inevitably imperfect world and to try to change small parts of that world—increased opportunity for women to work and to parent, more family-centered services available for those who needed them, more work with children in their own homes rather than in foster-care or institutional settings, and so on.

She thought about her lows and highs as a social worker over the years. Among the lows that vividly stood out for her was how the community, including many of her friends, expected her to "fix up" situations that reflected such social problems as poverty and racism at the same time that too many of those she served saw her as an ally of an unjust and inhumane society or even as their enemy. She remembered reading a book on social work that was subtitled *The Unloved Profession* (Richan, 1976). This phrase now struck her as so fitting. Perhaps that would be the theme of what she shared with Pam about her life.

Then Jill recalled the highs. She particularly thought of what she learned from those she served—the strengths they exhibited and how she learned to "pitch to those strengths" (was that what her first supervisor called it?) when she hung in there with them, tried to empathize with them and understand them, and helped to sustain them during their struggles. She delighted in recalling the many of them who had worked so hard on their own behalf and how she had been a part of that work. As she reflected she began to see flashes of faces—people she had served and grown to respect greatly as they worked to break vicious circles of child abuse, change behaviors and their environmental situations that contributed to child neglect, choose from their love to place their child in foster care, struggle with their adolescent's drug abuse, and so on. And she especially remembered the children. She recalled specific kids who seemed so in need and developmentally thwarted and who now were rearing healthy families of their own, working successfully, and seeming to thrive. What strengths they had! What capacity to work with the right help and resources! "Maybe social work is the 'strengthening' profession and I can use this theme to highlight the satisfactions of my career," thought Jill.

Pam arrived just as Jill had decided she would share both the highs and the lows with her. And she did.

WORK PHASE

This chapter covers the ability to sustain social work process through direct client contact in the work phase. This competence, as Jill Addams reflects in the above story, is critical. It is also complex. The theory and research of social work process attest to this critical and complex aspect of direct practice and suggest the particular skills of this competence.

Many models of short-term help evolve from the research finding that a great deal of early movement reaches a plateau or even goes downhill over time in the helping process (for reviews of this research, see Reid & Shyne, 1969, pp. 1-16). In other words, after the early establishment of a helping relationship, a contracting for work, and engagement in the helping process—just when the real work on adaptive growth in ecological interactions confronts the practitioner and client—the process often waivers and can regress. These blocks in the helping process led William Schwartz (1971) to conceptualize a particular set of skills for what he termed the "work phase" of help.

Schwartz conceived the work phase as a microcosm of the overall process, complete with its own beginning, middle, and end. These phases require a special adaptation of the generic skills that enable the helping process. These include sessional contracting; elaborating and clarifying aspects of the problem situation for ongoing assessment, service planning, and contracting; reaching for and empathizing with *more* of the feeling, both negative and positive; sharing one's own feelings; holding to work; providing information; and applying practice models for actual work with individuals, families, groups, organizations, and communities. These skills respond to the client's question: "What is being worked on?" They also answer the question that the practitioner must explore: "What can I do to enable the most effective work on this?"

Lawrence Shulman focused on a similar set of skills in his study of the helping process in social work (1977, 1984). This study found that particular skills correlated most highly with "building a helping relationship," while others correlated most highly with actual "helpfulness." It appears that once the relationship is established through initial focus on the work, the practitioner can best enable the necessary work through a related but different set of skills. For instance, Shulman discovered that the skills for building the helping relationship, ranked in order of correlation strength, were "sharing worker's own thoughts and feelings," "understanding the other's feeling," "defining the contract," "reaching for feelings," "providing working data," and "partializing the other's concerns." The helpfulness skills, or those that moved from problem identification to problem solving, were ranked as "supporting others in taboo areas," "understanding the other's feelings," and "sharing one's own thoughts and feelings."

Likewise, Robert Carkhuff's (1969) research on helping suggests the importance of phasic skills. Carkhuff placed these skills into two phases: facilitative and initiative. To enable exploration of problematic situations, the helper needs to build rapport through emphasizing one's humanity in the facilitative phase. To enable understanding of the situation that can lead to competent action, the helper needs to risk challenging the relationship through emphasizing one's toughness and self-confidence. In Carkhuff's model, then, the helper moves from expressing concern and understanding, through concreteness, genuineness, and self-disclosure, to confrontation.

The ability to sustain the work process through direct contact in this phase entails use of the skills deemed critical in this research. This chapter addresses this competence and these skills: (1) sessional tuning-in and contracting; (2) elaborating and clarifying; (3) empathizing; (4) sharing own feelings; (5) demanding work; (6) providing information; and (7) using practice models.

SESSIONAL TUNING-IN AND CONTRACTING

Sessional tuning-in involves many of the same concepts covered in Chapter 5. Likewise, sessional contracting uses those found in Chapter 7. Tuning-in requires sensitizing oneself to the potential concerns and feelings that may emerge during the contact—both one's own and the client's. And one particularly anticipates relevant developmental ecological life themes from applying what one knows about people in similar situations.

Contracting requires "beginning where the other is," or where the other begins subsequent contacts. Discovering what clients or others are working on, their urgent concerns in relation to the ongoing shifts in their experience, ensures that their agenda gets addressed. The practitioner assures that each session belongs to the one receiving help by listening hard to the client's concern.

Tuning-in well leads to responding directly to indirect communications. Contracting leads to focus on relevant work. Together, these skills provide the incentive for clients to risk working on the challenges they know are most difficult yet most important to them. As with all skills, there are no right or magic words to operationalize these. When we identify with our purpose and stance of enabling the other's adaptive growth and our mediating function, we find the words that seem to work best. In fact, a major principle behind all the skills of this phase is to risk genuine, more spontaneous responses. Behind any particular technique or skill, others need to know that we, as persons with a function, are fully with them in their struggles—supporting their reluctant efforts and challenging their best efforts.

After beginning the social work process, students often are uncertain about where to begin subsequent contacts. Often, they may continue to review past work or elicit reports on plans. In this approach, students tend to assume that the agenda for work was established in earlier contracting. They continue this agenda through work-phase contacts. Later, students move to sessional tuning-in and contracting by starting where clients are, discovering what they are working on, and addressing their agenda first. This skill includes reaching for and listening to the client's urgent themes of concern, information on what has occurred in the client's life between contacts, and the client's wishes and fears as a person in the process of becoming.

The student needs to increase the ability to pick up the life themes, messages, and patterns underlying the content that the other brings to the contact. Often at first, students begin to see in hindsight the relevance of the client's comments or digressions that confused them during the encounter. They can move to identifying and commenting on the themes and connections, particularly as they learn to discern the messages about concerns that tend to be embedded in less obvious contexts. In group and family meetings, they not only identify individual concerns but begin to help members connect with one another around their common themes. They can perceive how the group and family process reflects a microcosm of the themes and concerns in the lives of members outside the meeting and helps members identify these patterns for themselves.

Take, for instance, the following situation in a group meeting with adolescents. All of the members have been on juvenile probation for a series of offenses that include truancy, drug and alcohol abuse, and petty theft. A common goal for the group, which was contracted for in the earlier meetings, is their learning to develop more prosocial and fulfilling friendships. This is the third meeting of the group. At the last meeting they decided to work on the theme "discovering our problems in making good friends." Instead, the meeting begins with one member's tirade against "crooked politicians and cops." Several members pick up on this theme, and much of the early discussion focuses on their experiences with authorities they do not trust. No one appears displeased with the discussion, and it looks like it might continue for the remainder of the meeting. Using the skills of sessional tuning-in and contracting, what might you as the practitioner do at this point?

The first question you need to ask and try to answer is: What are they working on? Are they working or not working—avoiding their real concerns or working on an important theme in the group process and in their lives? Most likely, they are working on an important theme—their own agenda at this point—as they seem to devote much interest and attention to this discussion. The second important question is: What is the theme or concern they have initiated? In this example, the group members appear to focus on the authority theme. That is, they are sharing attitudes and patterns of perceiving authority (Anderson, 1984a).

The next question rises from this identification of the theme: How does this theme relate to the purpose and goals of this group? If the group is to develop into a mutual-aid system wherein members can help each other, the theme is very relevant. The group appears to reflect in *content* ("crooked politicians and cops") a concern in their *process* (How will authority operate in this group? Can we trust it here?).

If this is the recognized theme from sessional tuning-in, one possible response is as follows: "You seem to want to discuss your concerns about authority rather than the subject of discovering problems in making friends, which seemed relevant at our last meeting . . . I sense this theme is really important to you and may be related to your concerns about my authority in this group. Do you want to continue this discussion and include your thoughts and feelings about me as an authority in this group?" This response initiates sessional contracting that targets the members' agenda, an agenda that is embedded in their discussion of thoughts and feelings about those authorities they confront in their lives.

ELABORATING AND CLARIFYING

All of the models of problem solving in social work explicitly or implicitly note the importance of moving from problem identification to a fuller exploration and understanding of the problem (Compton & Galaway, 1984; Perlman, 1957; Reid, 1978). Elaborating and clarifying reflect these skills for working on clients' or others' concerns.

Elaborating and clarifying are the abilities to explore, draw out, and get the subjective and objective "facts" of the client's story. Students often begin by being hesitant and concerned about privacy and intrusion. They can be awkward about framing questions and fearful that the questions might sound accusing. They may not explore because they are uncertain about how to respond or use the information gained. With time, they should be able to offer support and explanation about the purpose of questions. They should also be able to clarify communications, to realize that messages sent to them and that they send are not necessarily the messages received. Students should learn to help clients elaborate their concerns by moving from general statements to specific expression of others' perceptions, feelings, behavior, and goals; by reaching inside silences through waiting them out and then inquiring or sharing what they might mean; and by using open-ended "what" and "how" questions to determine the meaning of events for clients. Also, they should find themselves using "why" questions and closed questions very infrequently and asking open-ended "how" and "what" questions fairly naturally in exploring, elaborating, and clarifying the facts of the client's story and situation.

Elaborating and clarifying skills further mutual understanding of the experienced realities of clients' situations for ongoing assessment, service planning, and problem solving. At their best, these skills promote mutual understanding—a "standing with" the client in his or her experience of the situation. Elaboration seeks information for this mutual understanding by asking questions designed to move from general statements to specific expression of the other's perceptions and by waiting out and reaching inside silences: "you say you can't talk to your boss about your fears of him (or her); how do you find yourself communicating these when you are face-to-face with him (or her)?"; "Tell me more about how you see this situation"; "What did you say and do and how did this affect the fight you had with your son?"; "I've been sitting here during this silence thinking that you had more you wanted to say about your feelings; am I correct?"; "I wonder what you are thinking and feeling during this silence."

In elaborating, "what" and "how" questions are much preferred to "why" ones. Likewise, open-ended questions work better than closed ones. To understand the person's experience of self-in-situation, and to increase the other's understanding of this interaction, "what" and "how" questions are more appropriate. "Why" questions promote simple explanations and imputing of "causes" to more complex situations. They tend to block rather than enable the understanding useful for acting in the situation. In addition, as Alfred Benjamin (1976) has noted, "why" questions are experienced as accusatory rather than as supportive of and/or challenging to mutual understanding. The child who had to explain misbehavior to a parent who said, "I don't understand; why did you do that?" is still there in the client who is asked, "Why do you let them do this to you?"

Closed-ended questions are those that can be answered "yes" or "no." Such questions as "Do you want to change jobs?", "Are you sure she did this for that reason?" and so on do not promote elaboration. Rather we ask open-ended questions, which cannot be answered "yes" or "no," such as: "What do you now think you want to do about your job?" and "What did you see and hear her do and why do you think she did that?"

Clarifying is closely related to elaborating. It is an important additional step in elaboration. Clarifying establishes what is mutually understood in elaborating. The meaning of elaborations, therefore, is clearly established through sharing what one understands and checking out whether this meaning is accurate for the client or other. The practitioner clarifies by finding ways to say: "I have this understanding of what you've said. How does this understanding relate to yours? How much are we sharing the meaning of what you see, think, and feel about yourself and this situation?"

In group and family situations, the practitioner uses elaborating and clarifying not only to promote his or her and the other's understanding but also understanding among members. For instance, in moving from the general to the specific, we can reach for intermember feelings behind individual member content and seek the relation of members' concerns outside the group or family to what happens within the family or group system. Questions can be directed to the group or family, as well as to the individual members. We can wait for inter-member understanding as they seek elaboration from each other. We can clarify not only the meanings of communications but also for whom messages are intended. We also can clarify whether the messages sent to other members were understood as intended. We can particularly clarify the shared group and family goals embedded in individual members' communications.

EMPATHIZING

Empathy is a generic and central skill of all parts of social work process. Clients' experience of another's understanding of their feelings is basic to the helping relationship. Chapter 6 on helping relationships elaborated on this principle of effective social work practice. The skills of empathy presented in Chapter 6 are also applicable to its use in sustaining the social work process through direct contact in the work phase.

However, in the work phase we use the empathy skills to assure that the discussion is meaningful, motivates clients, and helps them accomplish some relevant aspect of the work. For instance, we use empathy to invite them to invest their discussion with feelings, to help them get in touch with and understand their feelings as related to their situation and choices, and to integrate their perceptions, thoughts, and feelings into their choices and actions on their own behalf.

Thus empathy in this phase has some of the elements of responding to feelings necessary in the beginning of the helping process but also some *additive* elements (Egan, 1975; Hammond, et al., 1977). We reach for *more* feelings, positive and negative; we interpret *deeper* feelings when we put the client's feelings into words; we seek *more* understanding and *deeper* knowledge of the client's feelings as these relate to his or her perceptions, thoughts, and behavior; and in our interactions, we discriminate *more* accurately among the client's feelings and *more* actively and with *more* accurate understanding respond to the meaning of these feelings in his or her life.

Additive empathic skills can expand the client's meaning of the self-in-situation. They increase awareness of content by a deeper understanding of feelings and meanings that are only implied by and less conscious to the client. For example, a reciprocal response to a client who expresses anger at the withdrawal of a close friend would relate to the anger or resentment. An additive response may relate to the more vulnerable and tender feelings of hurt that could lurk just beneath the anger in the client's awareness. When the client increases awareness of *both* the hurt and the anger, he or she may be better able to choose and implement a course of action better suited to his or her needs.

Empathy in the work phase, then, includes not only reaching for more feelings, articulating the other's feelings, and displaying understanding of these feelings, but also interpretive seeking of their meaning. Research supports this critical interpretive nature of deeper, or advanced-level, empathy (Bergin, 1966; Carkhuff, 1969; Shulman, 1971; Speisman, 1959). Carl Rogers (1966, pp. 190–191) promoted this additive, more interpretive empathy when he suggested that we "not merely repeat [the] client's words, concepts, or feelings." Instead, we "seek for the meaning implicit in the present inner experiencing toward which the client's words or concepts point" as we dip "from the pool of implicit meanings just at the edge of the client's awareness." This empathy, as all empathy, involves helping clients to identify their feelings and translate the vague and undefined feelings and experiences into words and ideas. However, it also increases attention to implied deeper feelings and expanding the other's awareness of the meaning of these when these are at the edge of or just beyond this awareness. Hammond and colleagues (1977, pp. 141–152) present seven ways that we can use empathy to expand this underlying meaning. (1) We can assist others to identify relationships among feelings, behavior, and situations and make connections among common themes in these. (2) We can help others see how their beliefs (implicit assumptions, often inaccurate and dysfunctional) about themselves and others affect what they see, feel, and do. (3) We can increase others' awareness of their goals and ideals implicit in their feelings ("You feel ―― because ――, and you wish to ――."). (4) We can sensitize others to their major life themes, which may integrate the patterns in their perceptions, thoughts, and feelings. (5) We can help others recognize the underlying purpose of their behavior and feelings; that is, how these serve the purpose of achieving some goals (security, for instance) at the expense of others (growth, for instance). (6) We can increase others' awareness of nonverbal and postural meanings. (7) We can encourage others to take what responsibility they can for themselves in their situation ("You feel —— because you did not ——.").

Over time in the process with clients or others, students should more readily discriminate among others' feelings and respond with more accurate empathy. Empathic responses demonstrate understanding of clients through verbal and nonverbal expressions of the students' immediate experience of others' emotions. The student can put the client's feelings into words, articulating them slightly ahead of the other; reach for the positive and negative sides of ambivalent feelings; and connect feelings to work by relating them to the client's content and behavior in using services and taking action in the life situations. Progressing in this skill, students learn to understand and trust the underlying process of the client in its purposeful, yet irrational, emotional themes and to promote integration of the rational and irrational components in decision making and choice. They seek empathic understanding of situations in a way that expands the awareness and meaning for the other.

In families and groups, the practitioner's empathy can lead to intermember empathy in their interactions. The research on significant aspects of therapeutic group and family process views this intermember empathy as vital to outcomes (Anderson, 1975, 1978; Carkhuff, 1969; Lieberman et al., 1973; Olson et al., 1983). When members are helped to relate on a feeling level, they tend to connect naturally to each other with empathy and to deepen their ability to care about and help each other (Anderson, 1978). In families, this empathy is the prerequisite to giving and receiving love (Olson et al., 1983). Therefore, the use of this skill in families and groups also includes reaching for intermember feelings and understanding and seeking the shared meanings of these feelings in how members experience and relate to each other.

SHARING OWN FEELINGS

Sharing one's own feelings is the skill of presenting one's self to the client or other as a real human being. Research on the practitioner's sharing feelings (often under such synonyms as *self-disclosure*, *genuineness, authenticity*, or *transparency*) attests to the importance of this skill in practice and its special appropriateness to the work phase of social work process (Carkhuff, 1969; Dyer, 1969; Shulman, 1977). These studies find that, like empathy, the sharing of personal thoughts and feelings is a skill that correlates strongly both with developing a working relationship and with the actual outcome of help. It extends both the process and content for work. While experiencing the practitioner more as a person increases the human ties of the relationship process, the client often finds real help in the data provided by the practitioner's thoughts and feelings.

As students progress in the social work process with clients, they should be able to use the shared sense of purpose and general function as direction and protection for relating more fully as a person and less in a role. Then they can share their own feelings more spontaneously and genuinely with clients. These personal thoughts and feelings can relate to clients' themes or to the practitioner's own relationship process in the encounter. This includes support for clients' strengths through expression of belief in their ability to take some step or get through a difficult time.

Research provides a number of guidelines for how to share one's own feelings most effectively with clients. First, the feelings should be consistent with the purpose and function of the work and relevant to assessed client needs, as well as not detracting from the current focus (as in "You think you're having trouble with your mother-in-law; let me tell you about mine!"). Second, the feelings that seem most effective for increasing the client's exploration and understanding are those that have been consistently experienced, not expressed, since the beginning phase of the relationship. We share these positive and negative feelings most constuctively when they are tied realistically to the relationship and its purpose (not transferred from past relationships, not based on physical or sexual attractions, and so on) and related to behavior. A useful format is, "When you do this (describing the persistent action), I feel ―― (describing your curent inner experiencing)."

Third, we experience a range of emotions over time. For example, we may be aware of conflicting or ambivalent feelings. We express these most effectively when we share the conflict and seek its resolution in our relationship to the client or other. It is not unusual when we feel anger toward a client to feel guilt simultaneously with the anger. While we may feel so angry we want to strike out at the other, we can best express the range of our own feelings in such words as: "When you storm into my office like this, demanding to see me when I'm with someone else, I get so mad at you. I really don't want to feel such strong anger toward you. I'd like to try to resolve this. Let's discuss this." Or instead of telling a client simply, "I'm irritated because both you and I know that your drinking is a major problem for you and you've been avoiding discussing it," we might do better to share our multiple feelings: "I'm aware of feeling displeased about our work because for some time you've avoided talking about your drinking. Yet I'm also aware that your avoidance in part relates to me, and I'm concerned about introducing this topic because I know you may resent me for bringing it up. But it seems to be a real source of trouble for you, and I feel I let you down when I hold back and avoid this with you."

Fourth, directly related to the above, the most helpful feelings, positive and negative, to share seem to be those about the work together. These include the excitement at the client's efforts in his or her own behalf, the warmth of the support as the client faces the pain of struggle, the anger at untapped potential resources both in the client and in the environment, the respect for the client's choices and abilities we have come to appreciate, and so on.

DEMANDING WORK

Ambivalence and some resistance to work is practically inevitable during this phase of the social work process. Clients or others simultaneously experience wishes and fears for change in themselves and/or their situation. A part of them wishes for and moves toward understanding and adaptive growth. The other part resists, pulls back, and fears what is perceived as a difficult challenge.

Lawrence Shulman (1984, p. 78) wrote about this dynamic:

> Work often requires discussing painful subjects, experiencing difficult feelings, recognizing one's own contribution to the problem, taking responsibility for one's actions, and lowering long-established defenses . . . [It] may require a client to tackle a difficult task, to confront someone directly, or to put off immediate satisfactions. Whatever the difficulty involved, a client will show some degree of ambivalence. The amount of movement towards the work (the strength) as compared with movement away from the work (the resistance) will vary with each individual and the nature of the problem.

This ambivalence makes demanding work a most critical skill in this phase of the process. Demanding work is a special use of the balance of support and challenge—a skill covered in Chapter 6. As such, demanding work is not just a single skill or even a single set of skills. Almost all the skills in this phase demand work, if only in that their use reveals the message that you are there to help others work in their own behalf. However, a number of useful procedures help to support this work and challenge resistance to it more directly. As William Schwartz (1971, p. 11) proposed:

> The [practitioner] also represents what might be called the *demand for work*, in which role [he or she] tries to enforce not only . . . what we are here for but the conditions of work as well. This demand is, in fact, the only one the [practitioner] makes—not for certain perceived results, or approved attitudes, or learned behaviors, but for work itself. That is, [the practitioner] is continually challenging the client to address [oneself] resolutely and with energy to what he or she came to do.

The specific procedures for demanding work in the face of ambivalence and resistance include partializing clients' concerns; pointing out the illusion of work; confronting discrepancies between clients' words and deeds; and dealing with the authority theme by asking for negative feedback regarding the way clients are experiencing the work. These procedures pitch to clients' strengths in working toward their wishes, while relieving the fears behind resistances.

For instance, partializing clients' concerns helps to motivate them in situations they experience as overwhelming. We have probably all been in situations where we faced many demands all at once. We must finish writing a report, meet an appointment, get a haircut, take our car to the garage, and make three important telephone calls—all in one morning. Is it any wonder we might oversleep that morning, as if sleep would make such an overwhelming world go away? Then we find it even more overwhelming and potentially immobilizing as we now have less time to accomplish these tasks. In such a situation we could go back to bed for a nap after breakfast or we could partialize our problem, beginning with rescheduling tasks throughout the day or the week and working on those that take less of the time we have available now and/or those that we think absolutely must be done this morning.

We provide clients the support to manage and the challenge not to give up on tackling difficult problems when we help to partialize their concerns. This means seeking for the parts of the problem that can be dealt with one small step at a time. We help the client reduce the potentially overwhelming problem to smaller, more manageable proportions. The client's sense of urgency and our mutual understanding of capacity usually combine to highlight these parts and steps to take in partializing the client's concerns.

Pointing out the illusion of work involves detecting the pattern of illusion over a particular period of time and confronting the client with this observation. Work is marked by talk that is purposeful, consistent with the contract, invested with feeling, facing the challenge of life themes, and especially facing what others perceive as taboos. When we do not "feel" this talk in our guts, we need to suspect the illusion of work. Actually, the "illusion" is most often a "collusion," wherein we and the client tacitly agree to ignore our long periods of talk that are not purposeful, invested with feeling, or confronting the reality that has brought us together. When we have joined the ritual of resistance that comes from talking much and saying little, we can face the illusion in ourselves and risk challenging it by pointing it out to the client. We are ready to say: "We agreed together to work on this and we now seem to be avoiding the tough stuff. How come? What might we be afraid of here?"

Confronting discrepancies between clients' words and deeds can also challenge the illusion of work; for instance, confronting a married couple with these statements: "You know, when we started out, you both said you wanted help with how you get along with each other. It seems to me, however, that all we've talked about so far is how you get along with other people. You seem to be avoiding the real need in our work. How come? What seems to stop you from talking about your relationship to each other?" The best of confrontation comes from a real understanding of and support for the difficulty of work and the invitation to face the reality of discrepancies between what one says and what one does in relation to the work. Much of this discrepancy is natural. It reflects the ambivalences—the wishes and fears simultaneously motivating behaviors. Therefore, as a tool to increase the other's awareness of these ambivalences, confronting discrepancies should be as understanding and nonthreatening as possible. Whenever we tear at others' defenses, tear away others' masks, we will hear the rip. In fact, the confrontation here is most effective as additive *empathy*. That is, it reaches behind the "wish" intentions of the words to the "fear" intentions of the deeds whenever one talks about wanting to act and does not.

All of these procedures are related to dealing with the authority theme: the ambivalences the client inevitably experiences toward the practitioner, who is at once nurturing and supporting, demanding and challenging, and both a real person and one with a position in an often powerful social institution. Sharing such honest feelings with authorities is a major taboo in our culture. On the other hand, the withholding of these feelings can be a potent block to the work. Dealing with this authority theme requires reaching for the client's feedback, especially negative feedback, about the practitioner's role. Thus this obstacle to the work can be effectively dealt with by clarifying why we have done certain things, sharing where we are coming from, apologizing for mistakes we might have made, and expressing our concern for and investment in the other and the work.

PROVIDING INFORMATION

Providing information is a skill so ubiquitous in social work practice that it is often taken for granted. We are often involved in sharing a variety of information with clients or others throughout the social work process—the nature of our agency's services, our understanding of the client's concerns and feelings, some knowledge we think helpful to the other, and so on. During this phase such information can be crucial to clients' work, and it is important to attend to the information we provide and how we share it.

This sharing can include our own ideas about the client and his or her (or their) situation, our own values and beliefs that relate to the concerns being addressed, facts that add to the knowledge for decision making, ideas we have about ways to approach problematic situations (commonly called "advice"), and ideas about resources to meet specific needs, or "referrals." Whenever we provide such information, we would do well to remember some basic principles of communication. First, we should try to communicate this information in clients' language, in terms they can understand. Second, we should try to remember that information given is not synonymous with information received. That is, we need to check out what the other understood about what we communicated: "I want to be sure I was able to be clear in what I said. Would you please repeat in your own words what you heard me say?" Third, when we share our own values and beliefs or give advice, we should make clear that the information represents just one perspective—our own—and is not intended to be the answer for anyone: "I can't say this would work for you. I am not you. But I would likely ———." Fourth, a key factor in communicating is timing. One reason such information is more pertinent to the work phase is because by this time we have gained the client's trust. Timing also involves following significant leads from the other. When we follow the other's presentation of need or actual request ("How would you handle this?"), the client is more ready to receive this information with trust in our desire to help.

Students at first may find it difficult to provide information in language clients or others can understand. They may be reluctant to share their own ideas, values, and beliefs, feeling they are imposing judgments. Or they might share these too prematurely—not timed to client's need, readiness, or request. With experience, students learn to provide information meaningfully. At the appropriate time, they share data, facts, ideas, values, and/or beliefs relevant to clients' concerns and otherwise unavailable to them.

A special case of providing information is making referrals. This requires helping clients or others identify needs and resources, exploring their feelings and expectations about resources, and giving clear information. Students should check out a resource and know eligibility, the services actually provided, and the clientele served. They should be able to discuss clients' or others' previous experiences and feelings about similar resources, including their hopes, motivation, and personal priorities. There should be follow-up feedback from clients about their experience and its usefulness in order to clear up any misunderstandings in the information provided. In sharing any information, students should avoid giving advice or information in general terms; they should check out the meanings received in communicated data. Also, they should learn to qualify their information as one perspective—theirs.

USING PRACTICE MODELS

As practitioners engage in generalist tasks during intervention in the work phase, they face the need to use specific skills for influencing individuals, families, groups, organizations, and communities as well as the generic skills of social work process. The conscious use of practice models informs these specific principles and skills. In another source (Anderson, 1981), I present the variety of prevailing models. At a minimum in beginning practice, we need a theory base for each of the major systems through which we work: individuals, families, small groups, organizations, and communities. It is not within the scope of this book to present all of these potential formal practice models. However, as we study them and select those we wish to learn to use in more depth, we can develop a repertoire of approaches to inform the specific skills essential for generalist practice. These approaches combine with our understanding and use of the generic interactional model in our theories-in-use (Argyris & Schön, 1975).

The conscious use of practice models in our theories-in-use provides such guidelines as how to compose a group and enable its process in behalf of members; how to begin a meeting with marital partners (or other adult partners in a family), with a parent and child, or with the family as a whole; what strategies to use for organizational change; how to influence a community to change an existing service delivery system or to create a new one; and so on. In short, we have guidelines for why we are doing what we do and how we can best do it to accomplish the goals of our practice. As we consciously use this theory in our practice, we can consciously, even systematically, evaluate the theory and our use of it. We gain knowledge of which approaches to practice work best and which not so well. We learn more about which clients benefit most and how these models relate to particular needs and client systems' goals. This evaluation of why we did what we did with our colleagues, supervisors, consultants, and clients increases our competence in using practice models.

Students should be able to use identified practice models and to articulate the theories-in-use that base and shape their understanding and action. Over time, they will become selective about the clients who might benefit from their use of particular models and clear about the relationship of the approach to clients' needs and goals. They will be able to explain the purpose of the approach to clients and supervisors and get feedback.

At first students may be spontaneous and intuitive without understanding the "whys" and "hows" of what they do or could do in particular situations. In the early stages, they often need directions and prescriptions in their move toward greater independence in thinking things through, based on practice models, for themselves. Initial efforts to apply particular models in practice situations can be awkward and self-conscious. Eventually, practice models can guide students' activities in concert with spontaneity, intuitiveness, and feeling.

This practice theory minimally includes the generic interactional approach and models for work with individuals, families, small groups, organizations, and communities. With time, students can become selective about the variety of methods (e.g., individual, family, and group counseling; brokerage; advocacy; coordination; networking; and organizational and community development) and the approaches within methods (e.g., problem solving, task-centered work, crisis intervention, developmental group work, experiential family counseling, assertiveness training, locality development, etc.) that best address particular goals and targets in generalist practice. They will be familiar with a variety of methods and have the ability to use selective models and build on these. They will be able to explain the purpose of the method and model clearly and get feedback from client systems, colleagues, and supervisors about their efficacy.

CONCLUSION

The foundation competence of this chapter is *the ability to sustain social work process through direct client contact in the work phase.* The sustaining of work in this phase requires a set of seven generic skills. These are: sessional tuning-in and contracting, elaborating and clarifying, empathizing, sharing own feelings, demanding work, providing information, and using practice models. Through use of this competence and its skills, both social workers and clients attend to the parallel tasks necessary to improve the interaction of those served with their environment in the specific situations for which service was needed.

SUGGESTED LEARNING EXERCISE 8-1: DIRECT WORK-PHASE SKILLS

Take the situation used in the last chapter—Suggested Learning Experience 7-1—and summarize the presenting themes and your responses during three contacts in the work phase. Use the Educational Outcome Competence Rating form in the Appendix to assess your use of this overall competency and each of the seven skills. This is Competence #4 on the scale.

For any skills in which you rate yourself less than "unevenly developed," assess what has prevented you from more effective use. Consider obstacles within yourself, the helping situation, and the interaction between you and the situation. Develop a plan to address how you could work more on the effective use of these relevant skills.

9 Competence #5: Work Phase: Indirect Intervention

There is the story of the frog used in a college biology class. It seems that some professors have constructed a rather cruel experiment to demonstrate how organisms use their natural potentials and how these potentials may limit them in adapting to changes in the environment. In this ecological experiment, the frog is placed in a pail of water being heated on a stove. As the water heats, students can observe the actual physical changes in the frog as it adapts to maintain its body temperature. When the water reaches the boiling point and the frog has exhausted its furious adaptations, it dies. It appears that in its natural thrust to adapt continually to changes in the environment, the frog never thinks to alter this environment—by hopping out of the pail.

In social work we must help people alter their environments as well as aspects of themselves. We are always concerned about the "pail" as well as the person in our interactional perspective.

This chapter focuses on the skills in generalist direct practice that modify the interactions between people and their environments through attention to significant aspects of the environment. The overall competency concerns our ability to mediate between clients and resource systems during the work phase. Resource systems here refer primarily to the people on whom the client is dependent to meet needs and on the organizations designed to meet needs when the natural, less formal systems of people in the client's life break down or lack necessary resources. This chapter deals with mediating through indirect work.

In the interactional approach, mediating is the major function of all of the competencies and skills. This includes mediating between the client and the client's situation, between the client and agency, between

187

the client and others in his or her situation or as potential resources to meet needs, and between the client and the community. The first step of this mediation is to enable reciprocal interaction among the relevant parties. This includes connecting people with family members, peers, and others who share common needs and potential common goals, as well as organizations that have resources to meet assessed needs. William Schwartz (1961) saw this mediation as helping clients "negotiate" these resource systems. The first step in linking is one of enabling natural connections with resources. The second step may require more formal brokerage. In this referral and brokerage, clients are linked with resource systems, especially formal organizations, through the practitioner's influence with people in these systems—other staff, teachers, supervisors, and so on. The third step, if enabling and brokering do not work, is advocacy, which uses confrontation and social and/or legal pressure to achieve services or resources for the client. In this aspect of mediating, we take the side of our client against the system to bring about reciprocity in their interaction.

Thus two major skills constitute this mediating competency: linking and advocacy. Linking entails specific actions to bring together clients and formal and informal resource people in behalf of both clients and the resource system. Among the techniques for this linking with informal resources, or significant others in the client's life, are mediation and networking. A major methodology for linking to formal resource systems is referral. When clients' basic rights are violated in the interaction with potential service systems, advocacy becomes the primary skill we need to bring to this mediating work. This chapter presents these skills, techniques, and methodologies.

LINKING

Evidence is overwhelming and convincing that our survival and growth as human beings depend on human contact and support. Mutual aid and support are the primary keys to mental health and competence (Caplan & Killilea, 1976; Gottlieb, 1981). Support systems are the "continuing interactions with another individual, a network, a group, or an organization that provide individuals with opportunities for feedback about themselves and for validation of their expectations about others" (Caplan & Killilea, 1976, p. 4). They promote our growth by serving as buffers against stress and disease. This support comes from significant others: (1) helping us mobilize resources and master our emotional burdens, (2) sharing our tasks, and (3) providing extra supplies of money, material, time, tools, skills, and cognitive guidance to improve our managing of situations. Helping individuals cope more effectively with target problems in a way that increases adaptive growth requires a number of social work activities outside of immediate action with the client—all designed to establish ongoing environmental support systems.

Linking is especially significant in services to special populations who have experienced institutionalized oppression. Blacks, women, Asian Americans, Hispanics, and others survive and buffer the assaults of oppression through strong social supports and networks. In these situations, links to such social supports are not only strongly needed, but these networks are also among the strongest potential resources for services. Mutual aid is present and builds quickly when such interdependence in taking on the enemies of oppression exists. This common ground and the roots for mutual aid that grow in it make for fertile resources when extended families are linked to the needs of black children, for instance. Social supports and networks are fruitful resources when women join together in common concerns or when one looks for significant resources within ethnic minority communities. Two especially important methodologies for this linking are mediation and networking.

Mediation

Conflict with others is among the most stressful life events in the etiology of various illnesses and in difficulties in adaptive coping (Cobb, 1976; Dohrenwend & Dohrenwend, 1980). Interpersonal problems and conflict, involving family problems, divorce, child custody arrangements, and so on, account for a large majority of cases that social workers confront. Other stressors, such as landlord–tenant disputes, neighborhood conflicts, and merchant–consumer disagreements, often produce the anxiety and depression that fester and result in more serious problems. Social supports tend to break down in such conflict situations. Mediation is a set of conflict-resolution activities designed for intervention in such situations (Chandler, 1985).

Mediation has been defined as "solicitation of an agreement between two or more disputing parties by an agreed-upon third party" (Witty, 1980, p. 1). Mediation is a process that encourages two (or more) people in conflict to identify and communicate their needs and interests and helps them negotiate their own settlement by agreeing to a solution. In mediation, the processes of self-determination and social justice are paramount. Disputants are given the opportunity and support to create their own just and practical settlement. Unlike traditional counseling or therapy, this process does not target underlying personality dynamics. Rather, mediation helps participants identify and define their own needs and those of the other participants. Conflict resolution explicitly *empowers* participants with a problem—whether it is an interpersonal dispute, a family disturbance, a group dysfunction, or a neighborhood conflict—to find a mutually agreed-upon solution.

The mediation process is based on the techniques of three distinct phases (Chandler, 1985). These are (1) the forum phase, (2) the strategic-planning phase, and (3) the problem-solving phase.

The *forum phase* encourages and facilitates the participants' identification of their own interests and needs and communication of these to each other and to the mediator. The mediator begins with an exploration of the issues and gauges the appropriateness of the conflict for mediation. If appropriate, the mediator explains the mediation process and secures an agreement from the parties for his or her involvement. The mediator then begins information-gathering activities, which include both face-to-face interactions with all parties and/or individual, confidential conferences with one party at a time. This process is quite similar to the practitioner's assessment process. The social worker as mediator asks open-ended questions to elicit information from the participants and frequently acknowledges and reflects back the feelings and concern he or she is hearing.

In the *strategic-planning phase*, the practitioner examines all of the information gathered, reviews the natural history of the conflict, and examines the issues, positions, interests, and needs of the parties involved. This analytic stage is a conscious, strategic step in the mediation process in which the mediator may meet with the parties in private individual conferences and/or check with the participants if some issues remain unclear or the mediator feels that an issue has not been fully explored. Then he or she begins to develop a design, or specific plan of action, asking the disputants to become actively involved in the process.

For the social work practitioner, this stage is most similar to the intervention planning stage. However, in mediation, the process involves working with the disputants on practical solutions by preparing for a task called "principled negotiation" (Fisher & Ury, 1983). The principled-negotiation method of problem solving focuses on finding the basic interests of each participating party and the best options for both. By encouraging people to consider fair standards and examine their needs in the context of the other person's (or persons') needs, the social worker encourages a gradual consensus to emerge without "all the transactional costs of digging into a position only to have to dig yourself out" (Fisher & Ury, 1983, p. 14). The task at this point includes trying to get each side to develop a number of alternative ways to meet their own needs and the needs of the other participants. An example of this shift in a divorce situation might be the subtle change from "I want the livingroom sofa" to "I need a nice sofa for my apartment." At times during this phase the social worker as mediator becomes the agent of reality in the sense that he or she may help each side see the consequences of not finding a solution to the problem.

In the *problem-solving phase*, the practitioner works with the parties to improve the definition of the potential solutions to the problem. Through a variety of techniques, such as joint meetings, private conferences, and shuttle diplomacy, the social worker as mediator helps the parties negotiate their own resolution and draft a specific agreement. Usually this agreement is a specific, written solution that the disputants have developed themselves.

The mediator facilitates the communication and oversees the process, but the content is determined by the parties themselves. Once a positive climate has been established, the parties ready themselves to negotiate an agreement. The role of the social worker as mediator is to conduct "joint advocacy" and create an atmosphere of agreement. By seeking common ground to build the elements of an agreement, the mediation process begins to establish the individuals' sense of belonging to a family, group, or community.

This mediation methodology stresses mutual agreements in which both sides win. Rather than the adjudicative system with complex rules of procedures, mediation is an integrative and conciliatory process. The social worker as mediator is a nonjudgmental convenor who emphasizes the bonds among the participants and encourages broad discussion of the issues so that all viewpoints are expressed. This system for conflict resolution often prevents future conflict and stress for those interested in maintaining and enhancing their relationships.

Mediation has been proved successful with a wide variety of people. For instance, mediation works to solve disagreements among family members in parent–child and other domestic disputes. It clarifies issues for divorcing couples, and has been used extensively in child custody cases. It has also been used successfully to resolve disputes between students and teachers, teachers and school staff, and schools and parents (especially in cases of mainstreaming disabled children; see Gallant, 1982). Research also suggests that interpersonal conflicts among people involved in ongoing relationships are very amenable to negotiation and the possibility of compromise, since it is in the interests of both parties to arrive at a joint settlement (Tomasic & Feeley, 1982). For example, Tomasic and Feeley (1982) found that mediation is an effective and satisfactory method of resolving many types of minor interpersonal disputes. They reviewed more than 4,000 cases handled through mediation and found that 82% of the cases resulted in a successful resolution and agreement; 45% of these disputes involved family members or relatives.

Mediation Example

Consider the following case for mediation. You are the social worker in your county's Domestic Relations Office.

Carol and Bob have been sharing custody of 7-year-old June since their divorce 3 years ago. Carol married Ted a year ago, and Bob has been living with Alice for the last 2 years. Ted has called you to set up an appointment at the strong suggestion of a police officer who asked him to leave home after Carol made several calls for assistance when he had become violent. Carol became very frightened when she and Ted exchanged blows again during their last argument. She filed a restraining order to keep Ted from seeing her, from returning to their house, or even from telephoning. Ted had called Child Protective Services and said that Carol was neglecting June, leaving her alone for long periods of time and making her stay in her room for long periods of time when Carol was home. You talk with both Ted and Carol individually and find them receptive to mediation—Ted because he wishes removal of the restraining order and Carol because she wants Ted to stop threatening her.

In the first session, you learn that Ted's agenda is to keep the marriage together; Carol's is to end the marriage and all further contact with Ted. You learn that there have been previous instances of domestic violence in which the police were called. Also, Ted has filed reports of neglect with Child Protection Services (CPS) before. Agency personnel viewed these as spiteful, without merit, and therefore unfounded. This time, however, they investigated and filed a neglect petition with the court because June had witnessed the violence between Ted and Carol. Also, Carol had gotten previous restraining orders. She had filed for divorce several months ago, then withdrawn her petition. She reports that Bob, June's biological father, had filed for sole custody in the past but they had reached an agreement outside of court when Carol assured Bob that she was divorcing Ted and the violence would stop. Carol's greatest worry now is that she will be declared an unfit mother and that Bob will receive custody of June.

This first session reveals the difficulty in establishing a fully satisfactory negotiation by both parties. Ted is very interested in his relationship with Carol and wants to stay married no matter what. He is extremely frustrated and continues to contact Carol in violation of the restraining order—even though he says he does not want to go to jail.

Carol realizes from previous restraining orders how little protection they provide for her and women in situations like hers. She has changed the locks on her doors, as well as her telephone number, and is considering moving. However, Ted knows where she works and where June attends school and thus can maintain contact with both of them. Carol is highly motivated for mediation in this breakup of the relationship so she can avoid further harassment.

How might you proceed in using mediation with Carol and Ted? What is best for June? How can further violence be prevented? How might you need to involve the police, the court, and/or the Child Protective Services' social workers in this mediation?

Behind the conflicting interests, both want to continue their relationship with June (admittedly for Ted this is motivated by wanting to keep Carol in his life). You want especially to focus on June's needs in a way that prevents further violence. The goal here is more a successful outcome in June's nurturing and in ending the violence than a completed agreement between parties. You may ask them to develop a written agreement that focuses on what is best for June and what each of them plans to do both to assure what is best for June and to prevent further violence.

One caveat in this mediation, as in all mediation in conflicts that lead to domestic violence, is to make clear your own position against this violence. Both parties need to know that while you work with them toward enabling a full hearing for each in their negotiations, you find the battering of wives, children, parents, or anyone else intolerable and will use the full power of the law to halt such behavior. Here, mediation becomes full advocacy for the victim of violence.

Networking

Networking, or professional activities for work with "helping networks," has been informally used for many years (Froland et al., 1981). Natural helping networks (Collins & Pancoast, 1976) existed without professional intervention much longer. A great deal of evidence suggests that friends, neighbors, and relatives help each other (Campbell et al., 1976), volunteer their services for the sake of the community (Caplan & Killilea, 1976), and network as community members to develop and protect their communities (Warren, 1981). More recently, social work has evolved a methodology for informal and formal networking (Collins & Pancoast, 1976; Maguire, 1983).

Networking is "a purposeful process of linking three or more people together while establishing connections and chain reactions among them" (Maguire, 1983, p. 25). Strategies for networking evolve from research that clearly analyzes the structure, interactional patterns, and function of intimate, socially supportive network relationships. This analysis suggests specific strategies that strengthen networks where they exist, develop them when they are needed, and avoid intervention when they are working. This research implies that particular variables are significant in understanding their purposes, functions, and structure and their relation to health and mental health.

The purpose and function of networks are varied (Maguire, 1983):

1. Small, dense (frequent contact), culturally homogeneous, dispersed networks with strong ties maintain social identity in the midst of major life crises and stress.
2. High density and homogeneity of a network should increase the likelihood that network members are aware of and discuss their problems and agree about the best means for providing emotional support.
3. A more widely dispersed, larger network is more likely to supply a wider variety of material supplies and resources. (A high degree of density helps as well, because it supports communication within the network.)
4. When new knowledge or information is required, networks with some weak ties that bridge other networks seem best. One or more weak ties to different types of networks increase the chance of encompassing different opinions and new information, since close-knit personal networks tend to share similar opinions and information.
5. Networks for new social contacts can be established outside of an individual's close networks, but the reliability of the new social contacts is more likely to increase if they are first screened through one's personal or immediate social network.

Process within networks is also extremely varied (Maguire, 1983):

1. Networks are formed through "choice constraints" based on the relation of individual preferences to limited alternatives and resources.

2. Networks are maintained and changed in order to maximize rewards and minimize costs.
3. In friendship networks, intimacy, rather than length, increases the possibility of their maintenance.
4. The greater the multiplexity of roles in a network (friends, relatives, co-workers, neighbors, similar association members), the slightly less the intimacy of the relationship in network links.
5. Within roles, networks of relatives and childhood friends tend to be more intimate.
6. Kinship and work networks tend to be more constrained and to produce high density and low similarity.
7. Childhood ties and associations from more voluntary contacts are lower in density and higher in similarity than kinship networks.

Network structure takes various forms:

1. People diagnosed as "normal" tend to have 20 to 30 people in their personal network.
2. People diagnosed as "neurotic" have 10 to 12 others in their personal network and relate in a nonsystematic way to their networks when compared with "normals."
3. "Psychotics" and hospitalized psychiatric patients have the fewest contacts (4 to 5), although their networks appear quite dense (consisting almost entirely of family members); they also tend not to reciprocate support, guidance, and help.

In general, a great deal of research establishes the importance of social support networks in health and mental health (for a review, see Caplan, 1974). Social support networks are mediators of life stress and prevent serious mental and physical illnesses. In marriage, this moderation seems more true for men than for women. Women, whether single or married, derive their support primarily from friendship networks. Not only are rates of mental illness higher for men who are not married and for women without a close friendship network (whether married or single), but treatment prognosis is correlated. Single men and isolated women have a greater chance of improving less or becoming worse in mental health treatment.

In social work practice, networking can involve individual networking in intervention, family networking, networking with self-help groups, and case-management networking with organizations and communities. Generally, this networking involves three generic phases: (1) identification, (2) analysis, and (3) linking.

1. *Identification.* This phase identifies the potential for networking by gathering information useful for a network analysis. Potential personal or other resources are identified in relation to size, basis of relationship, capabilities, specific resources, and level of willingness to help the client.

2. *Analysis.* The second phase involves network analysis, or mapping. The analysis addresses frequency of contact, direction, duration, and intensity. The focus is on the strength of particular ties in the network in order to maximize their effectiveness and minimize the amount of time and energy required of network members (identified in the first phase).

3. *Linking.* In this phase the practitioner and client decide together who in the network to involve and how to involve them. This includes determining whom the client will involve, whom the worker might contact, and whom they both might contact together, as well as how this contact will be made (in person, by phone, or through the mail). Then the client may rehearse this plan. Finally, the plan for linking is implemented.

Networking Example

Consider how aspects of linking through networking might be used in the following direct-service situation (Anderson, 1981). Dora Down has eight children. Four are in school and four are preschool-aged. Ms. Down is having difficulty with her children and has become increasingly depressed since the birth of her last child 6 months ago. She has been keeping Dawn, her oldest child, home from school to help her care for the preschool children.

The school social worker has worked with the family because of the excessive absence of Dawn. In this work, the school social worker has referred Ms. Down to the neighborhood youth center for which you work.

Apart from the information you received from the school social worker, your earlier home visits with Ms. Down reveal that:

1. She feels overburdened by the menial chores of caring for so many toddlers.
2. She feels unproductive and uncreative.
3. She has no significant contact with other adults and desires such contact.
4. Her relationship with her husband has suffered.

In addition, your ecological assessment of Ms. Down's current interaction with her environment reveals that:

1. She does not have the resources to hire a caretaker to relieve her of the constant burden of child care.
2. The community has failed to provide a system of daycare centers available to all its members.
3. She perceives society and her husband as defining the role of women as constant caretakers of children and feels guilty because she is not fulfilled in this role.
4. She feels unable to cope with present family demands and perceives this lack of capacity as related to her own unhappy childhood experiences.

In your direct work with Ms. Down, you and she discussed these needs in relation to several possible resources. Together, you recognized that you could not change her childhood experiences, although Ms. Down wishes this were possible. Rather, you can promote her perceived capability and concomitant self-esteem by relieving her burden of constant child care, extending her role as a woman and her sense of self as a person, and developing a supportive social network for her. You determine the first step in this service plan is to secure some type of daycare service, even though no such service is currently available. You check with your agency and other community groups about the possibility of establishing a daycare program for Ms. Down and other mothers with similar needs. Your agency has limited financial resources. Several local church groups were willing to devote time and space to a daycare project, but they did not have funds for starting one. One church group had obtained federal funds and is planning to open a nonprofit daycare center within a year, but Ms. Down and her neighbors needed help immediately. *Ms. Down and her neighbors—* herein lies a significant key for networking in this situation.

How might you use networking to develop a resource to meet Ms. Down's needs as well as those of her neighbors? One possible network would be a cooperative daycare facility established by Ms. Down and her neighbors. You and she already know many neighborhood women with a need for daycare. They, like Ms. Down, are already involved in your agency's service through your work with them. As you discuss this possibility with Ms. Down, she gains enthusiasm about the idea and agrees to let you contact the people whose names you gave her to say that she would be telephoning them.

Five women attend the first meeting at Ms. Down's house. All of them commit themselves to work toward forming a cooperative day-care center. They decide to care for each other's children in their own homes on a daily volunteer basis and to appoint a daily secretary to keep track of the volunteered time. This decision is a deliberate attempt to keep everyone involved as an important and equal part of the group network. You are there as a resource to clarify communication, comment on their evolving group process, and furnish information on organizational tasks and child-care concerns.

In their second meeting, the co-op network decides that each member will volunteer for extra child-care duties 1 day per week. If a mother uses the service, she will tell the secretary the number of hours she left her children and with whom. The mother then is to spend the same amount of time caring for children of any mother in the co-op. Each mother also agrees to serve as secretary 1 day per week.

After a week of operation, the women realize that having a different secretary every day is causing confusion in record keeping. They decide that each will serve as secretary for a week and then turn the records over to the next person.

You encourage the group to set its own policies during weekly meetings instead of depending on you. As they gain confidence and skill, you lessen your involvement in the network and meet with them (only when asked) as a consultant.

As the co-op develops, the mothers also begin to meet as a support group. One of their major concerns becomes raising their consciousness as women and helping each other deal with oppression in the way their roles are defined. This mediation in Ms. Down's situation, through linking her to a cooperative network of neighbors, relieves her burdensome responsibilities *and* increases her self-esteem and consciousness as a woman striving to be more fully the person she was meant to become.

Referral

The skills for linking clients to existing formal resources, called "referral," is a three-step process: (1) locating the appropriate resource, (2) connecting the client to the resource, and (3) following-up and evaluating its effectiveness. Locating and selecting the resource involves a clear statement of the need; an investigation of the nature, operations, and quality of available resources in the community; and the exploration of the resource options and their consequences (including the "doing nothing" option) for the client.

Connecting the client to the resource requires skills for initial linking and for assuring the connection. Initial linking may best proceed in five steps (Weissman, 1976):

1. Giving the information to the other for contacting the resource. This works best when people already know what they need but have had difficulty locating the appropriate resource.
2. Providing the other with the name of a specific person to contact at the resource. This tactic may not work if the person specified is not available when the resource is contacted.
3. Drafting a brief written statement with the other to explain to the resource what the other wants. This helps when the problem seems complex and not easily defined.
4. Having the other call the resource while the practitioner is there.
5. Getting a family member, relative, friend, or maybe even the social worker to accompany the other when special problems are anticipated.

Techniques for strengthening the connections include:

1. Having the other call back to report on what happened during the initial referral contact.
2. Calling, with the other's approval, the resource to get reports on the progress of the referral.
3. Meeting with the other both before and after the initial referral contact.
4. Meeting with the other intermittently during the period in which he or she is involved at the resource.

The following-up and evaluation skill considers (1) whether the other is getting what he or she wants from the resource; (2) whether the problem is on the way toward amelioration or resolution; and (3) how the resource may serve in future linking through referral. This evaluation requires such contacts as checking with the other and the resource.

ADVOCACY

Advocacy as a concept has a long social work tradition. The history of social work is peopled by those who championed social victims and fought for human rights. However, advocacy as an operationalized skill for direct-service social workers lacks definitive development through this rich history. For instance, definitions of advocacy vary (Sunley, 1983), and its use has not been tested empirically. As Irwin Epstein (1981) has noted, "No empirical studies of social work advocacy have been published. . . . The literature in advocacy is confined to exhortations pro and con and to descriptive case studies" (p. 5). In his exploratory study, Epstein found two types of advocacy, consistent with the sequence proposed in Robert Sunley's (1983) work: case and cause (or class). Case advocacy targets unresponsive systems in behalf of a single person, while cause (class) advocacy operates in behalf of a number of people who are victimized by a particular system. In practice, Epstein found less than half of the advocacy to include specific efforts to develop clients' skills for self-advocacy. Also, the definition of the skill components of effective advocacy varied greatly, although there is some general agreement on the importance of acquiring specific knowledge about the interaction of clients and relevant systems, developing a planned strategy for influencing this interaction in behalf of the client, giving advice to the client about how to negotiate the system, and evaluating and following up on advocacy interventions.

In theory, NASW's Ad Hoc Committee on Advocacy (1969) defined case advocacy as "actively fighting on the side of the client to help meet needs, realize hopes, and exercise rights" (p. 17). The Family Service Association (FSA) (Manser, 1973) originally added cause advocacy to the definition in considering advocacy as a "professional service designed to improve life conditions for people by harnessing direct and expert knowledge of . . . needs with the commitment to action and the application of skills to produce the necessary community change" (p. 3). These definitions imply the risk involved in advocacy with the powerful in behalf of the less powerful. A recent conceptualization of advocacy incorporates this power differential, proposing it as "an attempt, having greater than zero probability of success, by an individual or group to make a decision that would not have been made otherwise and that concerns the welfare or interests of a third party who is in less powerful status than the decision maker" (Sosin & Canlum, 1983, p. 3). The advocacy skill, therefore, entails (1) pleading a case or cause, one's own or another's, (2) in a forum and a manner, (3) that increases the probability of accomplishing a specific goal. Such activity involves basic communication, analytical, and interactional skills (Schinke et al., 1985).

The oral and written communication skills for advocacy begin with effective pleading of a case or cause. The components of this effectiveness are its accuracy, feasibility, organization, and quality (Schinke et al., 1985). Accurate advocacy statements are technically correct; that is, they are informed by legal and other policies and codes and respond to the target issue. Feasibility is informed by the realistic understanding of resource limitations, political constraints, and bureaucratic resistance. Organization refers to the structure and internal consistency. Quality concerns the social work values reflected in the communication; that is, high-quality presentations are ethical, neither perjure nor demean others, and argue the merits of the issue honestly.

Advocacy as a skill also requires some significant analytical and interactional skills. When we advocate, we are not only pleading a case or a cause; we are doing so to achieve a different, more reciprocal interaction between the person, or persons, and a formal or informal resource system. This goal directs our analytical strategizing. This strategy includes selecting the most probable effective forum and medium for our communication: What would likely occur if we wrote a letter? Called a meeting? Whom should the letter target—a worker, a supervisor, and so forth? Who should attend such a meeting—those involved in the decision, the press, board members, and so forth? The determination of specific goals leads to the selection of appropriate targets. In turn, we plan and use strategies based on our own knowledge of what might best influence these targets. For instance, it is particularly important that we develop collaborative strategies prior to adversarial ones. This collaborative approach is less likely to increase the power struggle behind decisions demanding advocacy and therefore increase the likelihood of an acceptable decision.

In the interaction, we need to use all the principles of establishing helping relationships with resistant others in our involvement with those on whom we target our advocacy. Even when collaborative strategies falter and we decide upon a more adversarial stand, we must still respect the dignity and worth of those we are standing against. Such respect, as well as the attempt to empathize with those we perceive as enemies of our clients' rights, can be very difficult. Advocacy at best, however, is *enabling*—a calling upon the higher nature of others, even though those others may be averse to our plea. We cannot enable others to decide out of a sense of moral justice without reflecting our faith in this possibility in our interactions with them. We trust that the basis of this sense of justice is our interdependence. This mutual need for interdependence, as reflected in the common ground of clients' needs and the needs of systems to serve clients, is the basis on which advocacy begins and proceeds.

Case-Consultation Advocacy

A more subtle form of advocacy involves case consultation. In case consultation, the social worker tries to increase the responsiveness to a client's needs (rather than rights) in a way that increases the interaction between the client and potential resource. This includes contacts with teachers in behalf of a student's needs in schools, doctors and nurses in behalf of a patient's (or patients') needs in a hospital, employers in behalf of an employee, and so on. The skills for case consultation include an ability to begin with the agenda of the potential resource person, understanding his or her feelings about the perceptions of the client and his or her situation, articulating the needs of the client, identifying common ground, and challenging the obstacles to this common ground. The social worker also needs to mediate by preparing the client for more receptiveness to the potential resource. This entails beginning with the client's feelings and perceptions, identifying ambivalences and points of common ground, challenging obstacles to this common ground, and encouraging the client to view systems people in less stereotypical ways.

Advocacy Examples

The following vignettes provide examples of this advocacy through consultation and linking.

Josh is a fifth-grade student referred to the school social worker by his teacher, Ms. Andrews. He often creates classroom disturbances and recently led a group of boys from the room to beat up another boy on the playground. The early meetings with Josh produced a contract in which the goal of the work was to keep Josh out of trouble through focusing on his relationships with his classmates and with Ms. Andrews. Mediating consultation included identifying the common ground and pointing out obstacles to this common ground individually with Josh and Ms. Andrews: "Josh, you and Ms. Andrews both seem to want the same thing for you—your staying out of trouble and getting along better in school—but are not together on how best to accomplish this"; "Ms. Andrews, you and Josh both want him to stay out of trouble but you don't seem to have the same ideas about what he needs."

This work included some use of the mediation methodology. The social worker brought Josh and Ms. Andrews together to reach a mutual agreement on the specific behavior changes required. They also developed a plan regarding what consequences would result from specific misbehavior. In individual meetings with Josh, the social worker demanded work by encouraging him to view Ms. Andrews as a helper rather than a "mean teacher." In individual consultation with Ms. Andrews, the social worker encouraged her to break through her stereotype of Josh as a "bad boy" and to consider his developmental needs for attention and acceptance by peers as behind much of his behavior. As Ms. Andrews increased the attention she gave to Josh as a nurturer, including many rewards for his early attempts at controlling his misbehavior, Josh began to work harder to please, in his words, "such a super teacher."

This next example reflects work in a VA hospital ward for paraplegics and quadriplegics who had suffered spinal cord injuries (Lipton & Malter, 1971). The social worker entered the ward when the interactional conflicts in the common ground between patients and hospital staff were at an all-time low. The patients' care was very demanding, and the hospital staff often reacted with anger and inhumane actions because of their frustration and the escalation of conflicts. After Mr. Lipton, the social worker, began to know the concerns and needs of the patients through individual and group meetings, he consulted with hospital staff to increase reciprocal interaction with the patients in their decision making. Lipton reports the following exchange, which reflects one such consultation.

> I met with Nurse A. this morning and tried to prepare her for the complaints and feelings she might expect today in her meeting with ward patients. When I mentioned that a problem for the patients seemed to be the shifting around of nursing aides, she said she wished to keep them on the ward. She said, "They can't wait until they get off the ward." I asked her why. She said, "Because of the heavy work load and the constant demands and complaints of the patients." She added, "Of course, I would not tell that to the patients." I asked, "Why not?" She looked blank. I said, "I think it might be helpful to the patients if they knew why many aides don't want to work there. But I think if you tell them the truth they will be more likely to trust you. . . ." I informed Miss A. that many of the patients were very angry about the way things were on the ward. I asked, "How will you feel if they express a lot of anger toward you at the meeting?" Miss A. assured me that this would not be a problem for her. (p. 111)

In this exchange, Lipton reached out to the nurse in a way that showed concern for her needs and feelings. He did not overidentify with either patients or staff in this mediation. This interaction led to the nurse's leveling with the patients and not being defensive when confronted with their anger and complaints. She likely felt more able to trust and rely on Lipton now in improving her interactions with the patients.

When adversarial advocacy precedes such consultation, this exchange usually goes in a very different direction. Often this occurs because of identifying with clients against systems people rather than identifying with both and increasing the common ground between them. This mistake occurred in the following meeting between patients and a supervisory nurse:

> Both the patients and Nurse D. seemed to avoid the topic in the first few minutes. I suggested it would be helpful if both sides put their cards on the table. B. then asked directly why the Junior Red Cross girls were not allowed on the ward. The answer was that Nursing Service must decide where the girls could be more useful and it was decided that they could be more useful on other wards. B. said he thought that the girls could be useful up here. Nurse D. said angrily that she felt that the girls could be more useful elsewhere. There was a silence. I asked why. Nurse D. looked at me with anger and did not answer. I said, "Miss D., I think that it might be helpful if you gave some reasons so everybody will be able to understand better." She didn't answer. I said, "Miss D., I think the fellows have some ideas that the drinking and socializing might have something to do with it." She said icily, "Mr. Lipton, I will not assign them to the ward." There was a loud silence. I said, again putting my foot in my mouth, "Well, that settles that—except I guess the feelings of the patients are not settled." Patient Y. said, "Yeah, we got left out again." (p. 14)

This work increased rather than challenged the obstacles to interaction on the common ground of understanding patients' needs and serving them. Here, Lipton did not consult with Nurse D. in preparation, nor did he appear to prepare the patients for effectively advocating their own needs.

Consider the differences in the consultation below. In work with one quadriplegic patient, Lipton learned that he was angry at not getting turned over in bed at sufficiently frequent intervals during the night; he was afraid to verbalize his feeling and problem directly to the nurse; he was generally passive with authority figures; and he was interested in starting his own business upon discharge. The patient decided to try to assert himself to the nurse about the problem and asked Lipton to help explain this to her. Lipton needed to alert the nurse to the problem in order to collaborate with her in the work with the patient. In the past, this particular nurse had often become defensive and angry when Lipton brought complaints about her service to

her attention. At the same time, she identified strongly with her rehabilitation role. Here, Lipton reports:

"I told the nurse that I was working with L. this morning and that he has a
problem. He said he does not get turned enough at night," [and explained
the details]. "But he has a problem in asserting himself—he is afraid to tell
you about the problem. In fact, he said he never has really been able to
complain or argue with adults. But the interesting thing is that he wants to
go into business and that involves learning to speak up for himself. I
suggested to L. that it might be useful if he could learn to speak up for
himself here, and that you would be the one who could help him with his
nursing problem." The nurse said, "Sure, if he is going into business he has
to learn to open his mouth to people. What should I say to him?" [Lipton]
replied "Try something." She said, "Suppose I say something like this:
'Mr. Lipton told me that you are not getting turned enough at night. If
that happens, I am as concerned as you are about it. I want you to tell me
about these things if they happen . . .'" (pp. 117–118)

This appeal to the common ground in the consultation created the
interaction that could benefit both the patient's and nurse's needs.
How different this kind of advocacy would have been if Lipton had
attacked the nurse adversarily!

A Final Example: Linking through Networking and Advocacy

A final example represents consultative advocacy and efforts to force
various network links. This comes from the work of Lilian Wells and
Carolyn Singer (1985) in a demonstration project for delivering services to the institutionalized elderly. The service intervention led to
linking and strengthening the supportive qualities of various networks—those of the elderly residents and those of the institutional
staff—through a municipal system of nursing homes. Social work
students primarily delivered these services.

The project began with consultation with staff members and administrators. Staff were prejudiced toward and held stereotypes of the
families. They did not believe that relatives truly cared for the elderly
residents or wanted to be involved with them during the placement.
This attitude permeated the admissions process, wherein the emphasis
was on paper work with only the briefest contacts with families or even
with the prospective resident. Staff saw the family's contact with them
only as an avenue for unrealistic complaints about the relative's care—
and primarily designed to relieve their own guilt about the placement.

In consultation with staff and administration, the social workers received permission to provide a program of direct social work service in the home for prospective residents as well as their families. The goal was orientation to the institution to allow more effective coping with the move. This work fostered linkage between staff and family members.

Staff came to see that strengthening family involvement and the resident's capacity for decision making led to fewer adjustment problems for most residents, and thus to fewer problems for staff. Residents and relatives learned to communicate more effectively with staff and advocate their own needs more effectively. Both staff and family members tended to focus more on residents' strengths, despite their physical and mental disabilities. They also grew more aware that the elderly still have the need and capacity for participating in reciprocal interaction and relationships.

To develop network linkages further on the basis of this initial success, a social work student unit recommended groups for the relatives of new residents. Even with strong initial resistance by an administration that feared complaints would escalate, the students convinced staff that the relatives had so many common concerns, questions, and feelings that they would be a source of great support for each other. The groups would also serve as a more productive communication link to the nursing staff. Indeed, they did. Administrators soon observed the extensive mutual aid family members could give to each other and to residents in these groups—and the problems prevented for the institution in this contact with families. These groups became part of the institution's services, changing both attitude and policy.

Initially this project focused on improving the quality of support for residents and their families by strengthening internetwork linkages between staff and residents, families and residents, and staff and families. However, the need to develop mutual-support groups among residents themselves became apparent. Thus, as a counterpart to facilitating the families' involvement in the home, the student unit developed groups for the new residents to foster mutual support, deal with common concerns, and gain information and skills for institutional living. At times a long-term resident was involved in the project as a resource person and as a co-leader of the group, along with the student leadership. At other times, members of the group decided to continue as a self-help group without student leadership. In addition to the situational-transition groups for new residents, the student social workers developed a range of other groups based on special interests (such as groups for general discussion, drama, and current events) and initiated outreach programs for high-risk subgroups.

The majority of the residents and staff in the homes were women. Therefore, the interests and priorities of men tended to be overlooked. In one home, a student worked on a men's floor that had been marked by social isolation, inactivity, and apathy. Using a mediating approach, this student helped the residents to plan social activities for themselves and to develop organizational skills. He helped the men develop patterns of communicating, interacting, and resolving disagreements to overcome their fear of potential conflict with others, which contributed to their withdrawal and isolation. The residents took on tasks and responsibilities that they had not undertaken for years and developed friendships and common interests. Having gained some comfort, support, and confidence through their social activities, the residents pressed the home's administrators for a liquor license and for changes in the way that their trust accounts were handled. The student consulted extensively with one staff member to teach a respect for residents' self-determination as well as how to be a resource to implement the men's plans when the student left.

In one of the homes there was no residents' council, counter to government policy. At the request of the administrators, one student became involved in helping residents establish such a council, which would give them access to the administrators and help them formulate policy for the home. Although the administrators said they wanted a strong and active council, they felt threatened by such a formal organization and were afraid to permit independence and autonomy. The administrators thwarted the plans of the residents' council to raise money and tended to communicate only with those members of the council who were quiet and cooperative and who would create a good public image for the home. The student had to develop communication skills and strategic knowledge of the residents so that the residents could confront the administrators with the double messages projected and inconsistencies between what the administrators said they wanted and their behavior.

This case reflects the difficulty of developing an influential body of residents that can have an impact on a hierarchical, bureaucratic structure. It also illustrates the difficulty of changing ingrained attitudes of people who perceive the elderly as incompetent. Even those staff members who acknowledged the importance of considering residents' views found it difficult to hold to their intellectual stance consistently. Moreover, the staff found it difficult to implement policy that reflected residents' views. The social workers continued to facilitate interaction until the residents' council and the home administrators were able to work together effectively.

The cases above illustrate the role social workers can play in strengthening and maintaining the residents' links with their families, with other residents, and with the staff. The project also helped residents develop new linkages with the community. A community liaison worker from a school board asked if residents in one home could tutor immigrant children in a special education class and provide grandparent figures for the children. Most of these children had originally remained with their grandparents in their native countries when their parents immigrated. Later, when the children joined their parents, they left their grandparents behind and had to adjust to a new culture and language, as well as a different family structure. The role of tutor gave the residents a useful and productive function in the community. They were linked not only with the children but with teachers and the principal in planning and providing a unique service. The community's respect for their contribution and their warm relationships with the children heightened their self-concept and their stature in the home. This is a clear example of a network that has benefits for all its members.

The examples of this project suggest some significant summary principles for linking and advocacy through networking and consultation:

1. The central focus was always on meeting the needs of the residents and their families, and therefore the project's goal fell within the mandate of the institution. The common ground was established.

2. The approach involved collaboration with members of the system in exploring and in solving problems. This approach served to increase the problem-solving capacities of the members of all the network sectors. The advocacy involved consultation.

3. The social workers developed a climate that allowed the expression of differences, the examination and clarification of true issues, and the working through of conflict. They served all parties through mediating.

4. An important role for the social workers was to initiate and to show persistence in advocating for change in the services and policies of the organization. Advocacy came from persistence, not insistence.

5. The social workers contributed their substantive knowledge of the social and emotional needs of the elderly to the home's administrators and staff, teaching and demonstrating those skills required to meet these needs more effectively. The consultation on needs presented advocacy activities.

6. To ensure the maintenance of the networks established, the social workers modified attitudes, developed competencies, and influenced institutional change at the policy level. The advocacy for networking began as case and extended to cause.

CONCLUSION

The foundation competence covered in this chapter is the *ability to sustain work through mediation between clients and resource systems during the work phase.* Two general sets of skills operationalize this competence—linking and advocacy.

Linking entails specific actions to bring together clients and formal and informal resource people in behalf of other clients and systems. Students at first may be reluctant to link the client with significant others out of a need to be needed. The student learns to give up the need for client dependence and to work toward client independence. This entails encouraging clients to view systems people in new, less stereotyped ways; meeting with significant others to open up effective interactional and communication channels; referring clients to appropriate resources and monitoring the successful connection to informal and formal resource networks; coordinating the delivery of a variety of services to clients; and initiating family and small group services, when needed, to meet needs the individual client shares with other or potential clients.

Students may at first be reluctant to advocate clients' needs or may engage in adversarial advocacy before attempting more collaborative strategies. Eventually, students should learn to advocate for clients' needs in organizational and community systems, including their own agency, when their basic rights seem violated. Additionally, they should develop consultation strategies for organizational, community, or policy change in behalf of clients and others with similar unmet needs.

SUGGESTED LEARNING EXERCISE 9-1: LINKING

Develop a plan for linking, through mediation, networking, or both, in relation to a situation in the field. If not in a field practicum, select a situation of a friend, family member, or acquaintance and develop a strategy for them. Rate the effectiveness of the strategy by using the scale for Linking (Skill 17 under Competence #5) in the Educational Outcome Rating Scale found in the Appendix.

SUGGESTED LEARNING EXERCISE 9-2: ADVOCACY

In the situation used above, develop a plan for advocacy. Use the criteria described in the "Advocacy" section of this chapter to rate how well you draft a statement to plead the case. Include a statement of goals and strategies for increasing the common ground between the person on whose behalf you plan to advocate and the potential resource system. Consider consultation activities that might increase your mediating advocacy. Finally, rate your plan using the scale for Advocacy (Competence #5, Skill #18) in the Educational Outcome Rating Form in the Appendix.

10 Competence #6: Ending Phase

Jay Assume met with Lisa Blank for the last time. Jay, a social worker at Jewish Family Service, had been working with Lisa weekly for the past 3 months. Lisa, a 24-year-old, came to Jewish Family Service with a number of concerns. She had moved out of her parents' house 6 months before to lease an apartment with her boyfriend. After a week, the boyfriend left and Lisa remained. She worked as a clerk in a department store and had difficulty meeting expenses on her own. For 4 months prior to her first meeting with Jay, Lisa had ceased all contact with her parents, spent most of her time alone in the apartment, and found herself hardly talking to anyone but her customers at work. Her primary feelings reflected depression, including the symptoms of loss of appetite, inability to sleep, and withdrawal from interaction with people.

Jay worked with Lisa to increase her sense of self-esteem, to budget her limited income, and to increase her trust in people. They spent many interviews discussing her strengths as a worker and a woman managing on her own, her pain at being abandoned by her boyfriend, and her needs to get out of her apartment and meet people.

Jay and Lisa reflected upon their work together in this 13th and last meeting. Lisa reported feeling better about herself and her situation. She credited Jay and their work together for decreasing how often she cried. As she stated the meaning of their relationship to her: "You have understood me and I don't feel so alone in the world anymore." Jay shared how he saw Lisa talking more positively about herself and smiling more often in their interviews. He credited her for the way she used the relationship to share much about herself—both her hurts and her strengths. As he concluded, "You risked sharing much with me here and I know you can now risk getting closer to your friends and family." They ended with a brief hug, and both were filled with a sense of accomplishment as Lisa left.

No sooner had the door to the office shut when Jay suddenly found himself nagged by questions that interrupted his feelings of satisfaction: Why hadn't Lisa actually taken these risks during their work together? She has yet to contact her family or to reach out to any potential friends. Has the time she spends in isolation changed? She hasn't reported any activities outside of her apartment. Have her particular symptoms changed? Is she eating well? Sleeping? Actually experiencing less feelings of depression when not with him? Had they spent too much time talking about her feelings about herself and not enough focusing on actual changes in her behavior? How will I know if this work really did work for her? And finally, the most nagging question at all: Why didn't I think about raising some of these questions with her before she left?

"Oh well," thought Jay, "She really does seem to feel better. Isn't that enough? Maybe I'm too hard on myself." But he could not get rid of that sick feeling in the pit of his stomach. It bothered him for days.

This chapter deals with the last of the foundation practice competencies: the skills for ending and evaluation. More effective use of these skills may prevent the nagging questions and uncomfortable feeling that Jay faces about his work with Lisa. This chapter first considers endings; then it focuses on more formal evaluations as a part of ending the work. The specific process of ending for both clients and practitioners suggests some important principles and techniques. So do formal, more systematic evaluations of practice. While this chapter presents these principles and techniques in skills for ending and evaluations in two separate sections, these two processes occur simultaneously in the best of practice.

ENDING

The ending phase of social work process is powerful and difficult for both practitioners and clients. We all have orientations to significant separations in our lives that reflect the meaning of endings for us. The termination process in practice is a symbolic representation of these orientations. Often, these include our underlying feelings about the most major ending we face in life: death. Therefore, termination with individuals, families, and groups tends to proceed through the stages of the dying process identified by Elisabeth Kübler-Ross (1969). Practitioner and client may experience ending first as denial, avoidance, anger, regression, and flight, then progressing to a period of bargaining (when they give up holding on to the relationship but decide to still work together for ending). From this bargaining evolves the first step in facing the reality of the impending ending, as in dying, through depression, then grief, and finally to the acceptance, which leads to review, evaluation, and growth.

Both practitioners and clients might face endings with the pain of separation, the guilt of not living up to expectations, the regrets over unfinished business, and the denial of the work yet to be done—as well as the sense of accomplishment. The ending skills, therefore, begin in the practitioner's ability to tune-in to these feelings—in self, in client, and in the interactional helping process. This tuning-in increases such skills as initiating endings, responding directly to indirect cues to ending, empathy for the other's feelings, sharing one's own feelings, reaching for ambivalences, crediting the other, and enabling transfer of the other's learning.

Tuning-In

Tuning-in requires the same techniques covered in Chapter 5. Essentially, the practitioner needs to be aware of his or her own feelings about self, the client, and the work together as the time for termination draws near. Chief among the feelings to face in the self is the sense of responsibility for the outcome of the work: "How much guilt because of not having 'solved' significant aspects of the problem am I experiencing?" This can lead to a clearer recognition of what was done and might have been done *with* the client as well as what could not be done *for* the client.

Another key feeling to tune-in to is the regret for this "unfinished business." Such regret can spur a realistic attempt to use the ending to finish what might be completed in the time remaining. Again, the tuning-in might help the practitioner realize that not every problem can be "finished" and that one can only be a part—albeit a significant part at times—of another's ongoing life process and his/her need to solve one's inevitable problems in living.

Tuning-in prevents the practitioner's denial and avoidance of the ending and increases the skill in initiating termination. The practitioner initiates termination by pointing out the ending at the point appropriate for providing enough remaining time for effectively using this phase of social work process. Because of the difficulty clients have in facing their feelings about ending and their tendency to deny the ending to prevent experiencing these feelings, the practitioner must provide time and opportunity for these feelings to surface and be sorted out. The practitioner, therefore, needs to point out and remind the other about the impending ending in advance. This enables the initiation of the ending process for both.

Tuning-in to self and client in ending, as in all effective tuning-in, also increases the potential to respond directly to indirect cues. Clients often express fears and anger about ending, veiled in their verbal ("Will you miss me?") or nonverbal (lateness, missed appointments, etc.) communications. The practitioner needs to reach behind these indirect cues to encourage clients to express the anger (or fears) directly: "You have been joking today about my not having to spend parts of Tuesday afternoons with you in a few weeks, but I wonder if there is something more serious and important in this joke. You seem irritated about the fact that we will only meet for three more weeks. Are you feeling some anger toward me now?" This invitation is important, even if the client does not acknowledge the anger, pick up on it, or even acknowledge its existence. It speaks to the feeling and permits it to surface when the person is ready—freeing energies to participate more fully and productively in the ending phase of the work.

Empathy

This tying of feelings to the other's ending process is the basis of empathy for the other. Empathy, here, constitutes accurate acknowledgment of the client's ending feelings. We reach for the fears, the anger, the sadness often under the anger, *and* the hopes, the pride, and the appreciation about ending in the messages that reflect these feelings. When we tie these feelings to the client's experience of these endings, we increase the potential for understanding them together and permitting more rational consideration of the work that needs to be completed in the time remaining.

Sharing One's Own Feelings

Similarly, we help this process by sharing our own feelings. These include our personal reactions to the client's anger at us as well as our feelings about terminating the working relationship with the client. As the client hears our sadness, he or she may feel freer to risk honest emotional contact in ending. The shared emotions that first created and strengthened a bond between the practitioner and client were of value to both. This connection is still at work and increases the power to help in endings. While both may feel vulnerable because of the emotional meaning of the relationship, the practitioner has the function and needs the professional skill to risk talking about the meaning of the encounter together.

Reaching for Ambivalences

In this reaching for and sharing feelings, the practitioner especially needs to acknowledge *ambivalences*. When the client expresses the positives (the sense of accomplishment, for instance), the practitioner reaches for the negatives (the sense of loss); when negatives are expressed (i. e., the anger), the practitioner reaches for the positives (the appreciation). Similarly, the practitioner expresses both his or her own positive and negative feelings, perceptions, reactions, and evaluations. This assures the reality and honesty of the interaction and promotes respect for each other in the relationship that both have built.

Crediting the Other

One aspect of the skill of reaching for ambivalences is crediting the client. Crediting the other, the practitioner senses the positive feelings of accomplishment and directly acknowledges the other's strengths and skills for future problem solving. This skill supports the client's hopes for "going it alone" and helps alleviate the fears in ending. Even in situations in which important goals could not be achieved (practitioner or client ending before the work is completed because the social worker leaves the agency or the client moves from the area—or even when they decide together to end in the face of incomplete work), the client's learning what needs to be done and understanding the obstacles to accomplishing goals can be credited. In this crediting, the client has the opportunity to perceive the change in self and situation. There can be recognition of having "tried out the change for size" to "see how it could fit" into the client's interactional existence.

Transferring Learning

Transferring learning requires a special focus in which the practitioner and client together summarize and generalize what can be used from the work together in behalf of the other's future problem solving. The practitioner reaches first for the client's identification of what has been learned. This helps consolidate and integrate the learning and give cognitive direction for its use. The practitioner can add to the client's total ideas some other ideas that seem to fit. The practitioner can also share what he or she has learned from the experience together.

Also transferred is identification of areas for future work. This conveys to the client that the work will continue after the ending. The practitioner best confronts this future in a way that responds to the client's fears and wishes about facing future problems alone. Without in any way minimizing the other's fears that the going may be rough, the practitioner needs to convey a belief in the other's potential to tackle these.

Finally, the identification of the needs and skills for interaction in new support and resource systems is important. This transfer of learning involves specific attention to what the client wants to do, plans to do, and can do to increase the interactive match with significant others in his or her life. This may include transfer to new services or programs. In this transfer the practitioner particularly credits the skills the client has developed to recognize needs, reach out, challenge obstacles, and involve him- or herself in reciprocal interactions.

Students often at first deny their own ending feelings and may cut off service abruptly or without attention to clients' cues regarding their ending process. Later, students may be more tuned-in to one side of their own and clients' ambivalences, emphasizing either the positive or negative feelings about termination. Students should learn to use endings consciously and sensitively in behalf of clients. This entails pointing out endings in order to continue work in termination of the service; sharing their own feelings as a model of facing termination and to initiate the flow of positive and negative affect between themselves and clients during the ending phase; reaching for ending feelings, both positive and negative, and connecting these feelings to the substance of the work; crediting clients for their share of the work and transferring learning from this process; and asking for a review of the work as related to the goals and terms of the contract.

EVALUATION

Evaluation feedback is often central to the discussion noted in the previous section on ending. This evaluation entails focus on the practitioner's and client's feelings about the outcomes and how much they achieve. This is the evaluation that Jay does with Lisa in the vignette at the beginning of this chapter. In this section, however, evaluation refers to specific research skills. The evaluation skill requires the ability to use a systematic empirical process for determining the process and outcomes of one's own practice.

Students are prone to evaluating service and their work on the basis of their own and clients' feelings about the process. They tend to resist efforts at more systematic evaluation. Evaluation skills require that students objectify and systematize their assessment through the use of evaluation research. At a minimum, students need to develop instruments for pre- and posttesting client change. The student should develop scales to gather baseline data and to measure outcomes against baseline data. Therefore, students need to learn to operationalize goals into some measurable outcomes and to measure what parts of their practice approach influenced clients toward achievement of these outcomes, made little or no difference, or seemed deleterious. This requires the ability to operationalize the intervention hypotheses in their practice approaches and to evaluate process as well as outcomes in their practice.

The systematic evaluation of direct-service practice requires the ability to use single-system research designs (Bloom & Fischer, 1982). The use of single-system designs essentially involves the following ten steps:

1. Determining goals or outcomes—the dependent variable(s).
2. Determining process intervention to achieve the goals or outcomes—the independent variable—and formulating an intervention hypothesis that relates the independent and dependent variable: *If* I (process), *then* (goal or outcome).
3. Operationalizing the dependent variable (determining how changes in the dependent variable—goal or outcome—would be known if seen).
4. Determining an appropriate measurement for the dependent variable.
5. Measuring the dependent variable prior to intervention (the baseline).
6. Operationalizing the intervention (independent variable).
7. Determining an appropriate measurement of the intervention process.
8. Establishing a design for interventions and measurements.
9. Implementing the single system design.
10. Analyzing the data.

Dependent Variable

The first step—determining the dependent variable—comes from the outcome goals of the contract. These are the states toward which the client and practitioner have agreed to work. The basic question answered in contracting is: What needs changed and to what degree?

This outcome can include changes in feelings (less anxiety, more self-esteem, less fear, and so on); in behavior (more assertion, less isolation, more communication with a particular other, and so on); or in cognition (less negative evaluations of self, more positive evaluation of others, less catastrophic thoughts, and so on).

For instance, Jay in his work with Lisa in the vignette at the beginning of this chapter would likely indicate contracted outcomes as increases in Lisa's self-esteem and in her initiating relationships with others and decreases in her depression symptoms—sleep disturbances, loss of appetite, and time spent alone.

Independent Variable

The second step is often the hardest. This entails specifically noting what the practitioner and client will do to affect the goal or outcome. In short, we need to translate the intervention approach into observable behaviors and expected consequences. For instance, Jay's approach to increase Lisa's self-esteem might include specific crediting of her strengths (the independent or intervention variable). The hypothesis, or expectation, could be: "The more I (Jay) verbally identify a particular strength of Lisa's, the more Lisa will make positive rather than negative statements in our interactions." The ultimate outcome, of course, would be measurable differences in Lisa's feelings of self-esteem.

Operationalizing Measurement

Steps 3 through 5 are those covered most in the practice evaluation literature (Bloom & Fischer, 1982; Hudson, 1977; Jayaratne & Levy, 1979). In Step 3, we need to operationalize the dependent variables (major outcomes). "Operationalize" refers to specifying how we will know this empirical reality when we see it. For instance, if we were Jay, how would we know, by observation, that Lisa has increased her feelings of self-esteem? How would we know if she has increased her initiating relationships with others? Decreased her depression symptoms?

We first need to define the outcome variable in observable, behavioral terms. Self-esteem, for instance, could be defined as the ratio of positive to negative statements made about oneself. If this is our concept of self-esteem, as it might very well be for Jay with Lisa, then we would know (operationalize) self-esteem as the number of positive comments about self over the number of negative comments about self. Our operational definition would appear something like this:

Self-esteem operationalized

$$\text{Self-esteem} = \frac{\text{Positive comments about self}}{\text{Negative comments about self}}$$

In this definition positive self-esteem results in a numerator higher than the denominator; low self-esteem entails a higher denominator. Once we have defined the outcome variables in such a measurable manner, wherein we can count or quantify what we observe, then we move to Step 4.

Step 4 requires determining appropriate measurements for the dependent, or outcome, variables. This measurement can involve either formal, standardized scales or self-authored, often self-anchoring scales. A variety of standardized measurement tests and scales are available for many of the outcome variables of social work practice (see especially Buros, 1978; Hudson, 1982). For instance, Walter Hudson's (1982) scale, Index of Self-Esteem, if periodically administered, would be an appropriate tool for measuring the magnitude (extent, degree, and intensity) of Lisa's changes in self-esteem. This scale, like all of Hudson's scales, which are specifically developed for repeated measures in single-system evaluation research, is short; easy to administer, interpret, complete, and score; and has high validity and reliability.

Where goals involve changes in behavior, a self-authored scale is relatively easy to construct. For instance, a scale to measure positive and negative comments about self to determine self-esteem is simply one that counts and indicates the ratio of these statements. If Jay had recorded his first session with Lisa and counted these statements in both categories (positive/negative), he would determine the level of self-esteem by placing these numbers in his ratio:

Self-esteem measured

$$\begin{array}{c}\text{Level of self-esteem} \\ \text{(first session)}\end{array} = \frac{\text{4 positive comments about self}}{\text{19 negative statements about self}}$$

Where goals involve altering feelings, such as feelings about self, anger, depression, anxiety, and so on, we can construct a self-anchoring scale (Bloom, 1975). Here, we employ a five- or seven-point scale that represents varying levels of self-reported internal states. These states range from the absence of the troubling feeling or thought on one end to its maximum intensity on the other. To "anchor" these scales, we need to ask clients to imagine themselves experiencing the extreme degrees of the given feeling or thought and to describe what they experience. Then the descriptions can be placed on a continuum with these extremes and a midpoint. A self-anchoring scale for Lisa's depression might look like Figure 10-1.

Clients can employ such scales to record the extent of these troubling feelings and thoughts over time, often daily. This permits graphing the trends in the changes of these states to assess progress toward outcome goals and the effectiveness of specific interventions.

Step 5, already alluded to, requires using the measurement prior to intervention. This establishes a baseline. Baselining involves collecting information on the client's problem situation before intervention actually begins (Bloom & Fischer, 1982, pp. 267–285). The evaluation itself, then, entails analyzing subsequent data in relation to this baseline information. The comparison of observations and measurements to this baseline data throughout the intervention determines the degree to which interventions make a difference for the client—for good (in desired directions) and for ill (in undesired directions).

Figure 10-2 is an example of a graph that records baseline data and subsequent intervention data for Lisa's depression. It uses the self-anchoring scale suggested above and reflects the changes in her symptoms over the 13 weeks of work.

Graphs for demonstrating baseline measurements and the data analysis for evaluating the interventions that were used entail a horizontal axis denoting time intervals and a vertical axis denoting the magnitude of the behavior targeted for change. Figure 10-2 is an example of such a graph. In this instance, baseline data comes from a 3-week period, during which Jay likely assessed the problem/situation with Lisa and contracted for their work together. The interventions may have involved reaching for Lisa's feelings of anger and challenging her to initiate relationships with others. Week 9 may have involved a special intervention wherein Jay enabled a better social support network for Lisa by mediating between her and her parents in a conference set up

1	2	3	4	5	6	7
Least depressed (sleeping well, eating regularly, no crying)		Moderately depressed (interrupted sleep, varied appetite, crying twice a week)			Most depressed (not sleeping, not eating, crying 5 times a week)	

FIGURE 10-1 Example of self-anchoring scale for depression.

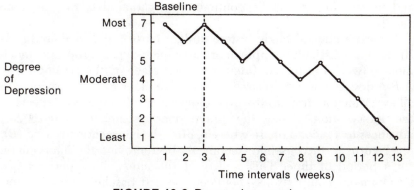

FIGURE 10-2 Depression graph.

for this purpose. We find ups and downs (as often occurs) in this early work and that the mediation within the family system appears to contribute significantly to more dramatic and consistent change in the desired direction. "Eyeballing" such a graph suggests a positive evaluation of this outcome and tests the efficacy of family mediation in the intervention.

This example demonstrates the significant elements of Steps 6 and 7. That is, specific interventions are used to operationalize the independent variable, and these are measurable. In this case, as in many, the measurement is ordinal—a "yes" or a "no," depending upon whether it was used. The degree of the intervention could also be noted on a five- or seven-point scale. This scale could list how well the intervention was used, with "very well" on one end and "very poorly" at the other point. This assessment is best when it includes the behavior description for the score, much as the self-anchoring scale does.

Designs

Step 8 constitutes the establishment of the most appropriate single-system research design. A number of excellent sources review these available designs (see Bloom & Fischer, 1982; Jayaratne & Levy, 1979; Tripodi & Epstein, 1980).

The four basic designs are the case study (*A-B*); experimental (*A-B-A; A-B-A-B; B-A-B*); multiple baselines and targets; and successive interventions. The case study design is analogous to the pretest-post-test design in research. In the single system evaluation model, the case study refers to gathering baseline data on the outcome variable (*A*) and intervening (*B*) while continuing to gather data on the same variable.

The experimental single-system designs (*A-B-A*, *A-B-A-B*, and *B-A-B*) are more difficult to apply in practice but, when appropriate, much more powerful in the confidence we can place on the findings. The *A-B-A* design in its first phase is exactly like the *A-B* case study one. In all experimental designs, the practitioner controls, or alters, aspects of the intervention. Thus, the practitioner/researcher using *A-B-A* advances to a second phase wherein, after the intervention is used (*B*), one returns to the baseline (second *A*) by removing the intervention for a period of time. This control of the intervention permits two simultaneous comparisons—between the first baseline and the intervention and between the intervention and the second baseline. Such a comparison would indicate more about what difference the intervention itself might have made on the outcomes.

The *A-B-A-B* experimental design is a replication or time-series control (Campbell & Stanley, 1963). This adds to the *A-B-A* design subsequent uses of the interventions (after its removal for a period). These subsequent interventions are symbolized in the second *B*. This series could extend for a period as in $A_1\text{-}B_1\text{-}A_2\text{-}B_2\text{-}A_3\text{-}B_3$.

The last experimental design refers to experimental repetition of the intervention (*B-A-B*). In this replication, intervention begins at once (*B*), followed by an interval during which no intervention is explicitly used (*A*), followed by another intervention period (*B*).

Multiple designs are of two types: baselines and targets. The multiple baseline design increases our potential for conclusions regarding interventions without any removing of the intervention from the client system. It can be used with one client system with two or more problems or goals (more appropriate for Jay's work with Lisa), or with two or more situations involving the same problem and goals. The diagram of multiple baseline design is shown in Figure 10-3.

As Figure 10-3 reflects and its use by Jay with Lisa suggests, the practitioner/researcher first identifies two or more problems and goals. For Jay, these would be increases in Lisa's self-esteem (A_1) and initiating contact with others (A_2) and decreases in her feelings of depression (A_3). In applying this design, Jay would measure the baseline condition of all of these problems of Lisa's (A_1, A_2, A_3). Then he would apply one intervention (crediting her—B_1) to one of these problems, while continuing to record on all problems. When a change occurs in the first problem (A_1—self-esteem), Jay would apply the same intervention to the second problem (A_2—contact with others)

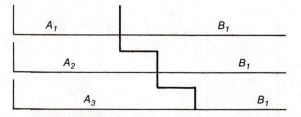

FIGURE 10-3 Multiple baseline design.

and note the changes. Jay could then determine with more confidence what effect his intervention had on each of Lisa's outcomes.

Multiple target designs with one client system are depicted in Figure 10-4, which would be even more appropriate for Jay's work with Lisa. It entails sets of two or more simultaneous designs involving different targets and interventions that are presumed to deal with conceptually related problems. As Jay used crediting to increase self-esteem (B_1), challenging to increase social contacts (B_2), and reaching for feelings of anger to decrease feelings of depression (B_3), he can gather three separate baselines on each outcome (A_1, A_2, A_3). This would lead to three graphs such as those in Figures 10-5, 10-6, and 10-7. The comparison of these three graphs reveals important patterns in the relationship of different interventions to each other and to desired outcomes (goals). While the evaluation cannot precisely determine causal connection, it could suggest intervention hypotheses. For instance, if social contacts increased before feelings of depression decreased, Jay might guess (hypothesize) with more confidence that challenging social contact does more than reaching for feelings of anger to decrease actual feelings of depression. Perhaps, too, Lisa's feelings of self-

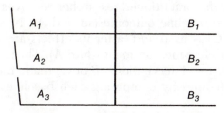

FIGURE 10-4 Multiple target design.

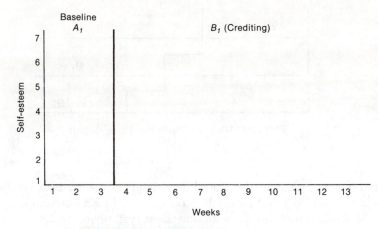

FIGURE 10-5 First target graph.

esteem increase greatly after social contacts. Jay could hypothesize here that crediting actual success may be more effective in increasing self-esteem than encouraging future behavior, such as making social contacts. In other words, the most meaningful crediting for increasing self-esteem might be "You did it!" rather than "You can do it."

Successive intervention designs consist of a series of designs that employ different interventions, each applied after the other in separate phases. Three common types of this design are A-B-C, A-B-A-C, and A-B-A-C-A. The A-B-C design is an extension of the basic A-B case study design with a new intervention added—C. The A-B-A-C design returns to measure the baseline data (second A) before introducing the new intervention (C). The A-B-A-C-A) design is the most rigorous of these and can suggest more specific causal connections. After the initial baseline (first A), an intervention (B) is introduced, presumably to the point at which the problem is showing a desired change from the baseline. Then, the practitioner/researcher removes the intervention and records the baseline outcome (second A). Next, an entirely new intervention (C) is used and, after its effects are observed, removed to a third baseline measurement (third A). The practitioner can then know which of two interventions (B or C) made the most difference, if any, in outcomes by comparing each baseline measurement with each other.

These four basic designs can be combined creatively in evaluating practice. Martin Bloom and Joel Fischer (1982, pp. 375–376) suggested

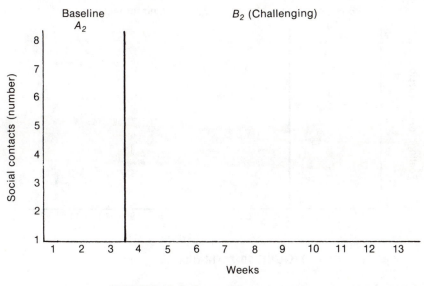

FIGURE 10-6 Second target graph.

a set of rules for the creative development and use of these designs. These include:

1. Use clear, direct baseline measures that are culturally and socially sensitive to the people involved.

2. Identify and use clear intervention hypotheses.

3. Let your practice hypotheses (at times "hunches"), based on the best information available, guide your action. Let the evaluation design follow from these decisions. Recognize you can add *A*'s, *B*'s, *C*'s, and *D*'s . . . *ad infinitum*. For every combination, however, you need to answer:

   a. Will changes from previous interventions be apparent or carry over? (Should you change baselines?)

   b. Will your choices of designs make clear the likely causal patterns among variables (intervention-produced outcomes)?

   c. Are your goals within the social and cultural definitions of what your client/system sees as desirable?

Steps 9 and 10 are closely related to selecting the design. Once the design is selected in Step 8, it needs to be implemented in Step 9. Step 10, however, requires separate knowledge to determine the most appropriate way to analyze the data collected in the design.

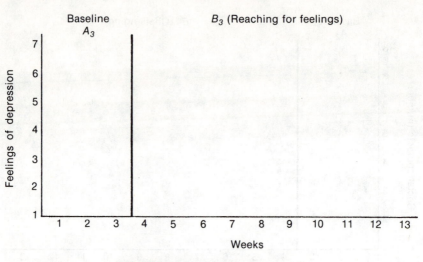

FIGURE 10-7 Third target graph.

Data Analysis

The analysis of data in single-system design research begins with "eyeballing," or visual analysis, and can advance through a series of statistical tests. This section summarizes these potentials and introduces the sources for appropriate tests. The intent in all forms of this analysis is to determine practical and, if possible, statistical significance of the interventions used. Practical or "clinical" significance refers to the magnitude of client system change and its social meaning (Hersen & Barlow, 1976). It suggests that the data reveal change in the desired direction that is observable by the client and those in contact with the client. Statistical significance involves some form of mathematical comparison of the change data.

The visual analysis of data is important to test for clinical, or practical, significance. Here, we examine data for trends from which we can infer the meaning of changes for good or for ill. There are several excellent sources that elaborate the properties to analyze in these trends (Bloom & Fischer, 1982, pp. 428–441; Gottman, 1973; Kazdin, 1976). Essentially, we need to study the data by visual inspection and infer the level (magnitude), direction (improvement or deterioration), stability (continuity or discontinuity), and general trends (within-phase "slope" or across-phase "drift") of change. We also need to assess, and maybe test further for (Gottman & Leiblum, 1974), whether the results may be "autocorrelated." That is, we can impute more significance to the interventions by assuring that the outcomes are not the result of natural, related changes that would have occurred with or without intervention. On visual inspection, a steady progression of change that seems to indicate success raises suspicion about the possibility of autocorrelation, or "serial dependency," and should be checked statistically (for this test, see Gottman & Leiblum, 1974). Without practical significance, any statistical significance is meaningless. However, without some statistical significance, much of what appears to be practical significance may be blind.

Among the statistical tests for significance, often used in sequence, are the "celeration line approach" (Gingerich & Feyerherm, 1979); the "proportion/frequency approach" (Bloom, 1975); and the "two standard deviation band approach using shewart charts" (Gottman & Leiblum, 1975). Other important sources to statistically determine the proportion and frequency of change are those that include tables of cumulative binominal probability distributions (Bloom, 1975; Bloom & Fischer, 1982). These compare the proportionate score and the frequency of observations and give significant statistical increases at the .05, .01, and .001 levels. We can, through our familiarization with these relatively uncomplicated statistical approaches, add readily to our tools for analyzing our data in single-system evaluation research. When the independent areas of practical and statistical significance combine and when our design holds strong operationalization of our intervention approach and determination of outcomes, we are not only more accountable to those we serve but more effective in our knowledge and skill for ongoing practice. Ending and evaluation skills together, then, constitute Competence #6—*the ability to enable effective termination during the ending phase of social work process.*

CONCLUSION

This last foundation competence covers skills for effective ending and systematic evaluation. The ending skills tap the potential of this phase of the helping process by tuning-in, reaching for ambivalences, crediting, and transferring learning. The evaluation skills assure accountability and professional competence development through creating and implementing single-system research designs. Together, these skills help to prevent the blind assumptions, self-doubts, and unfinished business that can arise for both the practitioner and the client (as it does for Jay in the vignette that opens this chapter). They assure the courageous and honest confrontation with and experience of the reality of social interaction that marks the best of all social work practice.

SUGGESTED LEARNING EXERCISE 10-1:
ENDING AND EVALUATION

Use either Jay's work with Lisa at the beginning of this chapter or an anticipated ending in your field experience and identify how you would use the ending skills and the single-system evaluation skills in this case. Select, identify, and give examples of those ending skills you believe most important for this work. Develop a single-system design that operationalizes outcomes and intervention variables, includes scales for baselining, and indicates how the data will be organized (through graphs) and analyzed. Evaluate the level on which you used these skills on the Educational Outcome Competence Rating form under Competence #6 in the Appendix.

11 Competence #7: Professional Development

Robert Mager, in the preface to his classic manual, *Preparing Instructional Objectives* (1962), tells the following fable:

Once upon a time a Sea Horse gathered up his seven pieces of silver and ambled out to make his fortune. He traveled only a short distance when he came upon an Eel, who said,

"Psst. Hey, bud. Where 'ya goin'?"

"I'm going to make my fortune," proudly replied the Sea Horse.

"You're in luck," suggested the Eel. "For four pieces of silver I'll sell you this speedy flipper. Then you'll be able to get there a lot faster."

"Gee, thanks," said the Sea Horse, as he paid the price, put on the flipper, and slithered off at twice the speed. Soon he came upon a Sponge who said,

"Psst. Hey, bud. Where 'ya going'?"

"I'm going to find my fortune," replied the Sea Horse.

"You're in luck," said the Sponge. "For three pieces of silver I'll let you buy this jet-propelled scooter so that you'll be able to travel a lot faster."

"Gee, thanks," said the Sea Horse, as he bought the scooter and went zooming through the sea five times as fast. Soon he came upon a Shark, who said,

"Psst. Hey, bud. Where 'ya going'?"

"I'm going to make my fortune," replied the Sea Horse.

"You're in luck. If you'll take this short cut," said the Shark, pointing to his wide open mouth, "you'll save yourself an awful lot of time."

"Gee, thanks," said the Sea Horse, as he zoomed off into the Shark's interior, there to be devoured.

Mager suggests: "The moral of this fable is that if you're not sure where you're going, you're liable to end up someplace else—and not even know the difference" (p. vii).

Another likely moral could be: We need to know where we're going but we also better be careful how we get there.

The text to this point should have given you some direction for the beginning mastery of significant generic foundation competencies in social work practice. This interactional competence model can provide some direction for where you go in future professional learning and development. Now I want to suggest some ideas about how you might get there.

Professional development requires both knowing what to learn and *how to learn*. This chapter suggests some guidelines for "learning how to learn" social work competencies and for evaluating your general competence for professional development.

This Competence #7—*the ability to use professional development activities*—is separate from but intimately related to all of the other competencies identified in this text. It is only through effective professional learning and development that all of the other competencies can be integrated into one's practice. This ability to use professional development for continually increasing competence for social work practice involves a number of skills. These include the skills for both deductive and inductive learning, risking personal disclosure and involvement in the learning process, assuring commitment to developing all aspects of competence in behalf of those served, accurate assessment of one's own learning needs, independent scholarship and inquiry, and the ability to engage in collegial learning activities.

Bertha Reynolds (1942), Charlotte Towle (1954), and Virginia Robinson (1978)—three people who contributed much to conceptualizing and teaching social work practice—have all written books focusing on the "learner" of professional social work practice. While each relied upon a different model of human growth and development, all three conceived learning in formal education as a significant personal growth process. The real mark of this process is the graduate's ability to continue to learn to increase professional competence, to integrate various learnings with each other and with practice experience. All essentially agree with Reynolds's original identification of the stages of this learning. The five stages are: (1) acute self-awareness of the strengths and limitations one brings to learning and the discrepancies between what one knows and needs to know; (2) a "sink or swim" adaptation to the demands of new learning; (3) an understanding of the problematic situation that compels new learning without the power to control one's own activity in it; (4) relative mastery in which one can both understand and control one's own activity; and (5) learning to teach what one has mastered.

Many of the skills discussed in this chapter are designed to achieve such a learning cycle. Most crucial are those that initiate learning—those that spur and lead to achievement of the self-awareness that opens us to the risks of giving up the old and taking on the new with which all meaningful learning presents us. These skills include the willingness to risk, the ability to accurately assess one's own learning needs, and the balance of deductive and inductive learning abilities.

WILLINGNESS TO RISK

All growth entails risk. Just as growth involves the risk of moving from current to higher levels of integration, so does learning in the professions. Risk, here, refers to the ability to expose one's practice, one's learning needs, and one's current questions, concerns, and ideas both to the self and to others. Rue Bucher and Joan Stelling (1977), in their sociological study of education for a variety of professions, found this willingness to risk as very significant for practice effectiveness. Yet most students in the profession were socialized toward cautious performance and away from this willingness to risk in their educational experiences! While they relied heavily on self-assessment of their competence weighed against standards of the practice they studied, they strongly resisted exposing their practice to others for potential constructive criticism.

Learning requires both acute consciousness of one's own practice and life experiences as well as the risks in exposing these experiences to others. Professional learning at its best is a discovery process. We discover the meaning of principles and concepts *for us* as a basis not just for learning them but for *using* them. This discovery of meaning takes place in dialogue—in our self-dialogue *and* in dialogue with others.

In the process of learning and discovering its meaning for us and others in our practice, feedback is essential. The willingness to risk basically entails our openness to feedback, including constructive criticism, within ourselves and from others. We can initiate this feedback by sharing our practice in recordings, in logs, in case presentations, and in other communications with faculty, consultants, supervisors, and colleagues. We also promote effective feedback for self-discovery through making our practice visible to others (observations, co-practice, videotaping, and so on). When we include our own questions, concerns, and ideas with this disclosure, we identify our learning needs as a focus for such feedback.

ASSESSMENT OF LEARNING NEEDS

This ability to assess one's own learning needs is vital for professional development. It requires an understanding of the competencies and skills demanded for high-level professional practice and the ability to appraise our strengths and limitations in relation to these standards. Like the Sea Horse in the fable that begins this chapter, we cannot assess where we are without knowing where we want to be. We need a model of competence outcomes against which we can appraise our current level of development and our specific learning needs.

This text presents one such model for evaluation in the Educational Outcome Competence Rating form in the Appendix. Such ratings can help you individualize your future working on those skills in which you rated yourself lower. As you seek meaning in these competencies and face your own feelings in relation to the content of these skills (especially those that readily accept or resist the use of these ratings), you will likely find it difficult to use such scales accurately. It is difficult to assess your application of content that you are newly confronting and not yet fully understanding.

However, this confusion itself needs to be identified. The major principle in all self-assessment is to be honest with yourself, to realistically perceive your understanding and your lack of understanding. The recognition of confusion is often the beginning of meaningful learning. Confusion confronts us both with what we do not know and with our need to know. As you assess your confusion, stay with it and struggle for understanding of any particular competence and/or skill—and you just may have begun a meaningful process of discovery that could lead to truly useful learning.

BALANCE OF DEDUCTIVE/INDUCTIVE LEARNING

We all have particular strengths and limitations in our learning styles. In general, there are three learning styles identified in professional learning. These are the deductive, the inductive, and the integrative (Bruner, 1966). The deductive learner prefers to start with concepts and theory and deductively apply those generalizations to understand practice principles and skills. The inductive learner prefers to begin with experience and to infer generalizations from this experience. Deductive learners have been called theoretically oriented; inductive ones, experientially oriented. Between these two extemes are integrative learners, who tend to balance deductive and inductive orientations and styles. While each of these learning styles holds some strong skills for professional development, the most effective learners, and perhaps the most effective practitioners in the long run, are the integrative ones.

Deductive learners like concepts. They find conceptualizing meaningful and easy. This strength leads them to digest theory, seek to integrate concepts, and formulate generalizations to understand reality. These learners tend to read and write well, to intimidate inductive learners with their knowledge, and to receive high grades in coursework. If this style is not balanced with strengths for inductive learning, they may not be able to translate what they know into what they do. They may resist actual practice experiences or intellectualize rather than honestly and emotionally confront their experienced discrepancies between what they know and what they cannot do.

Inductive learners like experiences, especially emotional encounters that bring meaning to their experiences. If deductive learners are thinkers, inductive ones are feelers. They tend to involve themselves with others readily and may demonstrate natural sensitivity and empathy. They would rather read novels than theories—if they have any strong motivation to read at all. When they do form ideas, often a struggle for them, these evolve from their experience and in their own terms. These ideas may not seem to relate meaningfully to synonymous concepts in the professional literature. Or they might assume similarity where complex differences in these ideas actually exist. If this style is not balanced with deductive learning strengths, they may not be able to link what they do to its actual consequences for others in practice or to formulate integrative guidelines to help resolve the inevitable confusion they confront in practice.

This discussion of the extremes is somewhat oversimplified. The extremes of these styles are very uncommon. Most learners fall on a continuum between these extreme types, possessing strengths and limitations for both deductive and inductive learning. These learners are those who benefit most from working on their limitations to achieve more balanced strengths. Learning social work is a continuous process of applying concepts to practice experiences and conceptualizing from this experience. This assures the integration wherein we relate perceptions, facts, and principles to provide direction in practice (Lowry et al., 1971).

The best integration relates our concepts to one another and to what we know, what we think and feel, and what we do. This learning comes from the discovery of theory and the discovery of actual problem solving, or what Jerome Bruner (1966) called "cognitive structuring." It is based on an attitude toward learning and inquiry that applies general principles to problems and draws general principles from problem-solving experiences. As he hypothesized: "It is only through the exercise of problem solving and the effort of discovery that one learns the working heuristic of discovery and the more one has practice, the more likely one is to generalize what one has learned into a style of problem solving or inquiry that serves for any kind of task one may encounter—or almost any kind of task" (Bruner, 1966, p. 618).

In fact, this suggests that we formulate useful principles for practice in a process that is always both inductive and deductive and often starts at both points simultaneously. That is, we confront the facts of our experience, constructing meaning from our theoretical concepts, whether these are our espoused models or our theories-in-use (Argyris & Schön, 1975). Then, we test these ideas against the experience, seeking principles and a symbolic integration of concepts in our theory. In this sense, we adhere to Kurt Lewin's axiom that "there is nothing so practical as a good theory" (Marrow, 1969).

We must, then, be able to assess our own learning styles accurately, with special attention to our inductive and deductive strengths and limitations. Then, we are in a better position to work on developing our limitations toward becoming the most integrative learner we can be.

The other three skills of this professional development competence are the commitments to competence, scholarship and inquiry, and collegial learning. These skills enable successful completion of the learning cycle from self-awareness to competence mastery. The commitment to competence requires considerable and continuous effort to increase and expand skill development. Scholarship and inquiry refers to the ability to engage in independent research and study. Collegial learning is the ability to learn from and teach others in group learning situations.

COMMITMENT TO COMPETENCE

The commitment to competence is largely reflected through work on the skills covered earlier—the willingness to risk, self-assessment of learning needs, and work toward balancing inductive and deductive learning abilities. Our continual effort to increase and expand our skills denotes a level of commitment to be as competent as possible as a social worker.

Research, however, has demonstrated that this commitment is directly tied to our early mastery of significant skills (Bucher & Stelling, 1977). The more we experience the mastery of skills and perceive our autonomy and responsibility in this learning, the more we become committed to both the profession and developing our competence for its practice. This mastery of and commitment to competence outcomes require as much practice as possible of the central, valued roles demanded in social work practice. These include simulated role-playing of problematic practice situations and actual field experiences. Whenever possible, our commitment to competence is both demonstrated and strengthened through autonomous and responsible experience in applying social work knowledge, values, and skills.

SCHOLARSHIP AND INQUIRY

The ability to research and study practice independently depends upon our motivation for such scholarship and inquiry and our academic learning skills. We can learn the skills; the motivation can only come from us. When we confront problems and independently study them to increase our professional learning, we find ourselves involved in what can be an exciting and creative search into the world of knowledge. We can enjoy the challenge that the inevitable new questions from answering current ones brings on.

With the motivation to begin, this process tends to be more self-initiated and rewarding. Such is how it must be in our ongoing professional development, especially when we leave the structure of formal education. With no term papers due, no library assignments harassing us, no tests to take, we are on our own to conduct inquiry into the problems we face and to pursue the scholarship that fulfills this inquiry. In fact, we might find libraries, books, journals, and so on are more our friends when we choose them through our own research rather than turn to them as requirements to complete assignments. This independent scholarship and inquiry—so important to competence development throughout our professional careers—begins in our developing this motivation and our capacities in our early learning.

COLLEGIAL LEARNING

Collegial learning skills constitute the ability to learn from and teach others in group learning situations. These begin in classroom participation and expand to a variety of formal and informal groups in later practice. Effective learners in groups are collegial learners. Webster's dictionary defines *collegial* as "marked by power or authority invested equally in a number of colleagues." Collegial learners balance autonomy and interdependence with others in achieving individual and group learning goals and engage in mutual-aid activities in the group process. The initiation of the ability for collegial learning requires some reframing of the traditional concept of education as one vested with knowledge and authority—the "teacher"—transmitting knowledge to those without knowledge and authority—the "students." The mark of this skill is the capacity to view one's self and others as potential resources for one another's learning.

This movement away from passive learning to active collegial learning is essential for professional development. When we share the goals of learning in groups we increase the potential for the feedback, coaching, modeling, and actual doing that is requisite for developing practice competence.

CONCLUSION

This seventh and last competence is the ability to use professional development opportunities. This competence begins in our formal education for social work and extends through lifelong professional learning. It involves such skills as our willingness to risk, self-assessment of learning needs, deductive and inductive learning capacities, commitment to competence, scholarship and inquiry, and collegial learning abilities.

The current level of skills for professional development can be rated by using the scales under Competence #7 on the Educational Outcome Competence Rating form in the Appendix. A rating of these skills can inform those areas worth working on. As these ways of learning competence are developed the actual mastery of practice competencies will likely increase. When this seventh learning competence is developed in conjunction with the other six practice competencies of this text, one may be in a better position than the Sea Horse in the fable beginning this chapter. One may better know both where one is going and how to get there in developing foundation competencies for social work practice.

Appendix: Educational Outcome Competence Rating

Person Rated: _____
Rater: _____
Position of Rater: _____

_____   _____
(Rater's Signature)   (Date)   (Signature of Person Rated)   (Date)

DIRECTIONS: Please use the scale below and rate the person's development of each of the twenty (20) skills listed under the first six (6) competencies and the seven (7) components of Competence #7. Also, use the scale provided to rate the person's development of the overall competence. Please rate by choosing the phrase below that accurately reflects your judgment of the person's current development of the skill:

Not known: You do not have the evidence needed to make a judgment.

Not developed: The person has not yet demonstrated the development of this skill.

Grasps in hindsight: The person grasps the idea and is beginning to recognize in hindsight how it might have been applied in a given practice situation.

Unevenly developed: The person demonstrated the skill at a beginning level. Performance is uneven. Further development needs time and practice.

Developed with some gaps: The person applies the skill quite consistently, but there are some gaps (e.g., not used with some clients, avoids some feelings, etc.).

Fully developed: The person has fully integrated this skill in his/her professional stance and style.

COMPETENCE #1: *Ability to tune-in to self, client (other), client's (other's) life situation, and the helping situation consistent with the social work perspective.*

Skill 1: Tuning-in to self

(RATE ACCORDING TO SIX-POINT SCALE IN OPENING OF APPENDIX)

Students often struggle with value differences. At first, they may not even recognize their own values. Self-awareness leads to accepting their own and the client's or other's values, understanding the sources for these values, finding the areas of commonality as well as differences, and respecting the client's right to be different. Students are especially able to demonstrate consciousness of their own humanness and choices and the common human elements and differences with clients of cultural, ethnic, racial, and/or sexual diversity.

This skill includes the ability to recognize similarities in as well as differences from the client's perspective. The student should be moving toward the acceptance of, and away from judging, differences in all client situations, but especially when the client's identity is related to a different ethnic, cultural, or racial background or to a different sexual orientation or preference.

Also, at first, students may experience, without clearly demonstrated awareness, a discrepancy between their personal values and professional social work values and ethics. Over time, this awareness increases and leads to more consistent use of the professional values of each individual's dignity and worth and capacity for self-determination, as well as the ideal of social justice in their thinking, feeling, and doing. They are aware of how their sense of purpose, conceptions of their practice, theories-in-use, perceptions of the client and of their own helping tasks, and own strengths and limitations reflect their use of professional values. These include consistent values of the "matching" purpose and "mediating" function of social work.

Finally, students develop over time an awareness of their own feelings toward the client or other and the work, both in preliminary tuning-in and through the work. This awareness leads to questioning and sorting out whether the particular feelings are realistic, provoked by the client as a defense to maintain distance, or generated from students' own unfinished business (e.g., an attraction toward certain people, an unrealistic need to parent, resentment of domineering or ineffectual people, a strong need to be liked, etc.).

Over time, students should be less fearful and more aware of any particular feeling in the self and in the client and should be able to identify and discriminate among the nuances of feelings they and others are experiencing.

Skill 2: Tuning-in to client

(RATE ACCORDING TO SIX-POINT SCALE IN OPENING OF APPENDIX)

Students often begin anticipating the client' needs and behaviors on the basis of stereotypes born in experience (or the lack of experience) with people of similar known characteristics. In tuning-in, students can begin to use their generalized ideas to sensitize themselves to the range of feelings and concerns on the potential client's part and be prepared to reach for them and respond to them.

Tuning-in to the client involves applying general knowledge to sensitize oneself to a client's life themes in relation to developmental needs, to culture-bound perceptions, and to the potential experiencing of the current life situation. In other words, the student learns to answer fairly accurately significant parts of the question: What might this current situation and initial experience with me *mean* to the client? This tuning-in can give students a better chance of responding to the real meaning of indirect communications rather than reacting defensively. Students tune-in in a tentative way, however, and are prepared to abandon preconceived assumptions about what the client may feel and experience and instead respond to the reality of the encounter.

Responding directly to indirect communciations entails the ability to recognize feelings accurately in the client's expression. This involves picking up and empathizing with expressed feelings, sensitivity to subtle or disguised expressions of feeling (e.g., the authority theme behind questions or anger), perceptiveness about nonverbal clues, ability to tune-in to probable feelings not quite expressed (e.g., the hurt beneath the anger), and perceptiveness about ambivalent feelings.

Skill 3: Tuning in to client's situation

(RATE ACCORDING TO SIX-POINT SCALE IN OPENING OF APPENDIX)

Students can apply knowledge more objectively in a preliminary ecological assessment. This requires the ability to recognize the potential range of factors and systems that may influence the client and his/

her situation. The factors may be: (1) biological (e.g., physical health); (2) psychological (e.g., vulnerability to separations); (3) social (e.g., family or peer-group pressures); (4) cultural (e.g., values); (5) economic (e.g., unemployment or underemployment); or (6) political (e.g., legal recognition of rights). The systems may be family or household, friends, school, work, neighborhood, extended family, social welfare, health, court, recreation, religion, and so on.

During the learning process, there is a tendency for students to emphasize one or a few of these factors to the exclusion of others. Students should develop a perceptiveness of all of these aspects and their interrelationships in the client's situations and an understanding of which of these are likely most relevant in transactions to a particular situation.

This skill involves using ecomapping as a tool to identify how these factors and systems might influence the client in potential areas of stress and as potential resources. Preliminary ecomapping entails identifying the major systems impinging upon the client and the likely nature of their relationship to each other and to the client in this particular situation. This tuning-in (always tentative) assures the use of the ecological perspective for a more comprehensive gathering of data about the meaning of the client's transactions with the environment in initial "generalist" assessment, service planning, and mediation. In situations marked especially by client diversity, the "dual perspective" is an additional tool that students use in preliminary tuning-in through ecomapping. The dual perspective pays special attention to the client's relationship in the immediate nurturing cultural environment and its systems and to the larger dominant, sustaining culture and its systems, as well as the relationship between these two cultural worlds. The student should use the factors, the client systems ecomap, and the dual perspective to identify the client's strengths and resources in the systems and to identify deficits, not in the client, but in those systems with which the client is interdependent.

COMPETENCE #2: *Ability to establish helping relationships that enable clients' active engagement in using services in their own behalf.*

Skill 4: Use of purpose and function

(RATE ACCORDING TO SIX-POINT SCALE IN OPENING OF APPENDIX)

Initially students may perceive the relationship as an end in itself, as in friendships. Or they may see the relationship as based in what they can do for the client and jump in to "fix" the situation by offering solutions without exploring the client's concerns, perception of needs, and life situation. This orientation to process takes on balance as students identify with and use the social work purpose of enabling growth in both clients and their environments through the mediating function. Then, their relationships to clients are marked by both the support of empathic understanding and involvement and the challenge of the reality of the client's needs and the purpose for their *work* together. The clarity of purpose and function and its consistent use frees the student to relate authentically and genuinely. With clear recognition that the relationship is totally for the client and that it demands consistent concern (not necessarily liking) for the client and others in his/her life situation, the student can begin to trust bringing more and more parts of the self to the encounter with the client.

Students move from jumping too quickly to provide a concrete service, or having difficulty in explaining their purpose and function without jargon, to a clear statement of purpose and function and a negotiating style. They should explore the client's concerns and wishes and explain what the agency and they can do. They should make a tentative plan for service, consistently checking out, evaluating, and renegotiating with the client the mutual understanding of the purpose; the goals; their respective functions, roles, responsibilities, and tasks; and the process.

Often students move from establishing warm, positive relationships to tuning-in and using the self in different ways to the fluctuating needs of the client. They should begin to tune-in more sensitively to the client's mood, become more comfortable with quietness, join the client's moments of enthusiasm, and understand and accept the client's distorted images and feelings (positive and negative) toward them without premature explanations or defensiveness. They should learn to empathize with the part of the client that resists change as well as the part that strives for growth; they should begin to see that working relationships are based on understanding, concern, and a shared sense of purpose and need not always be warm and friendly.

The use of purpose and function is marked by the ability to focus the work together with clients. A clear sense of purpose and direction maintains this focus and keeps the client on track. In focusing the work, students may show a beginning awkwardness or a need to establish a friendly relationship before getting down to business. They may be more comfortable in the friend role, thus promoting aimless discussion. Eventually, they may begin to bring the discussion back to focus. If the client is uncomfortable or avoiding the issues, they have some ability to discuss the client's discomfort and to risk facing or even creating necessary unpleasantness. A consistent sense of purpose should emerge.

Skill 5: *Integrated use of support and challenge*

(RATE ACCORDING TO SIX-POINT SCALE IN OPENING OF APPENDIX)

In relationships with clients, students must learn to accept the client, then begin to challenge, or make some demands—providing support along with the challenge. Some students go through periods of being too heavy on the support, or acceptance, side, or too heavy on the challenge, or expectation, side—perhaps achieving an integration with some clients but not with others. Eventually, they should develop a consistent style that incorporates both support and challenge in their relationships with clients (and systems people) that is marked by a sense of tact and timing.

In addition, this skill requires the ability to move back and forth across the subjectivity–objectivity line with clients (and systems people). This involves the capacity to empathize and feel with the other and the ability to step back and look objectively at the other, the self, and the interaction between them. This skill is particularly important and evolves when sharing the client's pain and helping the client take action on his or her own behalf.

This skill also includes the ability to achieve an active–passive balance. This combines passivity (or "contained activity") in letting the client struggle with his/her own themes, and activity in speaking up to suggest, advise, confront, or do for the client (other). Students may go through phases of being too active in giving suggestions, advice, or referrals and in doing for the client. Or they may be too passive, hesitant about making suggestions, giving opinions or information, and unwilling to do some things for some clients (others) at some times. Eventually, they should be comfortable with both activity and passivity, as based on an integrated style of both support and challenge and a clear sense of professional purpose and tasks.

Skill 6: *Responding to and with feelings*

(RATE ACCORDING TO SIX-POINT SCALE IN OPENING OF APPENDIX)

Helping relationships are grounded in the reality of feelings as much as in purpose and content. Students need to learn to develop empathic understanding of the client's feelings, to respond to these, and to share their own feelings. Early in their learning, students may tend to reassure clients prematurely or change the subject because of their discomfort in experiencing too much of the client's pain, anger, or fearfulness—or their uncertainty about how to respond. This should evolve into the ability to express empathy, put unexpressed feelings into words, and explore both sides of ambivalence. The ability to accept and deal with hostility, to tolerate anxiety, to stay with and reach for other's pain, and, in group and family situations, to draw upon the cues or feelings of other members also develops. Students should stop fearing feelings as irrational components of the client's behavior and struggling against these with logic. Rather, they should appreciate the purposive nature of irrational feelings and seek to understand and address them.

For instance, students will often move from giving up when faced with resistance from a client, to pushing, confronting, exhorting, advising, or getting into a battle with the client. Instead, they should be able to discuss the client's resistance, the meaning to the client of the helping process, and the fear and resentment inherent in change. They should recognize the need for defenses in the face of perceived threat and for periodic avoidance of stressful content. In other words, students should learn to respect the integrity of the human being and to see how feelings behind resistance reflect the client's efforts to maintain self-esteem in patterned approaches to interpersonal relationships and social demands.

Finally, students can share their own feelings about the client, the client's situation, and their process together. As students move from inhibition to spontaneity, their feelings are often first conveyed awkwardly—both bodily and verbally. At times students will assume the client would feel as they do. Or they will share personal experiences that interrupt the flow of affect and the focus on the other's experience. Students can eventually develop more sensitivity to the other's reaction to their own feelings and the ability to sense when the client is embarrassed, fearful of closeness, or resentful of the interruption. Then the student can reach for and share the positive and negative feelings involved in the relationship and current aspects of the encounter.

COMPETENCE #3: *Ability to begin social work process by engaging clients in service use through initial contracting, accurate and comprehensive assessment, and effective service planning.*

Skill 7: Contracting

(RATE ACCORDING TO SIX-POINT SCALE IN OPENING OF APPENDIX)

Students may at first struggle to clarify the specific purpose of service and be vague or too jargon-dependent in this statement of purpose. Similarly, they may not be able to give clients a clear idea of how they might help. Later, they may state their purpose and function without getting clients' reactions.

Students should be able to negotiate with clients an initial contract that focuses their work together. Contracting involves (1) clarifying purpose through a simple statement; (2) clarifying function and mutual roles and responsibilities through giving the clients a beginning idea of how they may help; (3) reaching for clients' reaction to and ideas about this purpose, function, and the nature of their work together (with special attention to the authority theme); (4) exploring the clients' most immediate concerns for which service was initiated; (5) prioritizing these concerns with clients to determine the most immediate concerns, goals, targets, and tasks; and (6) assuring clients that there are possibilities for change, no matter how small at first.

This skill includes the ability to enable problem exploration, to translate client wants and needs into target problems, and to establish relevant and feasible tasks for enabling the client to partialize and work on specific target problems.

Skill 8: Initial assessment

(RATE ACCORDING TO SIX-POINT SCALE IN OPENING OF APPENDIX)

Students at first are prone to view situations in simple cause-and-effect terms. They may believe that the situation would change if the client would only choose to act differently. Then, they may conceive the service as using their relationship to change the client. As students begin to understand the complex interactions among clients and their environments, they recognize the need for more ecological assessments and generalist practice.

Students should start where clients are in concerns and in contracting for service and develop understanding of clients' life situations from an ecological perspective and assessment. This assessment includes ecomapping the transactions between clients' needs and capacities and perceived stresses and resources in their impinging environmental systems. There is determination of the client's family's, other primary group's, organization's, and community's relation to the client's stressful life situation, in terms of both strengths and obstacles to meeting the client's service needs. The student uses the dual perspective for special consideration of these transactions and the goals and targets for intervention in behalf of clients when clients possess cultural, racial, ethnic, and/or sex differences subject to discrimination and oppression.

Skill 9: Service planning

(RATE ACCORDING TO SIX-POINT SCALE IN OPENING OF APPENDIX)

As students move from defining problems and intervention as the need for change in clients in assessments, they establish goals, targets, strategies, and methods for delivering service in more generalist service plans. These plans include when, why, and what goals they will work toward, with: (1) clients themselves in their own behalf and through which casework method; (2) client groups and family groups and through which methods; (3) organizations in behalf of individuals or groups of clients and through which methods; and (4) communities in behalf of groups of clients and through which methods. The plan would include the identification of specific theoretical approaches to direct the interventions. Often, the assessment and service plan is presented to clients in a written contract that specifies goals and tasks to achieve them.

This skill includes the ability to question and think critically about programs, theories, alternative approaches, and the effectiveness of interventions. This critical thinking, based on knowledge of approaches, should lead to ideas about changes and strategies to bring them about. The planning entails the ability to formulate ideas about the social work process and the steps involved in moving from initial contracting through termination. Initially, students should question the purpose and the process and cannot be expected to have a clear idea of what is helpful or why. They begin by seeing one useful step and move toward seeing a range of approaches. In the planning, students should work in partnership with clients in establishing clear goals and articulating first steps. They need to help clients select goals that maximize their motivation, capacity, and opportunity—moving away from being too protective or too ambitious in the goals decided upon in the service plan.

This skill also includes the ability to explicate the rationale for their service planning and intervention. This rationale entails identification of the agency policies, procedures, and programs and the practice theories that influence specific service planning and intervention and the critical assessment of these influences as they relate to effective service in specific client situations as well as to services to clients in general.

COMPETENCE #4: *Ability to sustain the social work process through direct client contact in the work phase.*

Skill 10: Sessional tuning-in and contracting

(RATE ACCORDING TO SIX-POINT SCALE IN OPENING OF APPENDIX)

After beginning the social work process, the student may not know where to begin subsequent contacts and may continue to review past work or report on plans. Often, students may assume that the agenda was established early, and this becomes their agenda for work-phase contacts. Students should move to sessional tuning-in and contracting by starting where clients are, discovering what they are working on, and addressing their agenda first. This entails reaching for and listening to the client's urgent themes of concern, between-session data, and the client's wishes and fears.

The student needs to increase the ability to pick up the life themes, messages, and patterns underlying the client's presenting content. Students begin to see in hindsight the relevance of the client's comments or digressions that confused them during the encounter. They move to identifying and commenting on the themes and connections as they learn to discern the messages that are embedded in other less obvious contexts. In group and family meetings, students begin to help other members connect with one another around their common themes.

Skill 11: Elaborating and clarifying

(RATE ACCORDING TO SIX-POINT SCALE IN OPENING OF APPENDIX)

Elaborating and clarifying are the abilities to explore and draw out the subjective and objective facts of the client's story. Students often begin by being hesitant and concerned about privacy and intrusion. They can be awkward about framing questions and fearful that the questions might sound accusing. They may not explore because they are uncertain about how to respond to or use the information gained. With time, they should be able to offer support and explain the purpose of questions. They also should be able to clarify communications, realizing that messages sent to them and that they send are not necessarily the messages received. Students should learn to help clients elaborate their concerns by moving from general statements to specific expression of their perceptions, feelings, behavior, and goals by waiting out silences and then asking what they might mean and by using open-ended "what" and "how" questions to determine the meaning of events for clients. Also, they should find themselves using "why" questions and closed questions very infrequently.

Skill 12: Empathy

(RATE ACCORDING TO SIX-POINT SCALE IN OPENING OF APPENDIX)

Over time, students should more readily discriminate among clients' feelings and respond with more accurate empathy. Empathic responses demonstrate understanding of clients through verbal and non-verbal expressions of the students' immediate experience of clients' emotions. The student can put the client's feelings into words, reach for the positive and negative sides of ambivalent feelings, and connect feelings to work by relating them to client's content and behavior. Progressing in this skill, the student learns to understand and trust the underlying process of the client in its purposeful, yet irrational, emotional themes and to promote integration of the rational and irrational components in decision making and choice.

Skill 13: Sharing own feelings

(RATE ACCORDING TO SIX-POINT SCALE IN OPENING OF APPENDIX)

As students progress in the social work process with clients, they should be able to use the shared sense of purpose and general function to relate more fully as a person and less in a role. Then, they can share their own feelings more spontaneously and genuinely with clients. These personal thoughts and feelings can relate to clients' themes or to their own relationship process in the encounter. They include support for clients' strengths through expression of belief in their ability to take some step or get through a difficult time.

Skill 14: Demanding work

(RATE ACCORDING TO SIX-POINT SCALE IN OPENING OF APPENDIX)

Students may lose track of the work after beginning. They may be fearful that demanding work of the client would entail expectations of them that they are not sure they can meet. Or they may settle for the illusion of work, especially with highly anxious, angry, or resisting clients, and collude in simply going through the motions of service. Students need to be sure that their relationship with the client produces work from clients in their own behalf. Demanding work requires partializing clients' concerns; pointing out the illusion of work;

confronting the discrepancies between clients' words and deeds; identifying the obstacles to balancing process and tasks in the work; reaching for discussion of taboo areas; identifying the feelings that appear to block discussion; and dealing with the authority theme by asking for negative feedback from clients.

Students can be very hesitant to use their authority to set firm limits in situations where the client is a danger to himself or others. There can also be a tendency to use power to punish when a client has been frustratingly uncooperative. In group and family process, the student can balance the authority of directing with the functions of providing, processing, and catalyzing.

Skill 15: Providing information

(RATE ACCORDING TO SIX-POINT SCALE IN OPENING OF APPENDIX)

Students at first may find it difficult to provide information in language clients can understand. They may be reluctant to share their own ideas, values, and beliefs. Or they might share these too prematurely—not timed to clients' need, readiness, or request. Students learn to provide information meaningfully; that is, to share, at the appropriate time, data, facts, ideas, values, and/or beliefs relevant to clients' concerns and otherwise unavailable to them.

A special case of providing information is the ability to make referrals. This requires helping clients identify needs and resources, exploring their feelings and expectations about resources, and giving clear information. Students should check out a resource and know about eligibility, the services actually provided, and the clientele served. They should be able to discuss clients' previous experiences and feelings about similar resources, including their hopes, motivations, and personal priorities. There should be follow-through feedback from clients about their experience and its usefulness, clearing up any misunderstandings in the information provided.

In sharing data, students should move from giving advice or information in general terms. They should learn to qualify their information as one perspective—theirs.

Skill 16: Use of practice theroy

(RATE ACCORDING TO SIX-POINT SCALE IN OPENING OF APPENDIX)

Students should be able to use identified practice theory approaches and to articulate the theories-in-use that base and shape their understanding and action. Over time, they will become selective about the clients who may benefit from their use of particular approaches and clear about the relationship of the approach to clients' needs and goals. They will be able to explain the purpose of the approach to clients and supervisors and get feedback.

Students may be spontaneous and intuitive without understanding the "whys" and "hows" of what they do or could do in particular situations. In the early stages, they often need directions and prescriptions but eventually move toward greater independence in thinking things through for themselves. Initial efforts to apply particular theory in practice situations can be awkward and self-conscious. Eventually, the thinking process can become sufficiently integrated and natural to guide the student's activities without the loss of spontaneity, intuitiveness, and feeling.

COMPETENCE #5: *Ability to sustain work through mediation between clients and resource systems during the work phase.*

Skill 17: Linking

(RATE ACCORDING TO SIX-POINT SCALE IN OPENING OF APPENDIX)

Linking entails specific actions to bring together clients and formal and informal resource people in behalf of both clients and systems. The student at first may be reluctant to link the client with significant others out of a need to be needed. The student learns to give up the need for client dependence and to work as much as possible for client independence. This entails encouraging clients to view system people in new and less stereotyped ways; meeting with significant others to open up effective transactional and communication channels; referring clients to appropriate resources and monitoring the successful connection to informal and formal resource networks; coordinating the delivery of a variety of services to clients; and initiating family and small group services, when needed, to meet needs that the individual client shares with other or potential clients.

Skill 18: Advocacy

(RATE ACCORDING TO SIX-POINT SCALE IN OPENING OF APPENDIX)

Students at first may be reluctant to advocate clients' needs or may engage in adversarial advocacy before attempting more collaborative strategies. Eventually, students should learn to advocate for clients' needs in organizational and community systems, including their own agency, when their basic rights seem violated. Additionally, they should develop strategies for organizational, community, or policy change in behalf of clients and others with similar unmet needs, including engagement in political action when necessary.

COMPETENCE #6: *Ability to enable effective service termination during the ending phase.*

Skill 19: Ending

(RATE ACCORDING TO SIX-POINT SCALE IN OPENING OF APPENDIX)

Students often at first deny their own feelings about ending and may cut off service abruptly or without attention to clients' cues regarding their ending process. Later, students may be more tuned-in to one side of their own and clients' ambivalences, emphasizing either the positive or negative feelings about termination. Students should learn to use endings consciously and sensitively in behalf of clients. This entails pointing out endings in order to continue work in termination of the service; sharing their own feelings to provide a model of facing termination and to initiate the flow of positive and negative affect between themselves and clients during the ending phase; reaching for ending feelings, both positive and negative, and connecting these feelings to the substance of the work; crediting clients for their share of the work and transferring learning from this process; and asking for a review of the work as related to the goals and terms of the contract.

Skill 20: Evaluation

(RATE ACCORDING TO SIX-POINT SCALE IN OPENING OF APPENDIX)

Students are prone to evaluate service and their work on the basis of their own and clients' feelings about the process. They tend to resist efforts at more systematic evaluation. Evaluation skills require that students objectify and systematize their assessment through the use of evaluation research. At a minimum, students need to develop instruments for pre- and posttesting client change. The student should develop scales to gather baseline data and to measure outcomes against baseline data. Therefore, students need to learn to operationalize goals into some measurable outcomes and to measure what parts of their practice approach influenced clients toward achievement of these outcomes, made little or no difference, or seemed deleterious. This requires the ability to operationalize the intervention hypotheses in their practice approaches and to evaluate process as well as outcomes in their practice.

COMPETENCE #7: *Ability to use professional development opportunities.*

This competence includes the skills for both deductive and inductive learning, the willingness to risk personal disclosure and interpersonal involvement in the learning process, commitment to developing all aspects of competence in behalf of those served, accurate assessment of own learning needs, independent scholarship and inquiry, and ability to engage in collegial learning.

Rate and explain each of these separately as not known, not developed, unevenly developed, developed with gaps, or fully developed:

1. Deductive learning
2. Inductive learning
3. Commitment to competence
4. Learning needs assessment
5. Collegial learning ability
6. Scholarship and inquiry
7. Willingness to risk

References

Abrahams, R. B., & Lantz, W. (1983). The consolidated model of case management and service provision to the elderly. *Pride Institute Journal of Long Term Health Care, 2,* 29–34.

Ad Hoc Committee on Advocacy. (1969). The social worker as advocate: Champion of social victims. *Social Work, 14,* 16–23.

Altschuler, S., & Forward, J. (1978). An inverted hierarchy: A case management approach to mental health services. *Administration in Mental Health, 6,* 57–69.

Anderson, J. D. (1975). Human relations training and group work. *Social Work, 20,* 195–199.

Anderson, J. D. (1978). Growth groups and alienation. *Group and Organization Studies, 3,* 85–107.

Anderson, J. (1981). *Social work methods and processes.* Belmont, CA: Wadsworth.

Anderson, J. D. (1982). Generic and generalist practice on the BSW curriculum. *Journal of Education for Social Work, 18,* 37–45.

Anderson, J. (1984a). *Counseling through group process.* New York: Springer.

Anderson, J. D. (1984b). Toward generic practice: The interactional approach. *Social Casework, 65,* 323–329.

Anderson, J. D. (1985). BSW programs and the continuum in social work. *Journal of Education for Social Work, 21,* 63–72.

Argyris, C., & Schön, D. A. (1975). *Theory in practice: Increasing professional competence.* Washington, DC: Jossey-Bass.

Attinson, Z. & Glassberg, E. (1983). After graduation, what? Employment and educational experiences of graduates of BSW programs. *Journal of Education for Social Work, 19,* 5–14.

Austin, C. (1983). Case management in long term care: Options and opportunities. *Health and Social Work, 8,* 16–30.

Avila, D. L., & Combs, A. W. (1985). *Perspectives on helping relationships and the helping professions: Past, present, and future.* Boston: Allyn and Bacon.

253

Bagarozzi, D. & Kurtz, L. F. (1983). Administrators' perspectives on case management. *Arete*, *8*, 13–21.

Bartlett, H. M. (1970). *The common base of social work practice*. New York: National Association of Social Workers.

Bartlett, H. M. (1971). Social work fields of practice. In *Encyclopedia of social work* (Vol. II) (16th ed.). New York: National Association of Social Workers.

Beistek, F. (1957). *The casework relationship*. Chicago: Loyola University Press.

Benjamin, A. (1974). *The helping interview* (2nd ed.). Chicago: Aldine.

Bergin, A. E. (1966). Some implications of psychotherapy research for therapeutic practice. *Journal of Abnormal Psychology*, *71*, 235–246.

Biggerstaff, M. A., & Kolevson, M. S. (1980). Differential use of social work knowledge, skills, and techniques by MSW, BSW, and BA level practitioners. *Journal of Education for Social Work*, *16*, 67–74.

Billups, J. O. (1984). Unifying social work: The importance of center-moving ideas. *Social Work*, *29*, 173–180.

Blizinsky, M. J., & Reid, W. J. (1980). Problem focus and change in a brief treatment model. *Social Work*, *25*, 89–93.

Bloom, M. (1975). *The paradox of helping: Introduction to the philosophy of scientific practice*. New York: Wiley.

Bloom, M., & Fischer, J. (1982). *Evaluating practice: Guidelines for the accountable professional*. Englewood Cliffs, NJ: Prentice-Hall.

Borenzweig, H. (1971). Social work and psychoanalytic theory: A historical analysis. *Social Work*, *16*, 7–16.

Brennen, E. C. (1978). Defining the basic curriculum. *Journal of Education for Social Workers*, *14*, 29–30.

Brill, N. (1973). *Working with people: The helping process*. Philadelphia: J. B. Lippincott.

Bruner, J. S. (1966). *Toward a theory of instruction*. Cambridge, MA: Harvard University Press.

Buber, M. (1970). *I and thou*. New York: Charles Scribner's Sons.

Bucher, R., & Stelling, J. G. (1977). *Becoming professional*. Beverly Hills, CA: Sage.

Bullmer, K. (1970). *Improving your interpersonal perceptual skills*. Bloomington: Indiana University Press.

Buros, O. K. (Ed.). (1978). *The eighth mental measurements yearbook*. Highland Park, NJ: Gryphon Press.

Campbell, A., Converse, D. E., & Rodgers, W. L. (1976). *The quality of American life*. Ann Arbor, MI: Institute for Social Research.

Campbell, D. T., & Stanley, J. C. (1963). *Experimental and quasi-experimental designs for research*. Chicago: Rand McNally & Company.

Caplan, G. (1974). *Support systems and community mental health*. New York: Behavioral.

Caplan, G., & Killilea, M. (Eds.). (1976). *Support systems and mutual help*. New York: Grune and Stratton.

Carkhuff, R. (1969). *Helping and human relations* (Vols. I & II). New York: Holt, Rinehart and Winston.

Carkhuff, R. (1983). *The art of helping* (5th ed.). Amherst, MA: Human Resource Development Press.

Carkhuff, R. R., & Berenson, R. (1976). *Teaching as treatment*. Amherst, MA: Human Resource Development Press.

Carkhuff, R. R., & Berenson, R. (1977). *Beyond counseling and therapy* (2nd ed.). New York: Holt.

Carroll, N. K. (1977). Multidimensional model of social work practice. *Social Work*, 22, 430–437.

Case Management Research Project. (1980). *A comparison analysis of twenty-two settings using case management components*. Austin: University of Texas School of Social Work.

Chandler, S. M. (1985). Mediation: Conjoint problem-solving. *Social Work*, 30, 346–349.

Chestang, L. (1970). The use of race in casework practice. In *The Social Welfare Forum, 1970* (pp. 110–121). New York: Columbia University Press.

Chestang, L. W. (1980). Competencies and knowledge in clinical social work: A dual perspective. In P. A. Ewalt (Ed.), *Toward a definition of clinical social work* (pp. 13–27). Washington, DC: National Association of Social Workers.

Cobb, S. (1976). Social support as a moderator of life stress. *Psychosomatic Medicine*, 38, 300–314.

Coelho, G. V., Hamburg, D. A., & Adams, J. E. (Eds.). (1974). *Coping and adaptation*. New York: Basic Books.

Collins, A. H., & Pancoast, D. L. (1976). *Natural helping networks: A strategy for prevention*. Washington, DC: National Association of Social Workers.

Combs, A. W., et al. (1969). *Florida Studies in the Helping Professions*. Gainesville: University of Florida Press.

Compton, B., & Galaway, B. (1984). *Social work processes* (3rd ed.). Homewood, IL: Dorsey Press.

Constable, R. (1978). The challenge of specialization: Issues in social work practice in education. *School Social Work Journal*, 2, 67–78.

Costin, L. B. (1981). School social work as specialized practice. *Social Work*, 26, 36–43.

Council on Social Work Education. (1982). *Curriculum policy for the masters degree and baccalaureate degree programs in social work education*. New York: Author.

Council on Social Work Education. (1985). *Report of task force on the future*. Washington, DC: Author. (Mimeographed.)

Cox, T. (1978). *Stress*. Baltimore: University Park Press.

Cummings, D. E., & Arkava, M. L. (1977). Predicting posteducational job performance of BSW graduates. *Social Work*, 21, 487–492.

Dea, K. L. (1971). *The instructional module*. New York: Council on Social Work Education.

Denzin, N. K. (1984). *On understanding emotion*. Washington, DC: Jossey-Bass.

Dohrenwend, B. S., & Dohrenwend, B. P. (Eds.). (1980). *Life stress and illness*. New York: Watson.

Dyer, W. G. (1969). Congruence and control. *Journal of Applied Behavioral Science, 5*, 161–173.

Egan, Gerard (1975). *The skilled helper*. Belmont, CA: Brooks-Cole.

Epstein, I. (1981). Advocates on advocacy: An exploratory study. *Social Work Research and Abstracts, 17*, 5–12.

Epstein, L. (1980). *Helping people: The task-centered approach*. St. Louis: Mosby.

Epstein, L. (1985). *Talking and listening: A guide for the helping interview*. St. Louis: Times Mirror/Mosby.

Erikson, E. H. (1963). *Childhood and society* (2nd ed.). New York: Norton.

Ewalt, P. (Ed.). (1980). *Toward a definition of clinical social work*. Washington, DC: National Association of Social Workers.

Fiedler, F. E. (1950). The concept of an ideal therapeutic relationship. *Journal of Consulting Psychology, 14*, 239–245.

Fisher, R. B., & Ury, J. S. (1983). *Getting to yes*. New York: Harper and Row.

Flexner, A. (1905). Is social work a profession? In *Proceedings of the national conference of charities and correction* (pp. 576–590). Chicago: Hildmann.

Froland, C. D. (1981). *Helping networks and human services*. Beverly Hills, CA: Sage.

Gallant, C. B. (1982). *Mediation in special education disputes*. Washington, DC: National Association of Social Workers.

Garvin, C. D., & Seabury, B. A. (1984). *Interpersonal practice in social work: Processes and procedures*. Englewood Cliffs, NJ: Prentice-Hall.

Gauthier, J. P. (1984). *Classification validation processes for social service positions: Executive summary*. Washington, DC: National Association of Social Workers.

Gaylin, W. (1979). *Feelings: Our vital signs*. New York: Harper and Row.

Gendlin, E. (1969). *Experiential psychotherapy*. Chicago: University of Chicago Press.

Germain, C. B. (1979). *Social work practice: People and environments—An ecological perspective*. New York: Columbia University Press.

Germain, C. B. (1981). The ecological approach to people–environment transactions. *Social Casework, 62*, 323–331.

Germain, C. B. (1984). *Social work practice in health care: An ecological perspective*. New York: The Free Press.

Germain, C. B., & Gitterman, A. (1980). *The life model of social work practice*. New York: Columbia University Press.

Gingerich, W., & Feyerherm, W. (1979). The celeration line technique for assessing client change. *Journal of Social Service Research, 3*, 99–113.

Gitterman, A. (1983). Uses of resistance: A transactional view. *Social Work, 28*, 127–131.

Goldmeier, J. (1968). A study of selected personality attributes and treatment preference of caseworkers and casework students. *Social Service Review*, 42, 232–240.

Gordon, W. E. (1969). Basic constructs for an integrative and generative conception of social work. In G. Hearn (Ed.), *The general systems approach: Contributions toward an holistic conception of social work* (pp. 5–11). New York: Council on Social Work Education.

Gordon, W. E. (1983). Social work: Revolution or evolution? *Social Work*, 38, 181–185.

Gordon, W. E., & Schutz, M. L. (1977). A natural basis for social work specializations. *Social Work*, 22, 422–426.

Gottlieb, B. (Ed.). (1981). *Social networks and social support*. Beverly Hills, CA: Sage.

Gottman, J. M. (1973). N-of-one and N-of-two research in psychotherapy. *Psychological Bulletin, 80*, 93–105.

Gottman, J. M., & Leiblum, S. R. (1974). *How to do psychotherapy and how to evaluate it*. New York: Holt, Rinehart and Winston.

Grisham, M., White, M., & Miller, L. S. (1983). Case management as a problem-solving strategy. *Pride Institute Journal of Long Term Health Care*, 2, 21–28.

Hammon, G. C., Hepworth, D. H., & Smith, V. G. (1977). *Improving therapeutic communication*. Washington, DC: Jossey-Bass.

Harris, G. E. (1978). *Training of public welfare staff in the use of service contracts in preventing and reducing foster care*. Richmond, VA: School of Social Work, Virginia Commonwealth University.

Hartman, A. (1979). *Finding families: An ecological approach to family assessment in adoption*. Beverly Hills, CA: Sage.

Hartman, A., (1983). Concentrations, specializations, and curriculum designs in MSW and BSW programs. *Journal of Education for Social Workers, 19*, 15–24.

Hartman, A., & Laird, J. (1983). *Family-centered social work practice*. New York: Free Press.

Hepworth, D. H., & Larsen, J. A. (1986). *Direct social work practice: Theory and skills* (2nd ed.). Chicago: Dorsey.

Hersen, M., & Barlow, D. H. (1976). *Single case experimental designs: Strategies for studying behavior change*. New York: Pergamon.

Hoffman, L., & Long, L. (1968). A systems dilemma. *Family Process, 8*, 211–234.

Hollis, F. (1980). Continuance and discontinuance in marital counseling and some observations on joint interviews. *Social Casework, 49*, 167–174.

Hosch, D. (1973). *Use of the contract approach in public social services*. Los Angeles: Regional Research Institute in Social Welfare, University of Southern California.

Hudson, W. W. (1977). Elementary techniques for assessing single client/single worker interactions. *Social Service Review, 52*, 311–326.

Hudson, W. W. (1982). *The clinical measurement package: A field manual.* Homewood, IL: Dorsey.

Imre, R. W. (1984). The nature of knowledge in social work. *Social Work, 32,* 41–45.

Jayaratne, S., & Levy, R. L. (1979). *Empirical clinical practice.* New York: Columbia University Press.

Johnson, P. J., & Rubin, A. (1983). Case management in mental health: A social work domain? *Social Work, 28,* 49–55.

Kazdin, A. E. (1976). Statistical analysis for single-case experimental designs. In M. Hersen and D. H. Barlow (Eds.), *Single case experimental designs: Strategies for studying behavior change* (pp. 92–119). New York: Pergamon.

Keefe, T., & Maypole, P. E. (1983). *Relationships in social service practice: Context and skills.* Monterey, CA: Brooks/Cole.

Keith-Lucas, A. (1972). *Giving and taking help.* Chapel Hill, NC: University of North Carolina Press.

Kierkegaard, S. (1968). *Fear and trembling and the sickness unto death.* (W. Lowrie, Trans.). Princeton, NJ: Princeton University Press.

Knapp, C. (1980). *Service contract use in preventing and reducing foster care: Final evaluation report.* Washington, DC: Administration for Children, Youth and Families, DHEW.

Kolevson, M. S., & Biggerstaff, M. A. (1983). Functional differentiation of job demands: Dilemmas confronting the continuum in social work education. *Journal of Education for Social Work, 19,* 26–34.

Kübler-Ross, E. (1969). *On death and dying.* New York: Macmillan.

Lamont, A. E., & Miller, E. P. (1983). The BSW at work: An empirical exploration. Paper presented at Council on Social Work Education's Annual Program Meeting, Fort Worth, TX.

Levinger, G. (1960). Continuance in casework and other helping relationships: A review of current research. *Social Work, 5,* 40–51.

Lieberman, M. A., Yalom, I. D., & Miles, M. B. (1973). *Encounter groups: First facts.* New York: Basic Books.

Lipton, D., & Balter, J. (1971). Mediation in a hospital ward. In W. Schwartz & S. A. Zalba (Eds.), *The Practice of Group Work* (pp. 41–62). New York: Columbia University Press.

Lowry, L., Bloksberg, L. M., & Walberg, H. J. (1971). *Integrative learning and teaching in schools of social work.* New York: Council on Social Work Education.

Mager, R. F. (1962). *Preparing instructional objectives.* Palo Alto, CA: Fearon.

Maguire, L. (1983). *Understanding social networks.* Beverly Hills, CA: Sage.

Mahler, R. (1982). Bacculaureate social work graduates. *Journal of Education for Social Work, 12,* 80–85.

Maluccio, A. N., & Marlow, W. (1974). The case for contract. *Social Work, 19,* 28–35.

Manser, E. (Ed.). (1973). *Family advocacy: A manual for action*. New York: Family Service Association of America.

Marrow, R. (1969). *The practical theorist*. New York: Basic Books.

Martinez-Brawley, E. E. (1986). Beyond cracker-barrel images: The rural social work specialty. *Social Casework, 67*, 101–107.

Maslow, A. H. (1970). *Motivation and personality* (2nd ed.). New York: Harper and Row.

May, R. (1958). The origin and significance of the existential movement in psychology. In R. May, E. Angel, & H. F. Ellenberger (Eds.), *Existence* (pp. 4–42). New York: Simon and Schuster.

May, R. (1969). *Love and will*. New York: Norton.

Mayer, J., & Timms, N. (1969). Clash in perspective between worker and client. *Social Casework, 50*, 32–40.

McLuhan, M. (1965). *The medium is the message*. New York: Random House.

Meares, P. A. (1981). Educating social workers for specialization. *Social Work in Education, 3*, 36–52.

Meyer, C. H., Garber, R., & Williams, C. W. (1979). *Specialization in the social work profession*. Washington, DC: Council on Social Work Education. (Mimeographed.)

Middleman, R. R., & Goldeberg, G. (1974). *Social service delivery: A structural approach to social work prcatice*. New York: Columbia University Press.

Milne, A. A. (1954). *Winnie-the-Pooh*. New York: E. P. Dutton.

Minuchin, S., & Fishman, J. L. (1981). *Techniques of family therapy*. Cambridge, MA: Harvard International Press.

Mitchell, K. M., Borzath, J. K., & Krauft, C. C. (1977). A reappraisal of the therapeutic effectiveness of accurate empathy, nonpossessive warmth, and genuineness. In A. Gurman & A. Kazin (Eds.), *Effective psychotherapy: A handbook of research* (pp. 724–738). New York: Pergamon.

Monat, A., & Lazarus, R. S. (Eds.). (1977). *Stress and coping: An anthology*. New York: Columbia University Press.

Mullen, E. J. (1969). Differences in worker style in casework. *Social Casework, 50*, 347–353.

Naisbitt, R. (1984). *Megatrends*. New York: Warner.

National Association of Social Workers. (1977). Special issue on conceptual frameworks. *Social Work, 22*.

National Association of Social Workers. (1980). NASW code of ethics. *NASW News, 25*, 24–25.

National Association of Social Workers. (1984). *NASW standards for clinical social work*. Washington, DC: Author.

National Conference of Social Welfare (1981). *Case-management: State of the art*. Rockville, MD: Project Share.

Norton, P. G. (1978). *The dual perspective: Inclusion of ethnic minority content in the social work curriculum*. New York: Council on Social Work Education.

Olsen, L., & Holmes, W. H. (1982). Educating child welfare workers: The effects of professional training. *Journal of Education for Social Work, 18*, 94–102.

Olson, P., McCubbin, H. I., and Associates. (1983). *Families: What makes them work*. Beverly Hills, CA: Sage.

Palmer, S. E. (1983). Authority: An essential part of practice. *Social Work, 83*, 120–126.

Pascal, B. (1965). *Pensées* (B. R. Smith, trans.). New York: Doubleday.

Perlman, H. H. (1957). *Social casework: A problem-solving process*. Chicago: University of Chicago Press.

Perlman, H. H. (1968). *Persona: Social role and personality*. Chicago: University of Chicago Press.

Perlman, H. H. (1979). *Relationship: The heart of helping*. Chicago: University of Chicago Press.

Pincus, A., & Minahan, A. (1973). *Social work practice: Model and method*. Itasca, IL: F. E. Peacock.

Pippin, J. A. (1980). *Developing casework skills*. Beverly Hills, CA: Sage.

Price, H. G. (1976). Achieving a balance between self-directed and required learning. *Journal of Education for Social Work, 12*, 102–112.

Procter, E. C. (1982). Defining helping relationships. *Social Work, 27*, 114–125.

Reid, W. (1970). Implications of research for the goals of casework. *Smith College Studies in Social Work, 40*, 140–154.

Reid, W. (1978). *The task-centered system*. New York: Columbia University Press.

Reid, W., and Epstein, L. (1972). *Task-centered casework*. New York: Columbia University Press.

Reid, W., & Shyne, A. (1969). *Brief and extended casework*. New York: Columbia University Press.

Reynolds, B. C. (1942). *Learning and teaching in the practice of social work*. New York: Farrar and Rinehart.

Rhodes, S. (1977). Contract negotiation in the initial stages of casework. *Social Service Review, 51*, 125–140.

Rice, D. G., Fey, W. F., & Kapecs, J. G. (1972). Therapist experience and "style" as factors in co-therapy. *Family Process, 11*, 142–160.

Richan, W. (1976). *Social work: The unloved profession*. New York: Columbia University Press.

Richmond, M. E. (1917). *Social diagnosis*. New York: Russell Sage Foundation.

Ripple, L., et al. (1964). *Motivation, capacity, and opportunity*. Chicago: University of Chicago Press.

Robinson, V. P. (1978). *The development of a professional self: Teaching and learning in professional helping processes—Selected writings, 1930-1968*. New York: Ames Press.

Rogers, C. R. (1957). The necessary and sufficient conditions of therapeutic personality change. *Journal of Consulting Psychology, 21*, 95–103.

Rogers, C. R. (1961). *On becoming a person*. Boston: Houghton Mifflin.

Rogers, C. R. (1966). Client-centered therapy. In S. Arieto (Ed.), *American handbook of psychiatry*, (Vol. III) (pp. 332–418). New York: Basic Books.

Rogers, C. R. (1975). Empathy: An unappreciated way of being. *The Counseling Psychologist, 5*, 2–9.

Rogers, C. R. Gendlin, E., and Barret-Leonard, G. B. (1967). *The therapeutic relationship and its impact: A study of psychotherapy with schizophrenics*. Madison: University of Wisconsin Press.

Rosenfeld, J. M. (1983). The domain and expertise of social work: A conceptualization. *Social Work, 38*, 186–191.

Rothman, G. C. (1985). *Philanthropists, therapists, and activists*. Cambridge, MA: Schenkman.

Sanborn, C. (Ed.). (1983). *Case management in mental health services*. New York: Haworth Press.

Schatz, M. S., & Jenkins, L. *Differentiating generic and generalist social work and advanced social work practice in the generalist perspective: A working paper on a Delphi study*. Fort Collins, CO: School of Social Work, Colorado State University. (Mimeographed.)

Schinke, S. P., Barth, R. P., & Blythe, B. J. (1985). Advocacy skills for social work. *Journal of Social Work Education, 21*, 27–33.

Schmidt, J. (1969). The use of purpose in casework. *Social Work, 14*, 77–84.

Schwartz, W. (1961). The social worker in the group. In Robert Morris (Ed.), *The Social Welfare Forum, 1961* (pp. 146–171). New York: Columbia University Press.

Schwartz, W. (1971). Social groupwork: The interactionist approach. In *Encyclopedia of Social Work* (Vol. II) (16th ed.) (pp. 1252–1263). New York: National Association of Social Workers.

Shields, S. A. (1985/86). Busted and branded: Group work with substance abusing adolescents in schools. *Social Work with Groups, 8*, 61–82.

Shulman, B. H. (1971). Confrontation techniques in Adlerian psychotherapy. *Journal of Individual Psychology, 27*, 167–175.

Shulman, L. (1977). *A study of the helping process*. Vancouver, British Columbia, Canada: University of British Columbia.

Shulman, L. (1984). *The skills of helping: Individuals and groups* (2nd ed.). Itasca, IL: F. E. Peacock.

Simons, R. L., & Aigner, S. M. (1985). *Practice principles: A problem-solving approach to social work*. New York: Macmillan.

Siporin, M. (1975). *Introduction to social work practice*. New York: Macmillan.

Siporin, M. (1980). Ecological systems theory in social work. *Journal of Sociology and Social Work, 7*, 507–532.

Social casework: Generic and specific: A report of the Milford Conference. (1974). Washington, DC: National Association of Social Workers. (Original work published 1929).

Social Work (1970). Special issue on "ethnicity and social work," *17*. p. 50.

Social Work Research and Abstracts (1981). Special issue on assessment, *17*.

Sosin, M., & Caulum, S. (1983). Advocacy: A conceptualization for social work practice. *Social Work, 28,* 2–28.

Specht, H. (1955). Managing professional interpersonal interactions. *Social Work, 30,* 225–231.

Speisman, J. C. (1959). Depth of interpretation and verbal resistance in psychotherapy. *Journal of Consulting Psychology, 23,* 93–99.

Stein, T., & Gambrill, E. (1977). Facilitating decision making in foster care. *Social Service Review, 51,* 502–513.

Stein, T., Gambrill, E., & Wiltse, K. (1974). Foster care: The use of contracts. *Public Welfare, 32,* 20–35.

Steinberg, R., & Carter, G. (1981). *Case management and the elderly.* Lexington, MA: Lexington Books.

Sunley, R. (1983). *Advocating today.* New York: Family Service Association of America.

Thomas, W. I. (1938). *Definition of the situation.* Chicago: University of Chicago Press.

Tillich, P. (1962). The philosophy of social work. *Social Service Review, 1,* 13–16.

Toffler, A. (1970). *Future shock.* New York: Random House.

Tomasic, R., & Feeley, M. (Eds.). (1982). *Neighborhood justice: Assessment of an emerging idea.* New York: Longman.

Towle, C. (1954). *The learner in education for the professions: As seen in education for social work.* Chicago: University of Chicago Press.

Tripodi, T., & Epstein, I. (1980). *Evaluation research in social work.* Homewood, IL: Dorsey.

Tropp, E. (1970). Authenticity in teacher-student communication. In M. Pohek (Ed.), *Teaching and learning in social work education* (pp. 13–26). New York: Council on Social Work Education.

Truax, C. B., Mitchell, K. (1971). Research on certain therapist interpersonal skills in relation to process and outcome. In A. Bergin and S. Garfield (Eds.), *Handbook of Psychotherapy and Behavior Change.* New York: John Wiley and Sons.

Vice-Irey, K. (1980). The social work generalist in a rural context: An ecological perspective. *Journal of Education for Social Work, 16,* 36–42.

Vigilante, J. L., et al. (1981). *Searching for theory: Following Hearn.* Garden City, NY: Adelphi University School of Social Work. (Mimeographed.)

Viscott, P. (1976). *The language of feelings.* New York: Arbor House.

Ward, E. L. (1983). A black perspective for social work counseling. In D. Devore & M. A. Schleisinger (Eds.), *Ethnic sensitive social work practice* (pp. 217–236). New York: Council on Social Work Education.

Warren, D. (1981). *Helping networks.* Notre Dame, IN: University of Notre Dame Press.

Wattenburg, S., & O'Rourke, T. (1978). Comparison of Master's and Bachelor's degree social workers in hospitals. *Social Work in Health Care, 4,* 93–105.

Weissman, A. (1976). Industrial social services: Linkage technology. *Social Casework, 57,* 50-54.

Wells, L. M., & Singer, C. (1985). A model for linking networks in social work practice with the institutionalized elderly. *Social Work, 30,* 318-322.

Wells, S. (1980). *Case management and child welfare.* Los Angeles: Region 9 Child Welfare Center, UCLA School of Social Welfare.

Westbury, I., Simon, B. K., & Korbelik, J. (Eds.). (1973). *Generalist practice: Description and evaluation.* Chicago: University of Chicago Press.

Witty, C. (1980). *Mediation and society.* New York: Academic Press.

Wood, K. (1978). Casework effectiveness: A new look at the research evidence. *Social Work, 23,* 437-458.

Index